The Challenge of Transition

Non-Governmental Public Action

Series Editor: **Jude Howell**, Professor and Director of the Centre for Civil Society, London School of Economics and Political Science, UK

Non-governmental public action (NGPA) by and for disadvantaged and marginalized people has become increasingly significant over the past two decades. This new book series is designed to make a fresh and original contribution to the understanding of NGPA. It presents the findings of innovative and policy-relevant research carried out by established and new scholars working in collaboration with researchers across the world. The series is international in scope and includes both theoretical and empirical work.

The series marks a departure from previous studies in this area in at least two important respects. First, it goes beyond a singular focus on developmental NGOs or the voluntary sector to include a range of non-governmental public actors such as advocacy networks, campaigns and coalitions, trades unions, peace groups, rights-based groups, cooperatives and social movements. Second, the series is innovative in stimulating a new approach to international comparative research that promotes comparison of the so-called developing world with the so-called developed world, thereby querying the conceptual utility and relevance of categories such as North and South.

Titles include:

Barbara Bompani and Maria Frahm-Arp *(editors)*
DEVELOPMENT AND POLITICS FROM BELOW
Exploring Religious Spaces in the African State

Jude Howell and Jeremy Lind
COUNTER-TERRORISM, AID AND CIVIL SOCIETY
Before and After the War on Terror

Jenny Pearce *(editor)*
PARTICIPATION AND DEMOCRACY IN THE TWENTY-FIRST CENTURY

Tim Pringle and Simon Clarke
THE CHALLENGE OF TRANSITION
Trade Unions in Russia, China and Vietnam

Non-Governmental Public Action Series
Series Standing Order ISBN 978–0–230–22939–6 (hardback) and
978–0–230–22940–2 (paperback)

You can receive future titles in this series as they are published by placing a standing order. Please contact your bookseller or, in case of difficulty, write to us at the address below with your name and address, the title of the series and the ISBN quoted above.

Customer Services Department, Macmillan Distribution Ltd, Houndmills, Basingstoke, Hampshire RG21 6XS, England

The Challenge of Transition

Trade Unions in Russia, China and Vietnam

Tim Pringle
Freelance Researcher

and

Simon Clarke
Emeritus Professor of Sociology, University of Warwick, UK

palgrave
macmillan

First published 2011 by
PALGRAVE MACMILLAN

Palgrave Macmillan in the UK is an imprint of Macmillan Publishers Limited, registered in England, company number 785998, of Houndmills, Basingstoke, Hampshire RG21 6XS.

Palgrave Macmillan in the US is a division of St Martin's Press LLC, 175 Fifth Avenue, New York, NY 10010.

Palgrave Macmillan is the global academic imprint of the above companies and has companies and representatives throughout the world.

Palgrave® and Macmillan® are registered trademarks in the United States, the United Kingdom, Europe and other countries.

ISBN: 978–0–230–23330–0 hardback

This book is printed on paper suitable for recycling and made from fully managed and sustained forest sources. Logging, pulping and manufacturing processes are expected to conform to the environmental regulations of the country of origin.

A catalogue record for this book is available from the British Library.

Library of Congress Cataloging-in-Publication Data

Pringle, Tim, 1959–
    The challenge of transition : trade unions in Russia, China and
Vietnam / Tim Pringle, Simon Clarke.
        p. cm.
    Includes bibliographical references and index.
    ISBN 978–0–230–23330–0 (alk. paper)
    1. Labor unions – Russia (Federation) 2. Labor unions – China. 3. Labor
unions – Vietnam. I. Clarke, Simon, 1946– II. Title.

HD8530.2.P54 2010
331.88—dc22   2010034191

10 9 8 7 6 5 4 3 2 1
20 19 18 17 16 15 14 13 12 11

Printed and bound in Great Britain by
CPI Antony Rowe, Chippenham and Eastbourne

Contents

List of Tables   *vii*

Acronyms and Abbreviations   *viii*

1 Introduction   1

2 State-Socialist Trade Unions in the Transition to a 'Socialist Market Economy'   6

Trade unions and employment relations under state socialism   6

The transition to a socialist market economy   11

Employment relations in a capitalist market economy   18

Industrial relations in a capitalist market economy   27

    Social peace and social partnership   *28*

    Industrial relations in the workplace   *34*

Conclusion   43

3 The Challenge of Worker Activism   45

Russia   46

China   56

Vietnam   65

4 Traditional Trade Unions Adapting to New Conditions   76

Collective agreements   79

    Russia   *79*

    China   *85*

    Vietnam   *96*

    Conclusion   *102*

Collaboration with state bodies   102

    The minimum wage   *105*

    Labour inspection   *109*

    Employment creation   *114*

The trade union and labour disputes   115

    Russia   *117*

    China   *120*

    Vietnam   *123*

Support for primary trade union organisations   131

Trade union elections   137

Extension of trade union organisation   140

    China   *140*

    Vietnam   *142*

    Russia   *144*

Conclusion   144

5 The Limits and Possibilities of Trade Unions in Transition   147

The Russian Health Service Workers' Trade Union   154

    Regional trade union organisations   *156*

    Primary organisations   *162*

Trade unions in the private sector   175

    Construction   *175*

    Metallurgy   *180*

    Auto industry   *185*

Dealing with multinationals   197

Conclusion   201

6 Labour Activism and the Reform of Trade Unions   202

References   *206*

Index   *213*

Tables

3.1 Official statistics of strikes in Russia   55

3.2 Strikes in Vietnam by enterprise ownership   67

Acronyms and Abbreviations

ACFTU	All China Federation of Trade Unions
ASM	Auto and Agricultural Machine Building Trade Union
BWAF	Beijing Workers Autonomous Federation
CCP	Chinese Communist Party
CEC	China Enterprise Confederation (former CEMA)
CEDA	Chinese Enterprise Directors' Association
CEMA	China Enterprise Management Association
CGT	Confédération générale du travail
CIA	Central Intelligence Agency
CLMS	Centre for Labour Market Studies
CPSU	Communist Party of the Soviet Union
CSR	Corporate Social Responsibility
CVTC	Vietnamese Confederation of Christian Workers
DOLISA	Department of Labour, Invalids and Social Affairs
DPE	Domestic Private Enterprise
EPZ	Export Processing Zone
FDI	Foreign Direct Investment
FES	Friedrich Ebert Stiftung
FIE	Foreign-Invested Enterprise
FNPR	Federation of Independent Trade Unions of Russia
FPAD	Federation of Air Traffic Controllers' Unions
GM	General Motors
GMD	Guomindang
GMPR	Mining and Metallurgy Workers' Union of Russia
GTZ	German Technical Cooperation
HCMC	Ho Chi Minh City

HR	Human Resources
HRW	Human Rights Watch
ICEM	International Federation of Chemical, Energy, Mine and General Workers' Unions
ICFTU	International Confederation of Free Trade Unions
IHLO	ITUC/GUF Hong Kong Liaison Office
ILO	International Labour Organization
IMF	International Metalworkers' Federation
IPZ	Industrial Processing Zone
ISITO	Institute for Comparative Labour Relations Research
ITUC	International Trade Union Confederation
IUF	International Union of Food workers
IWUV	Independent Workers' Union of Vietnam
JV	Joint Venture
KGB	State Security Committee
KTR	Confederation of Labour of Russia
KTS	All-Russia Confederation of Labour
MOLISA	Ministry of Labour, Invalids and Social Affairs
MOLSS	Ministry of Labour and Social Security
MPRA	Inter-regional Trade Union of Motor Industry Workers
NGO	Non-Governmental Organisation
NPC	National People's Congress
NPG	Independent Miners' Union
NPRUP	Independent Trade Union of Workers of the Coal-Mining Industry
NTCC	National Tripartite Consultative Committee
OHS	Occupational Health and Safety
POE	Privately Owned Enterprise

RKSP	Russian Confederation of Free Trade Unions
RPD	Russian Dockers Trade Union
RPLBZh	Russian Trade Union of Railway Locomotive Brigades
SEZ	Special Economic Zone
SME	Small and Medium Enterprise
SOE	State-Owned Enterprise
STEC	State Trade and Economic Commission
STK	Labour Collective Council
TCC	Tripartite Consultative Committee
TNC	Trans-National Company
TVE	Township and Village Enterprise
USSR	Union of Soviet Socialist Republics
UTS	Unified Tariff Scale
UWFO	United Worker-Farmers Organisation of Vietnam
VCA	Vietnam Cooperative Alliance
VCCI	Vietnam Chamber of Commerce and Industry
VGCL	Vietnam General Confederation of Labour
VKT	All-Russia Confederation of Labour
VND	Vietnam Dong
VSI	Vietnam Social Insurance
VTsSPS	All-Union Central Council of Trade Unions
VW	Volkswagen
WAF	Workers' Autonomous Federation
WFTU	World Federation of Trade Unions
WSC	Workers' Support Centre
WTO	World Trade Organisation
YFTU	Yiwu Federation of Trade Unions
YWLRC	Yiwu Workers' Legal Rights Centre

1

Introduction

Trade unions in state-socialist society were an integral part of the Party-state apparatus, supposedly representing the interests of the working class as a whole, as expressed by the Communist Party, rather than the interests of particular groups of workers. The transition from a command economy to a capitalist market economy transforms the employment relationship and so transforms the trade unions from being simply an extension of the Party-state apparatus into bodies that, at least nominally, represent their members in negotiation with employers and lobby within the political system to secure legal standards for decent pay and working conditions. As representatives of the interests and aspirations of employees, trade unions have the potential to play a very positive role in the construction of civil society in the post-socialist countries and so to play a central role in the democratisation process.

There has been surprisingly little research on the reform of former state-socialist trade unions, the most common assumption being that these trade unions are a hangover from the past that can be expected to wither away, perhaps to be replaced by new 'free' or 'alternative' trade unions, although there have always been those who regarded the traditional trade unions as 'genuine' trade unions that had achieved exemplary working conditions and welfare benefits for their members and who bemoan their decline with the development of a market economy, leaving workers unprotected. In fact the traditional trade unions have not withered away, nor have alternative trade unions been able to displace them. The traditional trade unions have been forced, under the pressures of globalisation and increasing labour unrest, to adapt their structures and practices to new circumstances. Our aim in this book is to assess the extent to which traditional and alternative trade unions have been able to respond to these challenges in three key post-socialist countries, Russia, China and Vietnam. Of course, the fate of the trade unions in these three countries is rather different from that in the former state-socialist countries of East-Central Europe, where the transformation of the trade unions has been more strongly conditioned by the relatively greater penetration of foreign capital, on the one hand, and the process of EU accession, on the other.

This book presents the results of a comparative study of the development of trade unions in Russia, China and Vietnam in the reform era. The two authors have been working with and researching trade unions and workers' organisations in these countries for almost twenty years and the present book builds on that research, but its principal source is a research project entitled 'Post-Socialist Trade Unions, Low Pay and Decent Work: Russia, China and Vietnam', directed by the authors and funded by the British Economic and Social Research Council under its Non-Governmental

Public Action Programme from 2005 to 2009. The research for this project was undertaken in collaboration with teams of experienced local researchers in the three countries in question, who carried out a series of case studies and prepared background, case study and analytical reports on which we have relied heavily in writing this book (this material can be found on the project website at go.warwick.ac.uk/Russia/NGPA). We are very grateful to all our colleagues for their work on the project. The research project was designed to focus on the best practice of trade unions in all three countries, to identify the possibilities of reform and the barriers encountered by serious attempts at reform, rather than looking at typical practice, which all too often is merely a continuation of past practice.

The aim of the project was to identify the possibilities and limits of trade union practice to improve the pay and working conditions of employees in these three post-socialist countries. These countries provided very favourable conditions for trade union activity to the extent that they have inherited large and wealthy trade union organisations from the state-socialist past. On the other hand, these trade unions remain encumbered by their past history as an arm of the Party-state, which has set limits to the degree to which the unions are willing or able to organise employees in opposition to employers. The trade unions in all three countries have had to respond to the double impact of the global penetration of capitalist production relations. On the one hand, capitalist globalisation has provoked, benefited from and accelerated the collapse of the state-socialist system. On the other hand, it has transformed employment relations, with the dismantling of social guarantees for urban workers and the opening of employment opportunities for the rural population, albeit often at very low wages with long hours and poor working conditions. While in principle these developments increase the opportunities for effective trade unionism, in practice it has not been the trade unions but the workers themselves who have mobilised to defend their rights and interests. Worker activism has been most pronounced in the sectors most open to the world market, where competitive pressure forces employers to intensify exploitation while labour shortages strengthen the hand of workers. The traditional trade unions, in the best of cases, have initiated reform only in response to rising worker unrest, under political pressure to maintain social peace.

At first sight the trade unions in Russia are radically different from those in China and Vietnam. The Russian unions have been independent of all political organisations for two decades, while the trade unions in China and Vietnam are still legally and constitutionally 'under the leadership of the Communist Party'. Russian trade unions function in a formally democratic political system and a liberalised market economy, whereas the Chinese and Vietnamese trade unions still function in an authoritarian one-Party state and in economies that continue to be subject to pervasive state control. The Russian trade unions enjoy freedom of association and the right to strike, while the Chinese and Vietnamese trade unions operate with a legally enforced monopoly of representation of employees. The right to strike is not protected in China and is severely circumscribed in Vietnam. While the Russian trade unions were admitted to the international trade union community through their affiliation to the International Confederation of Free Trade Unions (ICFTU) in 2002, the Vietnamese unions retain their affiliation to the Communist-era World Federation of Trade Unions (WFTU) and the Chinese reject all formal international affiliations, having until recently been ostracised by the bulk of the international trade union community.

Despite these important differences, the trade unions in all three countries have faced the common problem of adapting to capitalist market conditions. Under the state-socialist command economy, they were integrated into the Party-state apparatus as executors of state functions and Party policy. In a market economy dominated by capitalist employment relations, the trade unions have to take on the new role of representing employees in their relations with employers who have distinct and often opposing interests. In Russia the process of trade union reform has been directed by the trade unions themselves, as they seek to find themselves a place in the transformed polity and society. In China and Vietnam the process of reform has been undertaken under the direction of the Party. Yet the principal barriers to reform encountered in all three countries are the same – the conservatism of the trade union apparatus and the lack of confidence of workers in their trade unions. As a result, the tendency is to reproduce traditional patterns of bureaucratic working and collaboration with the employer as part of the management apparatus. The pattern of reform has been similar in all three countries, with an emphasis on strengthening and democratisation of workplace organisations and the extension of trade union organisation, with technical and organisational support from higher trade union bodies. The principal stimulus to reform has also been the same in all three countries, deriving not from initiatives imposed from above, which tend to degenerate into bureaucratic formalism, but from the pressure of worker activism from below, which requires workplace and local trade unions to develop their capacity to represent the needs and aspirations of workers. Reform is by no means a spontaneous response to worker activism but depends, crucially, on the initiative, imagination and courage of individual trade union officers who are committed to representing their members effectively.

A central issue throughout the state-socialist world has been that of whether the traditional trade unions can reform or whether the future lies with new alternative trade unions. In all three countries the balance of international opinion has shifted from the latter to the former point of view. Thus, the Russian trade unions were admitted to the ICFTU, alongside the two principal alternative federations, in 2002, and in December 2007 the International Trade Union Confederation (ITUC), successor organisation to the ICFTU, sought to open collaboration with the All-China Federation of Trade Unions (ACFTU), while bilateral and multilateral exchanges with the Vietnamese unions have increased despite the Vietnam General Confederation of Labour's (VGCL) continued affiliation to WFTU. In our view the issue is not one of 'either/or'. There is a risk that the new enthusiasm for collaboration will prove as unproductive as did the earlier adamant rejection of collaboration. On the one hand, the traditional unions continue to carry the legacy of bureaucratic state institutions. On the other hand, the alternative unions and informal worker organisations have not provided a sustainable alternative, in the face of state and employer intimidation, but they have been a crucial stimulus to reform. This observation informs our theoretical approach to the trade unions in this book. On the one hand, we take an institutionalist approach to theorising trade unions but, on the other hand, we regard the class struggle as the motor of history. Trade unions are self-interested organisations, but they have to pursue their interests in an environment conditioned by the practices and priorities of employers and the state and by the actions and aspirations of their members and their wider constituency.

The second chapter of the book examines the background to trade union reform by exploring the implications for trade unions of the transition from the state-socialist command economy to a 'socialist' and then a fully capitalist market economy. The most fundamental change is in the employment relationship, which is no longer a permanent relationship between the state and the worker but becomes a contractual relation between an employer and employee. This transformation implies a range of changes in the legal system regulating the employment relationship, including laws which regulate the terms and conditions of labour and laws which regulate the activity of trade unions. On the other hand, the transformation of the employment relation does not immediately change the social relations of the workplace, nor does it transform the role of the trade union in the workplace. Similarly, the transformation of the employment relation does not immediately transform the political role of the trade unions or their relationship to the state. We identify the subordination of the trade unions to management in the workplace and their subordination to the state in the wider society as the principal barriers to the radical reform of the trade unions in all three countries. We also argue that there is no reason for the trade unions to seek to transform themselves, nor any reason for their transformation from above. The only significant pressure for change comes from below, from the activism of workers seeking to realise their rights and aspirations in the face of their employers.

The third chapter explores patterns of worker activism in Russia, China and Vietnam. In all three countries the transition from the command economy to the market economy was accompanied by fears, if not always the reality, of unrest among displaced and impoverished workers in state-owned enterprises facing bankruptcy and privatisation, but this unrest could be contained within the existing political and trade union system. A much more serious challenge to the established order has been presented in China and Vietnam by the recent rapid growth of worker unrest, in the form of strikes and protests, concentrated particularly among rural migrant workers employed in predominantly non-union factories in the private and foreign-invested sectors of the economy. It has been this unrest that has underlain increasing pressure from the Party-state on the trade unions in these two countries to encourage them to reform in order to represent aggrieved workers more effectively and to channel their grievances into established conflict resolution procedures.

The fourth chapter examines in more detail the ways in which the traditional trade unions have adapted their activities and practices to the new conditions of the capitalist market economy. In all three countries the primary emphasis of the reform of workplace trade unions has been on the negotiation of collective agreements with the employer. However, the dependence of the workplace trade union on the employer has meant that, while there has been an enormous increase in the number of collective agreements signed, these very rarely provide any significant benefits for employees above those already prescribed by the law. This has meant that the efforts of the trade unions to defend and improve the conditions of their members have had to focus on the traditional methods of lobbying government for the introduction and enforcement of legislative instruments regulating the terms and conditions of labour, in particular the minimum wage and health and safety legislation, and lobbying the government to monitor the enforcement of legislation through the appropriate state inspectorates. We then examine the role of the trade union in the resolution of labour disputes, finding that the dependence of the trade union on the employer in the workplace and its commitment to maintaining social peace outside the workplace constitute serious barriers to its playing an effective role in conflict resolution, so that workers instead represent themselves, going through legal channels in the case of individual disputes and through alternative trade unions or informal organisation in the case of collective disputes. Finally, we examine the support provided to primary trade union organisations by the higher levels of the trade union, at trade union elections and at the ways in which the trade unions seek to organise the unorganised.

In looking at the adaptation of traditional forms of trade union activity to the new conditions in Chapter 4 we find examples of more innovative trade union best practice, although such best practices are few and far between in Vietnam and are largely confined to the local level in China. In Russia, freedom of association for the past 20 years has made it possible for workers to establish alternative trade unions which provide an organisational framework that makes it possible to advance beyond the sporadic and often fleeting achievements of the kinds of informal organisation that lie behind worker unrest in China and Vietnam. The alternative trade unions also present a serious competitive challenge to the traditional trade unions, forcing them to reform their own practices if they are to retain their legitimacy and their membership. Moreover, although the traditional Russian trade unions are severely constrained by their commitment to 'social partnership', enforced by their vulnerability in the face of the power of the state, they are not subject to the constraint of direct subordination to the Party, as are the trade unions in China and Vietnam. Thus, in the best of cases, the Russian trade unions have made significantly more progress in reforming their activities and practices than have those of China and Vietnam. In Chapter 5, therefore, we concentrate on presenting examples of trade union best practice in Russia, which illustrate the possibilities and limits of the reform of trade unions in transition. Finally, in a short concluding chapter we reconsider the connection between worker activism and trade union reform.

2

State-Socialist Trade Unions in the Transition to a 'Socialist Market Economy'

Trade unions and employment relations under state-socialism

The system of state-socialism was based on the state (in some cases nominally collective) ownership of the means of production and the planned allocation of resources to production units, which were assigned rights to acquire the necessary inputs of labour, raw materials and plant and equipment and were allocated production targets. Consumers could buy their basic means of subsistence in state shops at administered prices, but access to many goods and services, such as housing, consumer durables or vacations, was through administrative allocation, primarily through the workplace, rather than purchase. At various times, peasants had the right to sell the produce of their private plots in local markets, but otherwise the private sale of goods and services and the employment of wage labour by private individuals were more or less strictly prohibited. Production units were supervised by state bodies of the appropriate level, the largest units being supervised by national ministries, smaller units being supervised by the appropriate regional or municipal bodies.

Labour under state-socialism was an obligation to the socialist state imposed on all members of society, under the state-socialist principle 'from each according to his (her) ability, to each according to his (her) labour'. All employees were state employees, employed under terms and conditions determined by the state according to appropriate laws and regulations, who were assigned to work in particular production units. The terms and conditions of employment were determined by an extensive array of laws and regulations that determined pay, bonuses and overtime rates; working hours; holiday entitlements; health and safety; protection for women, children and the disabled; pension entitlements and so on. Employees received a state-determined wage or salary and additional bonuses paid at state-determined rates, which provided for their basic subsistence needs, while health, welfare and many other goods and services were provided through the workplace. In principle individuals were not free to choose their place of work, but were assigned to a workplace on graduation from school, college or university, release from prison or on completion of military service. The ideal was that the individual would remain attached to the production unit for his or her entire working life, although employees might be transferred from one unit to another in accordance with production needs, for example for the opening of a new plant, and it was common practice for the children of employees to join their parents' production unit, leading over time to the formation of 'labour dynasties'. In practice, particularly where there were labour shortages, production units might poach workers from one another, offering inducements for scarce or highly skilled workers to change their place of work, so that, particularly in the Soviet Union, there was in practice a shadow labour market and relative wages had to respond to the balance of the supply and demand for labour, with strategically important sectors, such as military industries, paying higher wages and employing more skilled and experienced workers, while the consumer goods and services sectors typically paid the lowest wages and employed the least disciplined and the least conscientious workers. Despite proclaimed gender equality, women were generally assigned to the lowest paid employment, particularly in the service sector, and enjoyed inferior opportunities for promotion, particularly once they had children.

China, Vietnam and the Soviet Union controlled the movement of population, particularly from the countryside to the towns. In the Soviet Union agriculture was forcibly collectivised in the 1930s and the rural population worked on state or 'collective' farms, although collective farmers were allowed to cultivate small private plots and sell the produce directly to consumers in the 'kolkhoz' markets. Agriculture was incorporated into the system of state planning, and wages and working conditions were determined by relevant laws and regulations so that the rural population, whether in state or collective farms, were wage workers and belonged to the relevant branch trade union. The peasantry constituted a labour reserve and rural–urban migration was controlled in accordance with the labour requirements of the national economy. Peasants were not issued with internal passports, necessary for internal movement, until 1972 and urban residence was controlled through the '*propiska* system' of residence permits. In China and Vietnam the rural population were considered to be peasants and so not a part of the working class, even in those periods in which agriculture was collectivised, and so not eligible for trade union membership. Rural living standards were far below those of the urban population and rural–urban migration was controlled, most strictly in China, so the rural population constituted an enormous labour reserve.

The production unit was the basic unit of state-socialist society, understood not as a set of means of production but as a unit of labour, a 'labour collective' (*danwei* in China), comprising all employees from the general director down to the lowliest cleaner, who were all equally employees of the state. The labour collective was the unit which paid wages and salaries, provided housing and social and welfare benefits, trained and educated its employees, and it was the primary unit of social control, embracing not only labour discipline but also personal life and domestic relationships. Social control and labour discipline were maintained through a system of incentives, including promotion and grade increases, the payment of bonuses, access to housing and consumer durables, vacations, social and welfare services, with deprivation of these benefits providing the corresponding punishments. Criminal and administrative penalties could be applied in cases of dereliction of duty or neglect of health and safety procedures, but dismissal was rarely employed as a sanction because dismissal would release the individual from the control of his or her native production unit and, at best, transfer the problem to another production unit or, at worst, leave the individual altogether outside the system of social control, to become an 'anti-social' element. Hence the legal protection from dismissal that was characteristic of state-socialist societies was not designed to protect workers so much as to ensure that they remained under the control of a production unit.

The production unit in a state-socialist society was managed, in theory, not for the benefit of the state, as owner, but for the benefit of the working class as a whole. In China the staff and workers were acclaimed as the 'masters of the enterprise', but this by no means implied that the production unit was under democratic workers' control. The interests of the working class as a whole were represented under state-socialism by the Communist Party, and this was embodied in the leading role of the Communist Party Secretary, heading the Party Committee of the enterprise, under the supervision of the Party Committee of the appropriate municipal, regional or national level, in monitoring the management of the enterprise. The dual system of control, through the state and Party apparatuses, and the dual authority of General Director and Party Secretary, contained the potential for conflict and confusion, which was resolved at various times and places by assigning primary authority to one or the other. But in practice state, management and Party apparatuses were so closely intertwined that they rarely pulled in different directions, and the demands of production were generally assigned absolute priority over all other considerations.

The management system under state-socialism can be characterised as 'authoritarian-paternalist'. The prosperity of the enterprise depended on the political connections and negotiating skills of the general director, which determined the resources available to the enterprise to achieve its plan targets, and the ability of the general director to organise production to achieve those targets. A prosperous enterprise was able to provide good housing and generous social and welfare benefits, the allocation of which provided an important instrument for managing the labour force and maintaining labour motivation, and credit for the prosperity of the enterprise was attributed to the director.

Trade unions had existed as workers' organisations prior to the revolution in all state-socialist countries. In Vietnam the trade unions played a leading role in the formation of the Communist Party and were mostly under Party control, but in China and Russia some of the strongest trade unions were politically aligned not with the Communist (Bolshevik) Parties, but with the opposition Guomindang (Mensheviks). In the latter cases a first priority after the revolution was to impose Party control over the trade unions, but even when this had been achieved the question of trade union independence remained an issue through the first decade after the revolution. On the one hand, some prominent trade union leaders pressed for the trade unions to play an independent role as representative of workers' interests in relation to enterprise management and even the workers' state. On the other hand, the Party leadership insisted that the trade unions should not represent the sectional interests of particular groups of workers, but should be subordinated to the interests of the whole of the working class, represented by the Communist Party. Eventually the latter view prevailed.

In the mature state-socialist society, trade unions were constituted as representatives of the interests of the whole of the working class, under the leadership of the Communist Party, and as such were an integral part of the Party-state apparatus, their structure closely mirroring that of the Party-state. In the Soviet Union the trade unions were organised on the territorial-branch principle, with one union for each industrial sector with its own regional organisations under the regional trade union council. In China and Vietnam there were branch unions for particular state-owned industries organised on a national basis, such as the railways, but the unions were basically organised on a territorial basis, with the hierarchy from municipal and county trade unions to the regional trade union, to the national union based in the national capital.

The trade unions played some role in the formulation of state labour, social and welfare policies, and even on occasion lobbied within the Party-state apparatus for improved wages, welfare and working conditions or for the introduction of particular laws and regulations, generally on the grounds of providing stronger incentives rather than pressing class interests. Similarly, the primary functions of the trade unions in the workplace were not to represent the interests of workers, but to maintain labour discipline, encourage the production drive and administer a large part of the state housing, social and welfare apparatus, the benefits of which were delivered through the workplace as a means of stimulating labour motivation. Thus the trade unions did not represent the workforce in opposition to management, but represented the workforce as a whole, all of whom were union members. The trade unions were primarily an instrument for controlling the working class, but they did play some protective role in the workplace, representing individual workers in the event of disputes over such management failings as the miscalculation of wages or pension entitlements or illegal punishment by the employer, or even in problems outside work such as housing problems, disputes with neighbours or marital difficulties. However, an aggrieved worker would more typically approach an appropriate manager or the Communist Party Secretary rather than a trade union representative to resolve a work-related problem.

In theory the trade unions were supposed to ensure that managers achieved their production targets through the rational organisation of production, rather than through the over-exploitation of workers, so they were supposed to enforce the protective clauses of the labour law or relevant regulations and to maintain minimal standards of health and safety at work. In practice these tasks often went by default as the priority of production over-ruled all other considerations. Overall, the role of the trade unions was to harmonise the interests of labour and management rather than to represent the interests of their members in opposition to management. The primary function of the trade union as a mediator was not to transmit the wishes of its members upwards, but to explain Party and management policy to its members. As far as most trade union members were concerned, the main role of the trade union was its allocation of housing, social and welfare benefits and material assistance. However, the trade union rarely got any credit for its beneficence. Since the trade union was responsible for the allocation of resources in short supply, it bore the brunt of complaints about the inadequacy of both the quantity and quality of provision and was always suspected of privileging managers and its own officials in allocation.

It is important to emphasise that state-socialist trade unions were fundamentally different from trade unions in a capitalist society, however much the latter might collaborate with employers and be integrated into corporatist structures of participation. State-socialist trade unions had a directive rather than a representative role and they played virtually no part in the regulation of the employment relationship, since the terms and conditions of employment were determined administratively by the state and embodied in a plethora of laws, resolutions, regulations, guidelines and directives. State-socialist countries embodied the rights of labour in an extensive array of protective legislation covering, often in minute detail, the terms and conditions of labour. However, this array of protective legislation by no means constituted an obligatory framework for the conduct of labour relations; instead, it served as a discretionary instrument for confining managerial authority within the limits of Party policy. The priority in the state-socialist system was production, and if adherence to the law impeded production, it was the law that had to give way. The law was not permitted to challenge the 'leading and guiding role of the Party', so 'in the hands of the Party élite, the law became a flexible tool… . Law proved incapable of restraining the powerful' (Hendley 1996: 4). Within the state-socialist system protective laws were not so much juridical instruments as ethical ideals, a conception of the law which persists today. A senior Ministry of Labour, Invalids and Social Affairs (MOLISA) official in Vietnam acknowledged that labour law was routinely violated, but described the Labour Code as 'what we would like to achieve, but not now', while a senior VGCL official similarly described the collective agreement as 'a statement of aspirations, while the individual contract is the basis of labour relations'. The Communist Party dream in Vietnam is that 'by 2020, all aspects of social life will be regulated by laws and codes' ('Realising Resolutions of the Ninth Party Congress', Tap chi Cong san (*Communist Review*), 20, 15 October 2004).

The transition to capitalism in the former state-socialist countries has transformed the environment in which the trade unions operate and has undermined, to differing degrees, the pillars on which their activity was constructed. In particular, the transition from a command economy to a market economy removed the enterprise from direct state control so that trade unions, at least in the workplace, ceased to be agents of the state regulation and control of the labour force, but instead mediated the relationship between the labour force and the employer. The corollary of this structural transformation was the transformation of the trade unions from governmental to non-governmental organisations, from agents of the state to representatives of employees, although in China and Vietnam, unlike Russia, the trade unions have continued formally to function as representatives of the interests of the whole of the working class, under the leadership of the Communist Party.

The transition to a socialist market economy

The first stage of the integration of the state-socialist regimes into the global capitalist economy in all three countries was marked by reforms in the system of economic management introduced in the mid-1980s, which were later rationalised as an attempt to introduce a 'socialist market economy'.[1] While private entrepreneurship and foreign investment would be permitted, or even encouraged, medium and large enterprises would remain under state ownership but would be freed to determine their own economic activity, subject to the penalties and rewards of the market. This involved the replacement of the administrative-command system by market relations and the devolution of decision-making to the enterprise. However, wage rates in state-owned enterprises continued to be determined centrally, although enterprises acquired some discretion in hiring and firing and in the payment of bonuses from their own funds.

According to the theory of the 'socialist market economy', the state enterprise continued to be a unitary body, securing the social reproduction of its labour collective and serving the interests of society as a whole. In the Soviet Union and China the transition to the 'socialist market economy' entailed a reduction in the authority of the Party in the workplace and the resurrection/introduction of workplace 'democracy' to supplement or replace the weakened monitoring role of the Party-state, to harness the initiative of workers and to check managerial corruption and incompetence.[2] In China, the Staff and Workers' Congress had been re-established in 1981, following the Yugoslav model, to institutionalise workers' participation in management (and to enhance the role of the workplace trade unions) and, in state

---

[1]   We use the term 'socialist market economy' to refer to the development strategy employed in all three countries until about the early 1990s. The term 'socialist market economy' was never officially adopted in the Soviet Union under Gorbachev, although it was used by commentators to rationalise the pragmatic reforms of *perestroika*. The term was only officially adopted in China in October 1992 at the XIVth Congress of the CCP, ironically just as the market economy was about to lose any 'socialist' characteristics, although it had already been used by Deng Xiaoping in an interview in the *People's Daily* as early as November 1979 (http://english.peopledaily.com.cn/dengxp/vol2/text/b1370.html). In Vietnam it was only formally adopted as the 'socialist-oriented market economy' at the Ninth Party Congress in 2001.

[2]   In both cases the introduction of representative institutions was strongly influenced by fears induced by the rise of Solidarity in Poland, although the initial plans had preceded the Polish events (Moses 1987; Wilson 1990).

enterprises, was granted extensive formal powers to approve (or reject) management's plans and managerial appointments (Henley and Nyaw 1986). In Russia the 1983 Law on Labour Collectives established the elected Labour Collective Council (STK) as an advisory body with very limited powers. The Law on State Enterprise (Association) of July 1987 strengthened the STK, which had the power to 'decide all production and social questions', although the Law simultaneously reaffirmed the traditional principle of one-man management. The extensive patronage network of unions and management, and the persistence of the state repressive apparatus within the enterprise, meant that in most cases the STK and the Workers' Congress remained firmly under management control (Clarke et al. 1993: 114–20; Goodall and Warner 1997: 586; Ng and Warner 1998: 81–94; Taylor, Chang and Li 2003: chapter Six; Warner 1995: 30), although some commentators in both Russia and China entertained hopes that the STK and Workers' Congress might be transformed into institutions of democratic workers' control. In Vietnam there was no such weakening of the role of the Party in state enterprises and the trade union and the Party organisation continued to work together with the Youth League and enterprise director in the 'group of four' which managed the enterprise.

The transition to a socialist market economy freed state enterprises from the detailed regulation that marked the administrative-command system of economic management, but it also created space for the creation of new private enterprises and for foreign investment. The initial idea was that new private enterprises would be permitted to fill the gaps in the state-owned economy, particularly in the provision of services and, particularly in China and Vietnam, in agriculture. It was expected that these would be small owner-managed enterprises with at most a handful of employees so, although they might provide low wages and bad working conditions, they would not mark a significant transformation of labour relations in the society as a whole and they did not raise any issues of trade union representation. As Deng Xiaoping noted reassuringly in an interview in 1979, 'the state-owned sector and collectively owned sector are still the mainstay of our economy' (http://www.china.org.cn/english/features/dengxiaoping/103388.htm).   Foreign investment was expected to be on a much larger scale, providing access to foreign technology, management skills and markets, but at first was confined to joint-ventures with an indigenous state enterprise in which the powers of the foreign owners were confined both by state regulatory bodies and by the social structure of the indigenous partner, including the inherited trade union organisation.

According to the theory of the 'socialist market economy' there is no conflict of interests between management and labour, because managers of state enterprises are not the representatives of capitalist owners, but the custodians of the interests of the enterprise as a whole. This led to a considerable ambiguity regarding the role of the trade union. Under the 'socialist market economy', the trade union was not supposed to represent the interests of employees in opposition to the employers, but was still supposed to represent the interests of the entire 'labour collective' (*danwei*), the enterprise as a whole. Nevertheless, article 2.1 of the 1990 Vietnamese trade union law defines the responsibility of the trade union to 'represent and protect the rights and legitimate interests of the workers', the Soviet Labour Code and the 1990 Soviet Trade Union Law assigned to the trade union responsibility for the 'defence of the labour and socio-economic rights' of employees, while in China the trade unions are supposed to 'represent the legitimate rights and interests of workers and staff members' (1994 Labour Law, article 7, and 2001 Trade Union Law, article 6), although at this time in practice in all three countries trade union membership was still confined to state enterprises.

The functional ambiguity of the trade unions was particularly apparent in the relationship between the trade union and the bodies established for the workers' participation in management in China and the Soviet Union, which were established unambiguously to represent the interests of the enterprise as a whole. In China the non-adversarial character of the trade union was emphasised by the fact that the trade union committee was mandated to serve as the executive of the Staff and Workers' Congress between meetings, although it has been suggested that one motive for establishing the Workers' Congress in parallel with the trade union was that it was seen as a 'less threatening avenue for democratisation' than more powerful unions (Wilson 1990: 265).[1] In Russia, the Labour Collective Council was established as a parallel structure to the trade union, duplicating many of its functions. However, this reflected the lack of confidence of the regime in the capacity of the enterprise trade union rather than any anxiety that the trade union would adopt an adversarial role (Moses 1987), and indeed it was the Labour Collective Councils, rather than the trade union committees, that were more likely to become a vehicle for workers' protest in the late 1980s (Christensen 1999). The duplication of functions did not last for long in the Soviet Union, since the powers of the Labour Collective Council were markedly curtailed by the 1990 amendment of the Law on State Enterprise and the institution itself was effectively abolished by the 1991 Privatisation Law.

The trade unions (and behind them the Party) in all three countries were well aware that the transition to a socialist market economy implied that they would have to play a more active role in representing the distinctive interests of workers in the transition. Reform stimulated workers' aspirations, which were often thwarted by increasing inequality and insecurity and, above all, a sense of injustice, leading to increasing levels of spontaneous worker protest outside and often against the official trade unions. In all three countries there were moves to declare the independence of the trade unions from the Party-state. In China the subordination of the trade unions to the Party-state has not gone without question. During the early 1950s the question of

---

[1] A number of commentators have suggested that the Workers' Congress system was introduced in the 1980s precisely to contain any display of independence by the unions (Ng and Warner 1998: 82–4). Ng and Warner (1998: 84–5) note the intense role conflicts implicit in this combination of functions.

the independence of the trade unions in the new China was a matter for debate, and the ACFTU vainly tried to assert an increased measure of independence again in the mid-1950s and the mid-1960s. The issue was raised once more in the 1980s, as the impact of economic reform made itself felt, with inflation eroding living standards and an increase in wildcat strikes and protests highlighting the failure of ACFTU to protect its members' interests in the face of economic reform (Howell 2003: 113). The eleventh ACFTU Congress in October 1988 called for 'the establishment of an independent, sovereign trade union with a high degree of democracy [and] which workers could trust' (*Workers' Daily*, 29 October 1988) including greater independence for the unions to enable them to head off the threat of independent worker organisations. The ACFTU did not publicly declare support for the student demands for negotiation with the government in 1989, but did make a cash-donation to hunger-striking students in Tiananmen Square, but the crackdown, which was particularly directed at independent worker organisation, immediately closed off the avenue of trade union independence and brought ACFTU firmly back under the wing of the Party (Wilson 1990).

In Russia the All Union Central Council of Trade Unions (VTsSPS) declared its independence of the Party-state as early as 1987, although at this time the change reflected the desire of the conservative trade union leadership to dissociate itself from more radical economic reform rather than any aspiration to transform the trade unions into more representative bodies. The independence of the trade unions from the Party was sealed in 1990, following the great wave of strikes in the summer of 1989, by the amendment of the Soviet Constitution and the passage of the Soviet Trade Union Law, which defined the trade unions as independent self-governing bodies and (perhaps inadvertently) allowed trade union pluralism. In Vietnam the trade unions declared a degree of independence from the Party-state at their 1988 Congress, at which they changed their name from the Vietnam Federation of Trade Unions to the Vietnam General Confederation of Labour, expressing their intention to broaden and democratise their activity and to extend their organisation from state enterprises to the private and collective (and later foreign-invested) sectors (Chan and Nörlund 1998: 184), although their role was still defined legally and constitutionally as being under the leadership of the Communist Party.

The fact that the ambiguous status of the trade union, as representative of employees and at the same time as representative of the enterprise as a whole, did not come to the fore is partly a result of the fact that trade unions still played no part in the determination of wages, but it is also indicative of the degree to which the trade union continued to be integrated into the management structure (Ashwin and Clarke 2002: chapter Eight; Chan 2000a: 39; Ding, Goodall and Warner 2002: 445–7; Taylor, Chang and Li 2003; Zhu Y. 1995; Zhu and Campbell 1996). Far from undermining this integration, the transition to a 'socialist market economy' if anything deepened the dependence of the enterprise trade union on management because the trade union was no longer able to rely to the same degree on the authority of the Party committee to back any assertion of independence from management, while it had not been able to develop a new basis for its authority in the collective organisation and collective representation of employees. For all the dramatic changes in the external environment in which enterprises operated, the social organisation of the state enterprise itself, and correspondingly the role of the trade union, barely changed at all.[1]

The idea that harmony could prevail in the socialist market economy was shattered in 1989 by the eruption of radical workers' protests in the Soviet Union and the willingness of workers to join, influence and defend the pro-democracy protests in China. In both cases, the workers' protest was launched outside and against the established trade unions, with the formation of independent worker organisations, bringing to the fore the fact that the official trade unions were not able to articulate the grievances of their members. The reaction of the Party-state to these events in Russia and in China was very different, which had important implications for the role of the trade unions in the transition to an unambiguously, even if in China as yet undeclared, capitalist market economy.

In Russia, having rejected conservative pressure for repression in 1989, Gorbachev sought to harness the workers' protests to generate pressure for '*perestroika* from below' through the reform of the trade unions, which implied the democratisation of trade union structures and an end to the 'democratic centralism' that had secured their subordination to the Party (Ashwin and Clarke 2002: 30–3). In the coal-mining regions new trade union elections were held with the aim of bringing the leaders of the strike committees into the trade union apparatus to provide the latter with new blood although, as the renewed strike wave of 1991 showed, the radicals who chose to enter the traditional unions were soon assimilated into the bureaucratic trade union apparatus (Clarke, Fairbrother and Borisov 1995: chapter Two). In practice the reform of the trade unions at the end of the 1980s had only a marginal effect, even the unions' official history acknowledging that changes on the ground were few and far between as officials continued in their habitual ways (Gritsenko, Kadeikina and Makukhina 1999: 316–20) and militant workers created their own strike committees and 'alternative' trade unions. More significantly, the strike waves of 1989 and 1991 destroyed the myth of the 'socialist' market economy and heralded the transition to a fully capitalist market economy in the wake of the collapse of the Soviet Union.

In China, the reaction to the workers' involvement in the democracy movement, which had not extended to large-scale strike action, was one of a tightening of control of non-governmental organisations and the severe repression of any attempts to organise outside the official trade unions. The official trade unions, which had acquired a degree of independence and some of whose cadres had participated in the

---

[1]   It is noteworthy that all the examples of trade unions independent of management that we have managed to find in China and Vietnam are in joint-ventures, where the trade union has the backing of a Party organisation that is itself independent of management.

protest actions, were immediately brought under much stricter Party control (Li 2000: chapter Three; Taylor, Chang and Li 2003: chapter Two; White 1996). The authority of Party secretaries in state-owned enterprises, which had been removed in 1986, was also reasserted at this time (Taylor, Chang and Li 2003: chapter Three). At the same time, however, the Party-state also appreciated the importance of the unions as a means of maintaining social and political stability in a period of rapid social change, so the official trade unions' status was increased. Their strict subordination to the Party did not necessarily imply that they would serve merely as an instrument of the state. President Ni Zhifu of the ACFTU noted after the Tiananmen events, anticipating developments to come, that 'the trade unions must avoid simply acting as agents of the government and work independently so as to increase the attraction to workers and enjoy more confidence from the workers, leaving no opportunity to those who attempt to organise "independent trade unions"' (Xinhua News Agency, 25 July 1989, cited in Ng and Warner 1998: 55). Thus, by 1992 the ACFTU was lobbying actively for measures to protect workers' interests and promoted its own position in debates regarding the legislative and policy framework of reform, with considerable success (Chan 1993: 52–5). In particular, ACFTU pressed strongly for the collective regulation of labour relations, against their regulation on the basis of individual contracts that was favoured by the Ministry of Labour, and provision for collective contracts was made in the new 1992 Trade Union Law (Clarke, Lee and Li 2004; Ogden 2000). The significance of the trade unions to the regime was endorsed when the ACFTU President, Wei Jianxing, who had made active efforts to strengthen the trade unions' influence and their role in protecting workers' interests since his appointment in 1993, was elevated to the Standing Committee of the Politburo of the Central Committee of the CCP in 1997.

The Tiananmen events in China initially brought reform to a halt, as the conservative elements in the leadership gained the upper hand. However, following Deng's Southern Tour in 1992, reform was resumed at an accelerated pace, with the official proclamation of the 'modern enterprise system', a euphemism for the 'modern capitalist corporation'. While foreign capitalists had already been welcomed and private capitalists encouraged, now state enterprises would be transformed into independent state-owned corporations. It was not long before corporatisation was followed by privatisation, as the shares in publicly owned corporations and Township and Village Enterprises (TVEs) began to be sold off, with only the commanding heights of the economy to be retained in state hands.

In Russia, too, the 1989 events strengthened the hand of the conservative opponents of perestroika but, after two years of prevarication, the failure of the putsch of August 1991 and the success of Yeltsin's counter-coup opened the floodgates of reform. In both China and Russia, the decentralisation of state management of the economy had stimulated the appetite of some enterprise directors for independence and provoked widespread dissatisfaction among workers, which was directed not at enterprise management, but at the state as the ultimate employer. The response of the state was not to reverse economic reform, to take matters back into its own hands, but to abdicate responsibility for the management of state enterprises and to initiate a programme of corporatisation and privatisation that would seal the independence of enterprise management and give them full responsibility as employers for their relations with their employees (Clarke 1990).

Vietnam initiated the process of reform (*doi moi*) in December 1986, but proceeded more cautiously than did China and the Soviet Union in the reform of state-owned enterprises (SOEs) as the legalisation of private enterprise resulted in a rapid growth of small businesses in agriculture and services. However, state-owned enterprises came under severe pressure at the end of the decade as they faced subsidy cuts in the wake of the withdrawal of Soviet aid. Between 1988 and 1992 almost a third of SOE workers, 800 000 people, predominantly women and mostly from small SOEs, were laid off without, it seems, provoking significant protest as many of them returned to the countryside or found jobs in the booming new private sector (Klump and Bonschab 2004: 31). The Vietnamese regime observed the political turmoil in the rest of the Communist world in 1989 and reversed its tentative political liberalisation, but did not experience significant worker protest and did not relax control of the state sector of the economy.

In Russia the soviet administrative-command system of management collapsed to be replaced by a 'wild market' system in which privatisation only gave juridical recognition to the *de facto* independence of state enterprises. In China, and more gradually in Vietnam, the transition to a 'socialist market economy' cautiously but inexorably developed into a transition to a capitalist market economy, with centralised regulation of the enterprise being replaced by managerial autonomy in economic decision-making. Whatever the form of its ownership, the reproduction of the enterprise was immediately conditional on its ability to cover its costs and to realise a profit to finance its future development, although bank lending and the accumulation of debt, including the non-payment of wages and social insurance contributions, continued to sustain many an unprofitable enterprise in all three countries. The institutions of workplace democracy were at least implicitly a barrier to managerial prerogatives, though management control of these bodies was rarely seriously challenged. Nevertheless, the first stirrings of independent activism within the Labour Collective Councils in the Soviet Union provoked their suppression. The significance of the Workers' Congress progressively declined in state enterprises in China, while they were never established in the private and foreign-invested sectors and were optional bodies with limited powers in joint-ventures. The erosion and abolition of the institutions of workplace democracy implied an increasing role for the trade union as representative of the interests of the employees of the enterprise in negotiation with enterprise management (Zhang 1997). However, to fill this role effectively would imply a fundamental transformation in the character of the enterprise trade union. This presented radically new challenges to the trade unions, which had to transform themselves from 'the transmission belt from the Communist

Party to the masses', in Lenin's phrase, to the representative of the rights and interests of the working class.

The new role of trade unions in representing the rights and interests of workers by no means implied that trade unions should represent those interests in opposition to the employer, let alone in opposition to the state. Thus, in China and Vietnam the trade unions remained legally and constitutionally under the leadership of the Communist Party and any attempts at independent worker organisation were severely repressed. In Russia the potential of trade union independence was neutralised by the commitment of the traditional trade unions to the principles of 'social partnership' with employers and the state to which they were forcefully confined by pressure from the Presidential administration and regional authorities.

Employment relations in a capitalist market economy

The transition from a 'socialist' to a fully capitalist market economy was marked by the gradual withdrawal of direct subsidies and the removal of the remaining administrative control of state-owned enterprises, institutionalised through their transformation into state corporations or joint-stock companies and increasingly by their subsequent privatisation. This meant that henceforth managers had to ensure the solvency, if not the profitability, of the enterprise on the basis of its economic activities, with insolvent enterprises threatened with bankruptcy and their employees with unemployment. Alongside the privatisation of state enterprises, the restrictions on private and wholly foreign-owned enterprises were eased.

Within the state-socialist system the interests of both management and the trade union were supposed to be identical and their identification was reinforced by the subordination of both to the Party-state. With the transition to a capitalist market economy, the interests of the parties diverge: the key interest of the employers is in maximising their profits. The prosperity of the enterprise is no longer a sufficient condition for the prosperity of its employees (or of the national economy): management may, and increasingly does, seek to secure the prosperity of the enterprise by selling off facilities, holding down or not paying wages and social insurance benefits, compromising workers' health and safety, laying off workers, intensifying labour and extending the working day. During the 1990s, the leadership of the Chinese Party-state was reluctant to unleash the managers of state enterprises for fear of consequent social unrest and reform was regularly checked by 'repairing measures' to keep management in check (Li 2000). In Vietnam the government trod cautiously in reforming the larger state enterprises, delaying privatisation and supporting insolvent enterprises through the banking system. In Russia the government showed no such restraint as the administrative-command system of regulation collapsed and enterprises seized their independence, but complete economic collapse and social turmoil was averted as insolvent enterprises were sustained by inflation, subsidised energy and the accumulation of debt.

The transition to a capitalist market economy had fundamental implications for the employment relation in state-owned enterprises. In place of the traditional employment for life as a servant of the state, the employment relation would become a contractual relation between the employer and the employee, and this is necessarily a relation between two parties who have conflicting interests, with clear implications for the role of the trade union. If state enterprises were to be competitive they also had to shed their obligations to provide housing and comprehensive welfare services to their employees, to be replaced by privatised and/or municipalised housing and contributory social and health insurance, depriving the trade unions of an important part of their traditional role.

The emergence of new private and foreign-owned enterprises had even more radical implications for the employment relation since many of these enterprises were operating in highly competitive labour-intensive sectors in which profits could only be made by holding down wages, neglecting health and safety, extending working hours and intensifying labour. These enterprises had none of the traditional institutions that had constrained management in state enterprises and many had no trade union even to pretend to defend the rights and represent the interests of their employees.

In all three countries a raft of legislation was introduced during the 1990s to regulate the employment relation, including labour laws which prescribed the minimum terms and conditions of employment in some detail, trade union laws which defined the role, rights and obligations of trade unions, and labour dispute settlement procedures. In all three countries provision was made for binding collective agreements to be signed between the employer and employee representatives, and in Russia and Vietnam, though not in China, the laws defined quite stringent conditions under which it was possible for a trade union legally to call a strike. In all three countries the passage of the legislation was by no means a formality, and the trade unions in each case were very active in pressing for their favoured clauses.

The dismantling of the administrative regulation of labour relations by the Party-state in China has been accompanied by the introduction of a new institutional framework for the regulation of industrial relations. The new legislative and institutional framework for industrial relations in China was initially developed piecemeal and experimentally through the issue of various instructions and directives before being consolidated in legislation in the early 1990s. This new framework has centred on the legal and contractual regulation of labour relations; a system for the tripartite resolution of labour disputes; the development of workplace 'collective consultation' between trade unions and employers and, more recently, a system of 'tripartite consultation'.

The 1950 Chinese Trade Union Law was extensively amended in 1992, to define the role of the trade union in representing the 'legitimate rights and interests' of the workforce, and amended again in 2001, in anticipation of the problems of rising unemployment expected to arise with China's entry into the WTO. The Trade Union

Law, in all its versions, determined the subordination of ACFTU to the leadership of the Communist Party, enforced the legal monopoly of ACFTU and prescribed the hierarchical subordination of all trade union organisations to ACFTU. The 1992 Law specified that the 'trade unions shall safeguard the legitimate rights and interests of the workers and staff members', but subject to 'protecting the overall interests of the entire Chinese people' (article 6) and determined that they 'shall assist the people's governments in their work and safeguard... the socialist state power of the people's democratic dictatorship led by the working class' (article 5). The Law also prescribed the action of the trade union in the event of a 'work stoppage' or go-slow, which was, 'together with the management or the parties concerned, [to] strive for a settlement through consultation on any demands made by the workers and staff members and *that are rational and can be met*, so as to restore the normal order of production as soon as possible' (article 25, our emphasis).

The 2001 revision was claimed by Zhang Chunsheng, Deputy Director of the Legislative Affairs Commission of the NPC Standing Committee, which had drafted the revisions in collaboration with ACFTU, to have been 'to better protect the rights of workers and maintain social stability while promoting reform and economic development." (*Xinhua*, 22 August 2001, cited in IHLO 2001: 1). The promotion of reform and economic development was defined as a central task of the trade unions, which 'shall take economic construction as the centre, adhere to the socialist road, uphold the people's democratic dictatorship, abide by the leadership of the Chinese Communist Party, adhere to Marxist-Leninism Mao Zedong Thought and Deng Xiaoping Theory, persevere in reform and opening' (addition to article 4). The revision strengthened the position of the trade union in 'consultations' with the employer and in mediating to protect workers' legitimate rights, empowered higher-level unions to participate in establishing a trade union organisation where none existed, and provided protection of trade union officers from dismissal without the agreement of the majority of the labour force or its representatives. The revision also introduced the principle of trade union elections into law: 'Trade union committees at various levels shall be democratically elected at members' assemblies or members' congresses ... . Trade union members' assemblies or congresses have the right to remove or recall the representatives or members of trade union committees they elected' (article 9) and provided for trade union participation in tripartite bodies. The revision also slightly modified the role of the trade union in the event of a work stoppage or go-slow, so that now it had not merely to 'strive for a settlement through consultation', but it 'shall represent staff and workers in consultation with the enterprise, institution or relevant party, and shall reflect the opinions and demands of staff and workers as well as raise solutions. The enterprise or institution shall strive for a settlement with the *reasonable* demands made by the staff and workers. The trade union shall strive hard in its task to assist the enterprise or institution to restore the normal order of production as soon as possible' (article 27, our emphasis).

The 1994 Chinese Labour Law was 'formulated ... in order to protect the legitimate rights and interests of labourers, readjust the labour relationship, establish and safeguard a labour system suited to the socialist market economy, and promote economic development and social progress' (section 1) and prescribed that 'trade unions shall represent and safeguard the legitimate rights and interests of labourers, and independently conduct their activities in accordance with the law' (section 7). The Law prescribed the form of the individual labour contract which should be signed between the worker and the employing organisation, and specified the conditions under which an employee can be dismissed. If the dismissed employee 'applies for arbitration or brings in a lawsuit, the trade union shall render him support and assistance in accordance with the law' (section 30). On the insistence of ACFTU the Law also provided for a collective contract, which 'shall be concluded by the trade union on behalf of the staff and workers with the enterprise; in an enterprise where the trade union has not yet been set up, such contract shall be also concluded by the representatives elected by the staff and workers with the enterprise' (section 33), but this does not legitimate the establishment of an independent workers' organisation. The Law set a maximum 8-hour working day and average 44-hour working week, but provided for a limited extension of working hours 'after consultation with the trade union and labourers', defined overtime rates (sections 36, 41, 44) and introduced a system of legal minimum wages (article 48). The Law also enjoined the state to introduce a social insurance system (article 70) and to develop social welfare provision (article 76). Responsibility for monitoring the enforcement of the Law was assigned to the Labour Department, but the 'trade union at various levels shall, in accordance with the law, safeguard the legitimate rights and interests of labourers, and supervise the implementation of laws, rules and regulations on labour by the employing units' (section 88).

The 1994 Labour Law also provided legislative foundations for the system of mediation and arbitration for individual and collective labour disputes, which had first been introduced in 1986. Conciliation committees, chaired by the trade union, were to be established in enterprises. If the dispute is not resolved through conciliation, it can be referred to the local (tripartite) Labour Disputes Arbitration Committee, which is chaired by the local Labour Department. A decision of the arbitrator can subsequently be appealed to the Civil Court. Disputes that arise around the conclusion of a collective agreement should be resolved on the initiative of the Labour Department and disputes around its implementation are immediately referred to the Arbitration Committee.

As in China, the new system of labour legislation in Vietnam was based on the definition and enforcement of the rights of employees as defined by the law, their contracts of employment and collective agreements, rather than on the explicit recognition and regulation of the conflicting interests of employers and employees. This approach defines the role of the trade unions as being to represent the rights and 'legitimate interests' (rather than the self-defined interests) of their members, with a

Labour Code that offers a high degree of protection to Vietnamese workers and a trade union law that encourages trade union organisation and the negotiation of legally binding collective agreements. Article 12 of the 1994 Labour Code, amended in 2002 (Socialist Republic of Vietnam, 1994, 2002), specifies that 'trade unions shall, in conjunction with state bodies and economic and social organisations, look after and protect the rights of employees; and inspect and supervise the implementation of the provisions of the laws on labour'. Article 2.1 of the 1990 Trade Union Law defines the responsibility of the trade union to 'represent and protect the rights and legitimate interests of the workers' and the trade union is responsible for monitoring the observance of relevant laws (article 9.1) and for representing workers in the negotiation of collective agreements (article 11.1) and in negotiations to resolve labour disputes (article 11.3), but the Law also makes the trade union 'responsible for liaising with the state in order to increase production, create jobs and improve the standard of living of workers'. Other articles similarly reaffirm the traditional participation of the trade union, 'under the leadership of the Vietnamese Communist Party' (article 1.1), in various aspects of enterprise and state management and reaffirm its responsibility for organising production competitions and sporting, recreational, tourist and cultural activities (Socialist Republic of Vietnam, 1990). The Labour Code only applies to those 'who are working on the basis of a labour contract'. This means that it does not apply to state employees and officials, members of co-operatives or those who are formally self-employed, though they may be in a sub-contracting relationship with an employer. Moreover, those on contracts of three months or less are not covered by social insurance or any collective agreements, although serial short-term contracts are prohibited: anybody working for more than a year is entitled to a long-term contract. In addition the union constitution excludes those with contracts of less than six months from union membership.

The collapse of the Soviet regime and the introduction of formally democratic institutions in Russia were reflected in the legal and institutional framework for industrial relations, which is on paper much more liberal than those of China and Vietnam, but these changes had already been initiated under Communist Party rule, prior to the collapse of the Soviet Union. The Soviet trade union federation, VTsSPS, was reconstituted as a new General Confederation of Trades Unions in October 1990, as a federation of independent trade unions in which the branch and republican union organisations had a greater degree of autonomy and in which the trade unions were formally separated from Party and state bodies, a separation which was confirmed by the USSR Law on Trade Unions of 10 December 1990. At the same time, it was decided to establish a Republican trade union organisation in Russia, the only Union Republic which had hitherto not had its own organisation. The Federation of Independent Trade Unions of Russia (FNPR) was founded in October 1990 as a voluntary association of trade unions 'independent of state and economic bodies, political and social organisations, not accountable to them and not under their control'. The 1990 Law on Trade Unions defined a legal procedure for the establishment of a trade union for the first time, providing legal protection for any properly constituted trade union, so allowing freedom of association and trade union pluralism.

The Soviet Union prided itself on the fact that the legal rights and protection accorded to labour were the most advanced in the world. The 1972 Soviet Labour Code minutely prescribed the terms and conditions of employment to be enjoyed by soviet workers. The code laid down pay norms and tariff scales; the (strict) conditions under which employees could be transferred to different posts; protection of workers from arbitrary dismissal; the length of the working day; the normal length of the working week; the length and timing of rest periods, meal breaks, days off and vacations, including special privileges for certain categories of worker; restrictions on night work, shift work and overtime; the payment due for any extra work undertaken; detailed health and safety provisions, and so on. However, these measures were not designed to protect workers so much as to check the tendency of management to seek to achieve the plan by intensifying labour and lengthening the working day to the detriment of the health of the labour force and at the risk of provoking conflict, rather than by organising work more rationally. At the same time, the irrationality of the soviet system meant that the plan could only be achieved by precisely such measures, particularly during the regular storming at the end of the month. Thus the contradiction between the extensive legal rights and protection enjoyed by workers and the reality of their situation was only an expression of the fundamental irrationality of the soviet system as a whole.

It might have been expected that the collapse of the soviet system would have been accompanied by an extensive revision of the legal regulation of the terms and conditions of labour and of the rights of trade unions to bring them into line with the changing economic and social reality. However, apart from the 1992 Law on Collective Agreements, some minor amendments to the Labour Code, concerned primarily with its application to changing property and contractual forms, and *ad hoc* and inconsistent Presidential decrees and government resolutions, the legal framework of industrial relations until the end of 1995 remained that of the soviet period. This is partly because this framework, which had proved its worth as a means of defusing conflict and regulating labour relations, was deeply embedded in the practice and expectations of trade unionists and workers. Thus the new alternative trade unions which emerged after 1987 continued to work within the traditional framework, seeking to achieve their aims not by building a membership-based organisation, but by employing lawyers and appealing individual cases to the courts, taking disputes out of the workplace and into the labyrinthine procedures of the soviet legal system. While trade unions and workers' organisations lacked the strength to enforce their rights within the workplace, the legal codification of those rights presented few limitations on employers. And while trade unions and workers' organisations continued to pursue disputes through the courts on an individual basis, with long delays and largely without effect, they were unlikely to develop effective workplace organisation.

Article 226 of the Labour Code, as amended in 1992, continued to define the trade union essentially as a part of the state: trade unions were to represent the interests of their members, but their rights were defined primarily in relation to their participation in the formulation, implementation and monitoring of labour legislation and their management of the state welfare and social insurance system. The extensive powers enjoyed by the trade unions were and remain powers delegated to them by the state to perform state functions rather than powers won by the trade unions in pursuit of their members' interests. The state has taken over some of these powers, for example in relation to the control of social insurance and the establishment of a state labour inspectorate, but the trade unions continue to administer the distribution of social insurance benefits and monitor health and safety and the law provides for the continued collaboration of the trade union with the new state agencies in monitoring the observance of labour law and health and safety regulations.

A second reason why reform of labour and trade union legislation was constantly postponed was the struggle for power and influence between the new and the old trade unions, new legislation being one of the daggers that the government could hold over the traditional unions. Following the 1993 Duma election, however, the situation somewhat stabilised, with the new unions having been marginalised and the traditional unions turning their attention away from politics towards the more routine defence of their institutional interests. The discussion of draft laws continued for a period of two years. Some of the drafts issuing from the Ministry of Labour in 1994 massively reduced the rights of trade unions and the protection accorded to employees, even managing to unite the leaders of the new and the traditional unions in their condemnation of the drafts, but it seems that these were intended more as shots across the bows of the traditional trade unions at a time when there was still some anxiety in government circles that they would constitute a significant oppositional force. During hearings and debate through 1995 final versions of the laws were agreed, and at the end of 1995 and beginning of 1996 new laws were introduced concerning trade unions, the settlement of collective labour disputes and, as a revision of the 1992 law, collective agreements, all of which at least maintained and in some cases strengthened the legal rights of trade unions and employees, but government hopes of revising the Labour Code were thwarted. The most contentious issue in the debates around the new labour legislation concerned not the rights of workers but the rights of trade unions, and in particular the privileges enjoyed by the unions affiliated to FNPR over the alternative unions. In all of these debates, FNPR emerged as the unequivocal victor.

A new Law on Procedures for the Resolution of Collective Labour Disputes came into effect in 1995, replacing the 1991 Soviet Law, which had in turn replaced Gorbachev's 1989 Law on Strikes that had been introduced as a panic measure following the 1989 miners' strike. Collective labour disputes only arise as a result of disputes around the conclusion or implementation of a collective agreement. Disputes with the employer where workers unite in support of their individual labour rights are defined as individual labour disputes of each individual employee with the employer and can only be resolved on an individual basis. This means that collective action, such as a strike, cannot be taken even in connection with issues such as the non-payment of wages, unless the collective agreement specifically provides for the timely payment of wages. Even in the case of a collective dispute, the procedures for the resolution of the dispute are strictly prescribed and are very restrictive, making it extremely difficult to organise a strike in conformity with the law, which requires a prior process of conciliation and arbitration and the consent of a majority of the labour force in every establishment affected by the strike decision, although a strike only becomes illegal when it has been judged to be such by the appropriate court. While everybody is guaranteed the right to strike and is protected from disciplinary sanctions for participating in a strike, a work stoppage only qualifies as a strike if it is conducted 'with the aim of resolving a collective labour dispute'. This means that a solidarity strike, a stoppage of work with political demands, or a stoppage of work with demands which do not relate to the collective terms and conditions of work, is not a strike and participants can be punished for absenteeism under the Labour Code. One result of the very restrictive legislation is that the recorded incidence of strikes in Russia is extremely low.

The new post-Soviet Russian Law on Trade Unions was not adopted until 1996. The general philosophy of the 1996 Law was one of social partnership within a framework of tripartism. Article 15.1 of the Law declares that relations of trade unions with employers and state bodies are 'constructed on the basis of social partnership'. The new Law confirmed trade union independence by removing the requirement for a trade union to register with state bodies, so that the state cannot refuse recognition to any trade union. The Law is also voluntaristic in principle, specifying the minimum of obligations on trade unions, leaving them to regulate their internal relations, including conditions of membership, forms of government, formation of primary groups and designation of their representatives according to their own constitution, which has only to meet a set of formal requirements. The sources and use of trade union funds and engagement in political activity are also determined by the union's own constitution, with no right of regulation or control by state bodies, apart from the formidable Russian Tax Inspectorate. Nevertheless, the Law provides for the suspension, banning or liquidation of a trade union for violation of laws or the Russian Constitution, which could include, for example, participation in an illegal strike. That this is no idle threat was shown by the case of the alternative Air Traffic Controllers' Union, which had been threatened with liquidation for supporting an illegal strike in a case brought in the Supreme Court, at that time without any legal grounds, by the General Prosecutor in November 1992. After a farcical trial, which was boycotted by the union leaders, the charges were thrown out, but the union was warned by the judge that a further strike would result in the union's liquidation (Clarke, Fairbrother and Borisov 1995: 339–71).

The revision of the Labour Code was postponed for even longer, as successive governments, in collusion with the International Monetary Fund and the World Bank, proposed ever more draconian neo-liberal revisions of labour legislation, which would remove almost all legal protection for the rights of workers and their trade unions, which were inevitably resisted by both traditional and alternative trade unions and blocked by the parliamentary opposition. A revision which strengthened the protection of workers was passed by parliament in July 1999, only to be vetoed by Yeltsin in November. Yeltsin's resignation and the election of a more compliant Duma in December 1999 put an end to the trading of unrealisable proposals and made it possible for the government to act. Eventually a compromise was achieved between the government and the FNPR which passed through parliament in December 2001. The compromise preserved most of the protective elements of the Soviet Labour Code,[1] while increasing the flexibility of labour contracts, but removed the trade union right to veto management proposals, though it preserved a trade union right to consultation, and, most importantly, it gave an enormous advantage to the traditional FNPR unions over the alternative unions in effectively confining bargaining rights and the right to strike to the representative of the majority of the labour force. It also substantially curtailed the already severely restricted right to strike by requiring that a legal strike required the support of a majority of the entire labour force of the enterprise, so banning strikes by particular sections or professional groups, which had been the primary form of struggle by the alternative trade unions.[2]

The general view outside the FNPR trade unions was that the new framework of industrial relations marked the triumph of the FNPR trade unions, which now enjoy a strongly privileged position as the legally sanctioned representatives of employees within a tripartite industrial relations framework. The Law on Trade Unions and the Law on Collective Agreements confine the right to participate in institutions of social partnership at the federal level to all-Russian trade unions, excluding most of the alternative unions, which are generally enterprise-based. At enterprise level the privileges of the FNPR trade union undermine attempts of employers in private enterprises to substitute their own house 'trade unions', but also restrict attempts of workers to establish their own forms of representation, typically in the form of strike and workers' committees. Similarly, the Law on Collective Labour Disputes recognises the legitimacy of properly organised strikes, with due notice and following

---

[1] In December 2009 the Constitutional Court struck out article 374 of the Labour Code, which protected primary trade union leaders from dismissal without the agreement of a higher trade union body, on the grounds that this provision violated the principle of equality of all citizens before the law.

[2] It is also necessary for there to be an agreed plan of essential work to be carried out in the event of a strike, making it impossible to have a legal strike where such a plan has not been drawn up and adopted.

a conciliation period, but only in the case of *collective* disputes, that is those concerning collective agreements. All disputes concerning issues not included in the collective terms of labour are regarded as individual labour disputes, even if they involve all the employees in an enterprise, which have to be pursued through the channels of resolution of individual disputes and strikes in such cases do not enjoy the protection of the law. Thus participants in wildcat and unofficial strikes or strikes over the non-payment of wages, where that is not included in the collective agreement, enjoy no legal protection.

Industrial relations in a capitalist market economy

The changes in the legal regulation of the employment relation in all three countries adapted the tradition of state-socialist regulation of industrial relations to the emerging capitalist market economy. As under state-socialism, the minimum terms and conditions of labour were specified in elaborate detail in the labour law. The legal minimum was to be supplemented by tripartite agreements at national, regional and sectoral levels and by collective agreements at the level of the enterprise. As in the past, this by no means meant that the real terms and conditions of labour in the workplace corresponded to the law and agreements. Employers continued to flout the law, forcing people to work long hours in unsafe and unhealthy working conditions, usually with impunity. Collective agreements as often as not specified terms inferior to those provided by the labour law and if agreements were flouted, employees had little or no redress. The continued strength of the legal protection of labour is not an indicator of the achievements of employees but of the weakness of employee representation, of the extent of the subordination of trade union organisation to enterprise management and of the inaccessibility of legal redress.

Labour disputes were to be resolved by conciliation, mediation and arbitration, with ultimate appeal to the courts, and priority was given to the resolution of labour disputes on an individual basis. The problem from an industrial relations point of view is that this bureaucratic-legal framework provides a mechanism of tension management through the fragmentation and bureaucratisation of conflict. It does not provide any effective mechanism of employee representation and conflict resolution. The result is that when conflict does erupt and overflows the bureaucratic channels provided there are no effective institutional mechanisms through which such conflict can be peacefully negotiated and resolved.

In all three countries, workers who choose to withdraw their labour in pursuit of a dispute enjoy little or no legal protection from dismissal and could face claims for compensation from the employer. Public order legislation and police intervention similarly restrict the right of workers to engage in other forms of public protest, such as pickets or demonstrations. Thus, for workers in all three countries there is very little space between accommodation to the demands of the employer and confrontation with the forces of the employer and the state.

The central issues in such a system of industrial relations are, first, how the rights and interests of workers are to be represented in establishing the legal minimum terms and conditions of labour and in negotiating collective agreements and, second, how such laws and agreements are to be enforced. In both cases the trade unions have neither the capacity nor the will effectively to achieve either. On the one hand, the trade unions' primary commitment to maintaining social peace prevents them from effectively representing their members. On the other hand, the trade unions' subordination to management in the workplace, where the violations take place, generally prevents them from effectively monitoring the enforcement of the law and agreements.

Social peace and social partnership

In all three countries the rights and interests of workers are nominally represented in negotiations at all levels by the traditional trade unions. In China and Vietnam the traditional unions still abide by the principles of democratic centralism, according to which decisions of higher union bodies are binding on lower bodies, but in Russia the unions are now constructed according to the principles of voluntary association, so lower-level bodies are in principle free to ignore the decisions of higher bodies, even if those decisions are democratically arrived at, though there is the ultimate sanction of suspension or expulsion, which has been applied on rare occasions to lower-level bodies which are chronically in default in their remission of affiliation fees. In all three countries, whatever the change in their formal status and their rhetorical commitment to assuming a representative role, the trade unions by and large continue to operate in their traditional bureaucratic ways. Left to themselves, there was no particular reason for the trade unions to change. Financially, the trade unions did not depend on their membership. The Russian trade unions initially disposed of the income of the state social insurance fund, which they administered, and had enormous property, including prestigious office blocks and associated hotels in the centre of every city, and virtually the whole of the domestic tourist complex. The Chinese and Vietnamese trade unions received a substantial income from a levy on state employers, regardless of trade union membership, were allocated government funds for particular programmes, and had substantial property and commercial interests. Trade union officials could enjoy a comfortable existence continuing to work in traditional ways, issuing instructions, passing around pieces of paper, writing reports, attending meetings, participating in ceremonies and celebrations and working with management to administer the social welfare apparatus of the enterprise. They had little interest in the hard and often dangerous work of encouraging the greater activism of enterprise trade unions or trying to organise the unorganised. Above all, they did not want to take the risk of articulating conflict that might provoke the social unrest that it was their role to neutralise and contain.

The primary commitment of the trade unions in all three countries is not so much to representing the rights and interests of workers as to maintaining social peace and harmony. In China and Vietnam this commitment is sustained and reinforced by the trade unions' continued subordination to the ruling Communist Party. In December 1992, at the Fifth Meeting of the Eleventh Executive Committee of the ACFTU, Hu Jintao, the member of the CCP Politburo who was in charge of the trade union at the time, made the Party's priority clear:

> The trade unions at all levels should assist the Party organs and government to mediate these conflicts. On the one hand, they should actively reflect the opinions of workers and staff members, promoting the improvement of reform measures; on the other hand, they should enhance workers and staff members' awareness of the overall interest, adopting a correct attitude towards the conflicts and difficulties in the course of reform, … the trade unions should strive to maintain national and social stability, guaranteeing the smooth progress of reform. (China Institute of Labour Movement 1993: 598–607)

The Communist Party does not supervise every last thing that the trade unions do, but it determines the unions' strategic priorities, prescribes the fundamental directions of trade union work and monitors trade union activity at all levels to ensure that it does conform to those directions. 'The trade unions accept the ideological and political leadership of the Party but are independent in their activities', as a senior ACFTU official put it to Clarke and Lee (Clarke, Lee and Li 2004: 243).

In Russia the situation became rather more complicated with the collapse of Communist Party rule and the political independence of the trade unions. Despite the legal and constitutional independence of the Russian trade unions, the state is not short of levers to influence their activity, quite apart from the threat of liquidation through legal processes. The trade unions inherited enormous rights and privileges, which the federal or regional government could withdraw more or less at will, as President Yeltsin showed when FNPR aligned itself with the parliamentary 'defenders of the White House' in their confrontation with the President in 1993, which culminated in Yeltsin sending his tanks against parliament. In response, Yeltsin removed the (very lucrative) administration of the Social Insurance Fund from FNPR and transferred it to a new state body, transferred the functions of FNPR for the administration of health and safety to the Ministry of Labour, temporarily forbade the check-off of union dues, cut off FNPR's telephones and froze their bank accounts, and renewed long-standing threats to require a re-registration of trade union membership and to confiscate the enormous property portfolio that FNPR had inherited from its Soviet predecessor, the right to which was only finally confirmed by the 1996 Trade Union Law. A chastened FNPR replaced its founding President, reportedly on the demand of the government (Connor 1996: 132), with the more conciliatory Mikhail Shmakov, who committed FNPR to a strategy of 'social partnership' with government and employers, within which the task of the traditional unions was not to mobilise and represent workers in defence of their interests, but to negotiate collective agreements and resolve disputes through the mediation, arbitration and conciliation procedures established by the new legal framework.

Social partnership provided the traditional unions with a means to reconstitute their traditional functions in a new form, being accorded participation in governmental processes in exchange for their contribution to maintaining social peace. Federal and regional government had an interest in establishing a framework within which they could negotiate social peace and use trade union endorsement to corroborate their claims to represent the interests of the mass of the working population, but the weakness of the trade unions meant that the latter had no levers to pressure the government to modify the course of reform. Thus 'social partnership' has consistently proved to be very one-sided, since the trade unions, lacking the confidence of their members, have had a very weak bargaining position.

The traditional Russian trade unions had committed themselves to a strategy of 'social partnership' at FNPR's 1990 Founding Congress, which adopted a resolution defining the basic tactics of the trade unions as involving the negotiation of general, tariff and collective agreements, to be backed up by demonstrations, meetings, strikes, May Day celebrations and spring and autumn days of united action in support of the unions' demands in negotiations and to enforce the subsequent fulfilment of the agreements. The official history of FNPR stresses that this was

> an extensive programme for the formation of social partnership as a particular type of social-labour relations, an effective mechanism of civilised regulation of those relations. (Gritsenko, Kadeikina and Makukhina 1999: 341)

The official history emphasises the continuity of 'social partnership' with trade union practices in the soviet past, arguing that the FNPR adopted it as a programme as a result of 'many years of positive experience' in the administration of socio-economic processes at enterprise, regional, branch and national level (Gritsenko, Kadeikina and Makukhina 1999: 341). The authors assert that

> In conditions of centralised administration of the economy with only state property, social partnership between enterprise administrations and different forms of worker participation in the administration of production… existed in the USSR. (ibid.: 506)

From this perspective, 'social partnership' has built on the traditional bureaucratic structures of participation of trade unions in management: the collective agreement at the level of the enterprise; collaboration of branch trade unions with the structures of economic management in relation to such issues as 'socialist competition', 'rationalisation and innovation', norm-setting, wage and bonus scales, health and safety, certification, training and retraining and the recruitment and retention of labour; the collaboration of regional trade union organisations with local government in considering issues of housing, social and welfare policy; and the involvement of the national trade union federation in the consideration of labour and social legislation and the formulation of the government's wages, social and labour policies. The fundamental difference from the soviet past is that the trade unions now collaborate voluntarily in the structures of social partnership, whereas in the past they did so under the leadership of the Communist Party. Nevertheless, such voluntary participation is severely constrained by the realities of power, as Shmakov declared to the FNPR General Council soon after his election as FNPR President in 1994:

> Today it is clear that a decisive, open confrontation with the regime would throw our trade unions into the backwaters of public life, would deprive them of all of the constitutional means of defending the interests of the toilers, and would be a real threat to the existence of the Federation and of FNPR unions as a whole. (quoted in Mandel 1995)

A commitment to social partnership by no means implied that FNPR renounced its right to oppose the government or employers, but only that it would pursue its opposition through constitutional channels and resolve differences through peaceful negotiation as a 'loyal opposition'. However, politically the traditional trade unions did not represent a united force. The principal division was between the unions in the relatively prosperous branches of oil and gas, chemicals and metallurgy, for whom the market economy provided opportunities for increasing relative wages, and the public-sector unions, most notably in health and education, whose members were suffering from low wages and high levels of non-payment of wages as a result of inadequate public financing. However, these differences are rarely fought out in the governing bodies of FNPR. In general, those branch unions that do not like elements of the FNPR programme tend to keep quiet in meetings, grumble in the corridors and ignore them in practice. These differences of branch interest have been reflected in the different political orientations of the various branch unions, ranging from the metallurgists, who were a mainstay of the liberal Yabloko, to the giant agro-industrial workers' union, which remained close to the Communist Party. These divisions prevented FNPR from becoming a unified political force and its attempts to align itself electorally with the centre-left opposition were unsuccessful, both because of internal divisions, the constituent unions backing their favoured political forces, and because of the repeated electoral failure of the centre-left (Clarke 2001).

Following the failure of the Fatherland coalition in the 1999 Duma election, FNPR had little choice but to endorse Putin's presidential candidacy and, following the triumph of United Russia in the 2003 election, to align itself increasingly with the 'Party of Power', United Russia, in the federal and regional legislatures. This alignment was sealed in collaboration agreements between FNPR and United Russia that were signed at federal level in 2004 and 2008 and replicated at regional level. Under the 2008 agreement United Russia committed itself to supporting FNPR's long-standing programmatic demands, including the demands that the minimum wage should be set at the level of the adult subsistence minimum, that the minimum pension should be set at the level of the pensioner subsistence minimum and that minimum social standards should be defined by a Federal Law. In exchange, the FNPR committed itself to recommending that its member organisations support the regional and local associations of United Russia at elections at all levels (*Vesti FNPR*, 3, 2008: 7–14).

Under Shmakov, the FNPR has pursued a consistent strategy of participation in tripartite structures at federal, regional and branch levels, of the peaceful negotiation of collective agreements at the enterprise level and of collaboration with state bodies in the formulation and implementation of social and labour policy at all levels, supporting its position by lobbying parliament and the government at federal and regional levels for the introduction of laws and regulations which would protect the privileges of the trade unions and the interests of workers and by monitoring the enforcement of those laws, primarily through collaboration with state inspectorates and the judicial system. Trade unions at all levels have been encouraged to negotiate tripartite agreements with government and employers' organisations and collective agreements with employers, but have been strongly discouraged from supporting their negotiations or seeking to secure the enforcement of agreements with threats of strikes or industrial unrest. The FNPR showed that it was able to channel dissatisfaction into peaceful forms of symbolic protest through its annual May Day parades and 'days of action' to support its negotiating position with the government. The FNPR saw its successful lobbying over the 2001 revision of the Labour Code as a vindication of this strategy, by contrast to the more militant tactics of the alternative trade unions, which saw them marginalised. Social partnership is above all a commitment to maintaining social peace, in exchange for recognition by the employer and the state as respected partners. Shmakov made his position clear in his report to a meeting of the FNPR General Council attended by Putin on 16 February 2000, 'the trade unions consider a strike to be a "failure" of social partnership. *Either social partnership or class struggle!*' (*Vesti FNPR*, 1–2, 2000: 10, original emphasis).

The FNPR had committed itself fully to the democratic process, but Putin's KGB vision of a 'managed democracy' did not provide for the existence of any independent political forces which could potentially provide a nucleus of opposition. At the meeting of the General Council of FNPR at which Putin had sought FNPR's endorsement in the 2000 Presidential election he had declared that 'the trade unions should have a worthy place in society' and appealed for the collaboration of the trade unions with the state in monitoring working conditions, promising government support for this, but he also warned the trade unions that 'to demand what cannot be fulfilled is to inflame social tension' (*Vesti FNPR*, 1–2, 2000: 1–6, 38–9).

By the turn of the new century membership of the FNPR trade unions had fallen by almost half, while a patchy economic recovery was leading to a sharp reduction in social tension and the demobilisation of political opposition, which enabled the Putin regime to treat the trade unions with growing disdain. The FNPR strategy of achieving its fundamental aims through social partnership at the federal level was steadily eroded as the federal government relinquished its residual role as social guarantor and divested itself of almost all its responsibilities in the sphere of labour, assigning responsibility for setting public-sector pay to regional and municipal governments and disengaging from a national programme for health and safety at work. This process was crystallised in the abolition of the Ministry of Labour and the absorption of its residual functions into the Ministry of Health in 2004, which deprived the trade unions of their social partner on the government side. If the trade unions were to enjoy a greater social and political weight they had to establish their legitimacy as representative of their members and this depended, above all, on the reform of trade unions in the workplace.

Throughout Putin's presidency there were rumours of threats to FNPR, and Shmakov's leadership, emanating from the Presidential Administration. In 2001 there was a proposal, reliably reported to emanate from the Presidential Administration, to establish a new trade union federation for the company trade union organisations of Russia's largest corporations, a proposal that was only thwarted by the timely intervention of ICFTU and International Federation of Chemical, Energy, Mine and General Workers' Unions (ICEM) and the agreement of FNPR to support the adoption of the revised Labour Code. In October 2008 Shmakov was warned that he would be removed from office if he did not cancel a Day of Action, called as part of the ITUC's global day of action for decent work, on the grounds that the demonstration was an insult to Putin, whose birthday coincided with the assigned day, and that it was part of an international conspiracy, the demonstration having been planned in Washington DC, where the ITUC General Council had met in December 2007, and in Brussels, ITUC headquarters. The demonstration was only allowed at the very last moment, with the precondition that FNPR include demands for recognition of Abkhazia and South Ossetia in their set of slogans for the action, which were the only slogans shown on the main TV channel.

The FNPR is even more vulnerable to political pressure at regional level, where it depends for any effectiveness that it might have on the support of the regional administration, and this dependence has only increased with the devolution of decision-making powers and the management of the public sector to regional and municipal levels.

The continued dependence of workplace trade unions on enterprise management has meant that the unions have been unable to secure the confidence of their members or to mobilise them in significant numbers in support of trade union demands. As a result, the trade unions have been very dependent on harnessing the powers of state bodies to secure any improvements in the living and working conditions of their members through legislative and administrative means, including putting pressure on employers to sign and abide by branch, regional and collective agreements, and so have been dependent on maintaining the favour of the political authorities and state officials. In exchange for such favour, the trade unions are required to commit themselves to the preservation of social peace. The strategy of social partnership has therefore locked the traditional Russian trade unions into a vicious circle. Lacking the confidence of their members, they are forced to rely on partnership with employers and the state to achieve their ends, which obliges them to make every effort to contain conflict, dissuading their members from taking collective action in pursuit of their demands in order to resolve conflict through bureaucratic and legal channels, so demobilising their members and further undermining their members' confidence in the union.

The vicious circle of social partnership has proved quite as successful in persuading the Russian trade unions to commit themselves above all to maintaining social peace as has the subordination of the trade union to the Communist Party in the case of the Chinese and Vietnamese unions. Nevertheless, however one-sided 'social partnership' might be, it does leave more space for trade unions at all levels to develop their own strategies and tactics for representing their members than does direct subordination to the Party-state and so, as we shall see, we find many more examples of good practice among Russian trade unions than we do among Chinese and Vietnamese trade unions.

The alternative trade unions in Russia have generally followed the opposite path, taking militant action in defence of their members' interests, and their fate shows just how dangerous such a path can be in the Russian political environment. We have already noted the political marginalisation of the alternative trade unions after 1993 and their effective loss of rights of representation and the right to strike in the 2001 revision of the Labour Code, but whenever they have engaged in militant action they have been met with a virulently hostile press and heavy legal and administrative pressure, including dire threats of prosecution. Members of alternative trade unions are systematically victimised by their employers and activists dismissed on spurious pretexts. More recently, alternative trade union leaders have regularly and mysteriously been threatened and assaulted in the street, in what in many cases appear to have been co-ordinated actions. Although Russian workers in principle enjoy freedom of association, in practice they have little more chance to exercise this right than do their Vietnamese and Chinese comrades. They have the legal right to establish and belong to alternative trade unions, but as soon as they do so they open themselves to the victimisation from which Chinese and Vietnamese workers are to some extent protected by the anonymity of their informal organisations.

Industrial relations in the workplace

The transition to a capitalist market economy fundamentally transformed the environment in which enterprises operated and radically changed the objectives of management, but it did not have any immediate impact on the social structure of the enterprise or the forms of management of labour, which changed much more slowly. In particular, it barely touched the dependence of the trade union on management and so the functions of the trade union in the workplace. On the one hand, trade union facilities and a substantial proportion of the resources which the trade unions distributed to the workforce continued to be provided by management. On the other hand, the workers had always considered the trade union to be a part of the management apparatus and had little conception of the trade union as representative of their own interests. If a worker had a grievance he or she was far more likely to take it to his or her line manager than to the trade union. The result has been that workplace trade unions have continued predominantly to function as a branch of the enterprise administration, carrying out their traditional personnel and social and welfare functions. Most enterprise trade union leaders retain the traditional conception of their role: to improve the conditions of their members by collaborating with management to increase productivity, maintain labour discipline, enhance the culture of labour and to support management's lobbying of state bodies for funds and privileges. In return they expect management to do its best to maintain employment and living conditions, to preserve the social and welfare infrastructure of the enterprise and to continue to provide the social and welfare benefits that the labour force expects. The trade union president has continued to be a member of the management team, and indeed the trade union president often combines the role with that of a senior manager, in China and Vietnam frequently as the personnel or human resources director. Collective agreements continue typically to be drawn up in close collaboration with the management, without any semblance of bargaining. If a trade union leader displays unwelcome signs of activism, as has occasionally been the case in Russia, the management can deny facilities to the union and withdraw the social and welfare benefits that the union administers and that the workers expect to receive from the union, undermining support for any radical leadership and forcing the union back into the traditional mould.

Even in Russia, only in exceptional circumstances has a radical workplace trade union organisation been able to mobilise its members and extract significant concessions from management and even more rarely has such a trade union been able to sustain its activism over a significant period of time. In such cases a traditional workplace trade union cannot expect support from higher trade union bodies, committed to the maintenance of social peace, and so is likely to turn to an alternative trade union for support, but the expectations of the members even constrain militant alternative trade union organisations. Thus the role of the trade union in coal mines controlled by the Independent Miners' Union soon became indistinguishable from that in mines controlled by the traditional Independent Trade Union of Workers of the Coal-Mining Industry (NPRUP). Independent Miners' Union (NPG), just as much as NPRUP, had to ensure that its members received the social and welfare benefits that they looked to the trade union to provide. Whether a coal mine was controlled by NPRUP or NPG essentially became a decision for the mine director, not for the coal-miners themselves.

The dependence of the trade union on management is not so much a matter of the corruption of trade union officers, although this is not unknown,[1] as of the structure and orientation of the enterprise unions, which encourages identification of the trade union with management's priorities. It is not so much that the trade union is subordinated to management as that the trade union is an integral part of the management apparatus.

Although the trade union under state-socialism was supposed to be the 'transmission belt' between the Communist Party and the masses, it was characterised by a very low level of involvement of the trade union membership and this has persisted into the reform era. Most of the work of the trade union was traditionally conducted by the president or within the trade union committee, with the membership having little involvement and little information about what the trade union actually did, and this remains the case in the vast majority of enterprises. Union dues are collected by check-off and it is the president and the union committee who decide how to allocate those dues, reporting back to the annual conference of the trade union. Although members of the trade union committee and representatives of subdivisions are required regularly to report back to and consult with the members in their workplaces, in most cases this is at best a formality, with meetings, if they take place at all, bureaucratically organised and poorly attended. Trade union conferences are also usually under the firm control of management and the trade union apparatus. Surveys in all three countries regularly show not only that workers have little confidence in their trade unions, but also that a significant proportion does not even know whether or not they are trade union members.

Surveys in Russia have generally shown that the population as a whole has little confidence in trade unions, although they have usually rated them higher than politicians or private businessmen. There is a difference between the evaluation of trade unions as political actors and the evaluation of the activity of the trade union in the workplace. Nevertheless, a 1998 survey found that 58 per cent of union members did not trust their union officers to look after their interests at their place of work (Rose 1998). In a 1995 survey, 41 per cent of employees saw the director and administration as their defenders, 16 per cent themselves, 13 per cent the union and 13 per cent nobody. Even trade union leaders were as likely as the trade union to see the employer as the employees' defender, and Directors saw the defensive role of the union as negligible. Almost two-thirds of employees and almost half of the enterprise trade union leaders thought the influence of the trade union in defending employees was insignificant, only a third of employees thinking that the union could ever fight

---

[1]   The 2001 trade union law in China introduced a prohibition on the appointment of close family members of senior managers as members of the trade union committee. This was because it had become common, particularly in joint-ventures, for the general manager to appoint his wife (or occasionally her husband) as trade union president. Even if this did not bring harmony to the relationship between management and trade union, it brought a significant addition to the household budget!

for their interests. Over one-third of the employees saw the trade union as an aid to management in resolving production problems and strengthening labour discipline, one-third saw it as a means of defence against the administration and half of those questioned saw distribution as the most important function of the trade union (Chetvernina, Smirnov and Dunaeva 1995).

A survey of 1454 presidents of trade union primary organisations in nine Russian regions in May 2001 (data is available at go.warwick.ac.uk/russia/trade#Survey) found that only one in five, mostly in larger enterprises with over five hundred members, held the post as a full-time position, the remainder having to do their trade union work on top of their regular job (across FNPR as a whole only 3.4 per cent of presidents of primary organisations are full-time officers (*Vesti FNPR*, 3, 2009: 28)). Although trade union officers are protected by the law, a part-time president is particularly vulnerable to management pressure. Part-time trade union officers are legally entitled to time away from their jobs on average pay to perform their trade union duties, but this has to be negotiated with management and is sometimes included in the collective agreement. Three-quarters of the trade union presidents were, or had previously been, managers, professionals or senior specialists, while only 5 per cent had previously been skilled or unskilled workers. Nearly all the part-time presidents were paid by the employer, although a quarter received some payment from trade union funds, while a quarter of full-time presidents received some payment from the employer. The low status and limited career prospects of the position are indicated by the fact that trade union presidents were disproportionately female when compared with the workforce they represented, while over a third of presidents were close to or beyond pension age. On average the trade union presidents had worked in the same enterprise for the past 18 years, so they were well embedded in the informal networks of the enterprise, and over a quarter had been in their trade union post since the soviet period. In a majority of enterprises with fewer than five hundred employees the trade union had no premises and no equipment, not even a telephone, so that the trade union depended entirely on using the employer's facilities to meet or to communicate.

Almost half of the income of all primary organisations, net of wage costs, was devoted to providing material assistance to members (for weddings, funerals or medical treatment, for example) and over a third was devoted to 'mass-cultural work' (providing vacations; organising celebrations, sporting and cultural events; giving new year presents and so on). Very little was spent on training and informational activity or on obtaining legal advice, for which primary organisations rely heavily on the regional trade union bodies. Almost nothing was devoted to the 'solidarity fund', which serves, among other purposes, as a strike fund.

Providing material assistance and organising mass-cultural work are very time-consuming activities and generally fill the working day of the trade union president and his or her associates. Quite apart from the organisational work involved, there is a constant stream of supplicants coming into the trade union office asking about the availability of vouchers for vacations, particularly for children in the summer, or pleading for financial help to arrange a funeral, purchase medicines, pay for an operation or carry out repairs to their home. Many people turn to the trade union for help with problems quite unrelated to work, for example, marital problems or trouble with the neighbours. This is the traditional work of the trade union, and trade union officers often remark that it is the most satisfying part of their job because they feel that they are able to provide people with real help. It is also the most congenial because it does not involve their having to make any demands of management and so avoids conflict.

We have already noted the personal dependence of the trade union president on the enterprise director and of the trade union on the administration for facilities and resources. In the soviet period the nomination of a candidate for the post of trade union president would usually be agreed between the Party secretary and the enterprise director, and it is still usual for the director to play a role in the nomination of the trade union president, often in consultation with the regional trade union organisation. It is very rare, except in situations of endemic conflict, for a trade union president to be elected against the wishes of the enterprise director.

In the vast majority of enterprises and organisations, senior managers, right up to the director, remain members of the trade union, and so are eligible to attend trade union meetings and to serve as trade union officers or delegates to trade union conferences: according to the Russian Labour Flexibility Survey data in 1997, the administration belonged to the trade union in 72 per cent of surveyed enterprises, and in a further 23 per cent part of the administration belonged to the trade union (data provided by the Centre for Labour Market Studies of the Institute of Economics of the Russian Academy of Science). It is not uncommon for enterprise directors to be elected as delegates to the regional and national conferences of the branch trade unions and they sometimes serve on elected union bodies, particularly in the public sector. One defining characteristic of the alternative trade unions is that they exclude managers, generally defined as those with disciplinary powers, from their ranks.

In the Institute for Comparative Labour Relations Research (ISITO) survey the vast majority of enterprise trade union presidents described their relationship with management as being basically collaborative or even amicable, even in enterprises in which current wages were not being paid, with fewer than 5 per cent describing the relationship as conflictual, the latter being significantly more likely in privatised enterprises under outsider and especially under foreign control. Relations were significantly more conflictual where the president was paid from trade union funds than where the president was paid by the enterprise, and trade union presidents who were or had been skilled workers were much more likely to describe relations as more or less conflictual, and those who were or had been managers more likely to describe relations as collaborative.

In China, in spite of some shift of emphasis in the designated primary role of the trade union, the predominant functions of the trade union at the workplace still tend to be management functions (Biddulph and Cooney 1993; Chan 2000a: 39; Ding, Goodall and Warner 2002: 445–7; Li 2000: 192; Zhu Y. 1995; Zhu and Campbell 1996). Formally, the principal function of the trade union is 'to take economic development as its central task', encouraging workers to increase productivity, enforcing labour discipline and conducting extensive propaganda on behalf of management. 'Protecting the rights and interests of employees' is usually interpreted as monitoring managerial practices, and particularly the work of the personnel department (to the extent that the trade union does not itself do that work), to ensure that it conforms to all the relevant laws and regulations, and implementing the social and welfare policy of the enterprise: visiting sick workers, dealing with personal problems, distributing benefits, organising picnics and arranging celebrations, which in practice occupies most of the time of trade union officers. For most trade union cadres at the workplace, the idea of representing and protecting the legitimate rights and interests of their members in opposition to the employer is something that is unfamiliar, if not entirely alien, to their traditional practice and to their traditional conception of their role, which is to serve the interests of the enterprise. One trade union chair explained the problems to Qi Li:

> You know, it is difficult for us to do union work because we are sandwiched between management and workers. When workers complained their wages were too low, we couldn't negotiate this issue with the director face to face and force him to raise wages. The reason is very simple, if this factory was bankrupt, the workers would lose their rice bowls. The only thing we can do is to convey workers' requirements to management. Whether or not there will be raising of wages will finally be determined by the director. Concerning the issue of reducing staffing, what we can do is to do ideological work with the workers, asking them to give us their ideas, letting them know that there will not be an 'iron rice bowl' in a market economy, if they have bad job performance, they will run the risk of being made unemployed. (Li 2000: 195–6, translation amended)

However sympathetic the trade union cadres may be to the plight of their members, the Chinese enterprise trade union is so closely integrated into management that it is not unfair to characterise it as 'just a branch of management' (as a senior officer of the Chinese employers' confederation described it), and its role is still not so much to represent workers as to explain to workers why the company cannot increase their wages or why redundancies are unavoidable or even desirable for the prosperity of the company. It is not unknown for trade unions to go beyond justifying management practices to the workers to confronting workers on behalf of management (Cooke 2002: 21). Ding, Goodall and Warner concluded that, although Chinese unions are sometimes able to protect workers' interests, overall, 'Chinese unions function more as an offshoot of the HR department, and are primarily concerned with supporting managerial interests' (2002: 447).

This situation can be attributed to a number of factors. Trade union officers are largely drawn from the ranks of management. A full-time trade union president is paid by the employer and normally enjoys the status (and salary) of a deputy general director of the company;[1] the personal careers of union leaders revolve around the positions of party cadre, union leader and enterprise manager;[2] they are usually members of the Board of Directors or the Supervisory Board of the company; and they (rightly) regard themselves as members of the senior management team. Whether or not there is a formal election of the trade union chair, the latter is normally appointed by management (Li 2000: 190). The majority of trade union representatives at every level similarly tend to be managers or team leaders, rather than one of the employees whose interests they are now supposed to represent. As one regional industry trade union leader explained to justify the practice, 'workers normally nominate the person who can best represent them' (Clarke, Lee and Li 2004: 243).

The situation in the private and foreign-owned sectors in China is even worse than that typical of SOEs and former SOEs described above. The massive expansion of ACFTU membership in the private sector since 2003 has been based on close collaboration of higher-level unions with management in the establishment of trade union organisations in order to meet recruitment targets and so, not surprisingly, many of these union organisations exist only on paper, nominally headed by a senior manager, who perhaps even signs a collective agreement, but otherwise are completely inactive.

The situation is no different in Vietnam, where state and former state enterprises are still managed by the 'group of four' (general director, Communist Party Secretary, trade union president, Youth League President) and the trade union still sees its role in entirely traditional terms as being one of personnel management, rather than of employee representation. It is common in Vietnam for an HR manager or deputy director to take up the position of union chair and VGCL officials see no problem in this practice. Mr Chinh, Director of the Socio-Economic Department of VGCL, explained: 'being an HR manager does not affect the work of a union chairman. In fact, it is an advantage because an HR manager is closer to the employers so they can talk more easily to them. They also understand the law better and have a stronger voice in the company'.

---

[1]   This prescription was introduced alongside the introduction of the Workers' Congress system, with the intention of recruiting competent leaders for trade union work (*Qiye zhigong daibiao dahui zanxing tiaoli* (Interim Provisions on Workers' Congress) Beijing: Falu chubanshe, 1983).

[2]   According to a survey in Zhejiang province, 41.5 per cent of the surveyed union leaders were recruited from managerial cadres, 35.8 per cent were from full-time party cadres, 5.7 per cent were from technicians and 5.6 per cent were from other positions, whereas only 11.3 per cent of them were from rank-and-file workers (Baek 2000).

Workers do not see it the same way. In an article in *Lao Dong Daily* in March 2006, a worker participating in a strike said: 'the union chairman in our company is a deputy director. Of course, they have to protect the company's interests not ours.' Another worker criticised the union: 'instead of protecting us, the union guy in my company spies on workers and tells the director our mistakes.' A VGCL official acknowledged the subordination of the union to management, telling us 'union leaders are all part-time, they rely on the employers for job and income and they dare not go against their boss'. Inevitably, where formal unions are unable to represent workers, workers would resort to some sort of alternative leadership.

Workers we interviewed in a Taiwanese enterprise which had experienced a major strike in June 2007 had a sceptical view of their union. The union had been set up in 2006 with the warehouse manager as union chairman and HR manager as vice chair. But most workers had never attended any union meetings and had no idea how the union committee was elected. One worker told us: 'I heard that one day all managers, including line leaders, were invited to a lunch. After the lunch, a union committee was elected and their names were placed on the company bulletin board the next day.' When asked whether any worker has approached the union leaders to express their demands, our informants burst into laughter: 'are you kidding? He [union chair] is a manager. If I open my mouth, the next day I am gone. And you know who would sign my dismissal decision? The union vice chair – the HR manager.' The workers had no more confidence in the higher-level union: 'I saw them [district union officials] visiting the company several times. But they never talked to us. They went straight into the managers' office then left. I guess they left with an envelope. You say, should we trust them?' When the strike broke out, a woman whom we suspected of being the informal strike organiser called the provincial union, district union, the local Department of Labour, Invalids and Social Affairs (DOLISA), and the press informing them about the strike, but the workers only trusted DOLISA to represent their interests. 'I have seen people from the district union, the People's Committee, the police visiting the company. They talked to the managers in the office then left. There is no doubt that the management has given them good bribes otherwise all their violations would have been discovered a long time ago. Only DOLISA people have never been here so we only trust them', said the strike organiser.

Lack of confidence in the trade union is not confined to workers. A Korean employer said: 'Previously, we depended on the enterprise union as the bridge to workers but it is clear that workers do not trust the union. They planned the strike but the union did not know until it happened. Now, we had to approach the workers ourselves to understand their concerns and demands to prevent future strikes.'

In Russia, the removal of the Communist Party from the workplace only increased the dependence of the trade union on management, since under the soviet system any rare display of independence of the trade union from management depended on the support of the Party. On the other hand, the Communist Party continues to play an important role in binding the trade union to management in state and former state enterprises in China and Vietnam. In the past in China, the Party organisation played an important role in ensuring that management and the trade union pulled in the same direction. Enterprise reforms have led to some reduction in the formal authority of the Party over management,[1] but the Party can compensate by exerting its influence through the trade union (Chan 2000a: 44; Warner and Ng, 1999: 306). The Party played a very important role in inaugurating the system of collective consultation, but once the process is set in motion its implementation is left largely to the initiative of management and the enterprise trade union. Nevertheless the trade unions still benefit from the Party's support at enterprise, as at national, level. For example, where there is a Party organisation, it will review the collective agreement and may persuade a reluctant management to accept the union's proposals. Although we might expect the Party equally to persuade the union to moderate its excessive demands, a senior ACFTU official interviewed in 2002 did not know of any case of the Party opposing the trade union's proposals for the collective contract (Clarke, Lee and Li 2004: 243). This is probably more an indication of the self-moderation of the trade union than of any predisposition of the Party to oppose management. Thus the absence of a Party organisation in private and foreign-invested enterprises in China leaves the trade union even more dependent on management than it is in state enterprises. This is part of the rationale for proposals from VGCL in Vietnam that Party organisation should be extended to enterprises in the private and foreign-invested sectors.[2]

In the Soviet Union the Party organisation was distinct from both management and the trade union, to keep a check on both, but in China and Vietnam it is common for senior managers and the trade union leader to double up as the Party leaders in the enterprise. In one Chinese enterprise, in which the General Manager was the Party Secretary and the trade union president his deputy, the former commented that 'having the General Manager as Party Secretary and trade union president as Deputy Party Secretary produces balance'. Where the trade union president is also the Party Secretary, which we have only found to be the case in joint-ventures, this gives the trade union president considerable authority to ensure that the foreign management respects all the relevant laws and regulations.

The identification of trade unions with management priorities is institutionalised in China in the Workers' Congress system and appears to be further reinforced by the

---

[1] The Party formally lost its authority over SOE managers in 1986, but its role in SOEs was partially restored from 1989, in the wake of Tiananmen (Li 2000: 105–07).

[2] In the 2007 Communist Party Resolution on the Working Class, drawn up in collaboration with VGCL, the Party sets a target of 'recruiting the majority of workers in the non-public sector as Party members by the year 2020' and 'establishing Party cells in all enterprises'. Later, Directive 22–CT/TW of the Central Party Secretariat, issued on 5/6/2008, emphasised the role of the union in 'containing and limiting illegitimate strikes' while replicating successful models of Party cells and social organisations in enterprises. As a result, VGCL increased the scale of political training for workers. The HCMC Federation of Labour, for instance, provided political training to 3500 workers in 2007 (Do 2008).

widespread practice of substituting a meeting of the Workers' Congress for the trade union members' congresses that are required by the Trade Union Law (c.f. Goodall and Warner 1997: 586). The Congress usually meets between one and four times a year, with the trade union committee serving as its executive body between meetings. While the constituency of these bodies is virtually identical in traditional enterprises that have full union membership, their functions and powers are very different. The Congress of Worker Representatives is not a trade union body, but an instrument for the participation of workers in the management of the enterprise. As such, the Congress expresses the unity of the enterprise as a whole and does not accommodate separation, let alone conflict, of interests between the management and workers. Therefore, this substitution of the Staff and Workers' Congress for the trade union members' congress, and confusion of two supposedly different institutions in the mind of trade union cadres and members, tends further to weaken the trade union's function as a representative organisation of workers vis-à-vis management. Moreover, decisions of the Congress are not binding on the trade union. Finally, a large general meeting is not a substitute for democratic channels of representation because it is not an appropriate forum for the careful and serious consideration of proposals regarding important and often complex issues, which may involve divisions between different sections of the labour force as well as divisions between the employer and employees.

The close integration of the trade union into the structure of management, and the traditional identification of trade union officers with the priorities of management, underlies a tendency for the trade union to seek to reconcile any differences of interest between employees and management within its own structures and so guarantee that its negotiations with management will be consensual.

The corollary of trade union identification with management in the workplace is the identification of the trade union with management priorities at higher levels. This is particularly the case in Russia, where the trade unions are constituted on a branch rather than a territorial basis, so that the branch unions at regional and national levels represent the workers of a particular industry and see their best prospects to be not through representing workers in opposition to management, but in representing the interests of their industry in relation to national and regional government. Indeed, in the absence of strong employers' organisations, during the 1990s it was the trade unions that filled the gap and represented the employers' interests both in lobbying government and in participating in regulatory bodies for their industry. Where employers' organisations have been created, in many cases these were originally established on the initiative of the relevant trade union, as a means of creating a social partner and as a means of more effectively representing the industry as a whole.

Conclusion

In all three countries, the new industrial relations system that has developed alongside the transition to a capitalist market economy does not represent a radical transformation, but an adaptation of the traditional state-socialist system of industrial relations to new conditions. Thus, in most state and former state enterprises the trade unions can continue with their traditional practices, functioning as a branch of the personnel department, primarily administering the provision of social and welfare services to employees and pensioners of the enterprise, and in the best of cases providing the employer with channels for employee consultation. The trade union sees the prosperity of the employer as a necessary and even sufficient condition for the prosperity of the employees and so collaborates with the employer in all manner of programmes and activities designed to improve the moral and physical qualities of the labour force, to foster innovation, encourage labour motivation and improve labour discipline. Although the trade union is supposed to monitor the implementation of labour and health and safety legislation, it will often overlook violations if management claims that it cannot afford to repair premises, provide statutory benefits or even pay wages on time.

In all three countries the political position of the trade unions depends on their ability to maintain social peace, expressed in Russia in the trade unions' wholehearted commitment to a strategy of 'social partnership' and imposed in China and Vietnam by the subordination of the unions to the Party. The higher levels of the trade union in all three countries accordingly see their role not so much as supporting and mobilising their primary organisations as collaborating with state bodies, lobbying for the introduction and enforcement of legislation and collaborating with state inspection and control bodies. In Russia such lobbying takes place in public, by lobbying legislators and through participation in tripartite bodies at federal and regional levels, backed up by petitions, protests and demonstrations. In China and Vietnam such lobbying mostly takes place behind closed doors since the trade unions are still integrated into the Party-state apparatus, although the trade unions own large-circulation newspapers which they can use to press their favoured policies.

In accordance with their commitment to harmony, social peace and social partnership, the trade unions in all three countries give absolute priority to the judicial resolution of disputes, through the successive stages of mediation, arbitration and appeal to the court, with strikes being seen as the very last resort in Russia and Vietnam and being entirely excluded from the trade union agenda in China.

In this situation, the reform of trade unions can only be reactive, in response to conflict initiated independently by aggrieved workers, in order to demonstrate the trade unions' capacity to contain and resolve such conflict peacefully. The key driving force of trade union reform has correspondingly been the pattern and intensity of industrial conflict. Such conflict does not immediately result in trade union reform, but it creates the space in which enterprising and energetic trade union officers can undertake reform initiatives and it imposes political pressure on the trade unions from above to reform their practices in order to maintain social peace more effectively.

3

The Challenge of Worker Activism

We have already seen that the initiatives to give the trade unions more independence in representing the interests of their members in the early stages of reform in all three countries were determined primarily by the real or potential threat of worker activism and the emergence of independent worker organisation, exemplified by the rise of Solidarity in Poland, the strike wave across the Soviet Union, centred on the coal-mining regions, and the developing support of Chinese workers for the student-led democracy movement in July 1989. On the other hand, legal and constitutional changes had little impact on the activity of trade unions on the ground. The transition from state to market regulation of the activity of enterprises led to radical changes in the orientation of management, now seeking to maximise profits rather than fulfil central directives, but the social structure of the enterprise, and the role and function of workplace trade unions, barely changed. Higher trade union bodies had little leverage over their primary organisations and had no interest in encouraging changes which might stimulate rather than contain conflict, while few trade union officers had any interest in changing their ways of working. Pressures for change could only come from below, from the activism of workers themselves.

In all three countries the traditional trade unions have been very cautious in response to worker activism, generally seeking to marginalise and discredit independent worker activists, often colluding with employers to get such activists dismissed and with state bodies to secure their repression. However, once worker activism gets beyond the stage of a few disgruntled individuals it becomes more difficult to ignore or repress. In Russia, worker activists established workers' (strike) committees and later alternative trade unions, while trade union legislation gave their activists some protection against victimisation, and the alternative trade unions in many cases presented a serious challenge to the traditional unions, to which the latter had to respond by reforming their own practice. Although alternative organisations have no legal standing in China and Vietnam, and attempts to create them are very firmly repressed, informal networks among traditional SOE workers and more or less informal associations based on place-of-origin among rural migrant workers have provided the framework within which independent labour activists have been able to mount increasingly well-organised strikes and protests. Freedom of association is not often something that is granted, it is something that has to be won, and although workers in China and Vietnam do not have legally protected freedom of association, in practice they have won the space, if not the right, to organise themselves informally and the Party-state has come to understand that such informal organisation cannot be countered successfully by repression, but only by reforming the trade unions so that they can play a more effective role in representing the rights and interests of workers. In all three countries, therefore, it has been worker activism that has played the major role in pushing forward trade union reform, both directly in the challenge that it poses to the traditional unions, and indirectly, through the pressure that it induces the government and/or Party to put on the traditional unions to encourage them more effectively to represent workers in order to maintain social peace. Before looking at the steps taken to reform the trade unions, in this chapter we will look at the forms and patterns of worker activism in Russia, China and Vietnam in the reform era.

Russia

The Russian revolution had been based on the urban industrial working class, centred on the large factories of the major cities, whose workers remained very active in pressing their demands on the revolutionary regime through the 1920s, with organised workers' opposition to the government persisting into the 1930s until it was ruthlessly suppressed under Stalin. Nevertheless, soviet workers' resistance to arbitrary, incompetent or unjust management remained constant and pervasive, dissipated and diffused through the informal relations of the workplace. Spontaneous work stoppages by small groups of workers seem to have been fairly common throughout the soviet period, but these very rarely reached the attention of the public or the authorities. If they did draw official attention, not only the workers responsible, but also the managers and Party and trade union officials who had allowed the situation to arise would equally be penalised, which gave the latter a very strong incentive to cover up any forms of protest or resistance. Thus Vladimir Klebanov, who came to the attention of the West when he protested publicly and was arrested in Moscow in 1978 (Haynes and Semyonova 1979), had had a small organisation in the Bazhanov mine in Makeevka in the Ukrainian Donbas since the 1950s, which was tolerated by the management so long as it restricted itself to economic issues and was not publicly known (Simon Clarke, interview with Vladimir Klebanov, Moscow, 16th March 1992). Most people in the Soviet Union knew of cases of demonstrations or even riots which extended beyond the limits of the workplace, but these were rare, and until the Gorbachev years were always suppressed by force, the most brutal being in Novocherkassk in 1962, when at least 25 protestors were killed, so worker opposition only very rarely took on an organised or public form.

The disruption caused by the early phase of perestroika, and particularly by Gorbachev's wage reform, provoked a growing number of small wildcat strikes, which were usually settled rapidly in the traditional soviet way, with immediate concessions designed to placate and isolate the striking workers, although a strike at the Yaroslavl Motor Factory in December 1987 grew beyond the authorities' control, and lasted for a week (Mandel 1991). At the January 1987 Plenum of the Central Committee of the Communist Party of the Soviet Union (CPSU), Gorbachev opened the flood gates of 'democratisation' and at the Nineteenth Party Conference in June 1988 he effectively signed the Party's death warrant by announcing the transfer of executive power to elected soviet bodies, unleashing a wave of political activity and the formation of initiative groups and oppositional political organisations, mostly mobilising around politically safe issues such as the environment but, in a few cases, also harnessing growing worker discontent. The partially democratic elections to the new USSR Congress of People's Deputies in March 1989 provided a focus for concerted political mobilisation.

During 1989 informal democratic activists sought to establish closer links with workers' organisations, but most of the small workers' organisations that had emerged were anarcho-syndicalist in orientation, with a strong distrust of intellectuals and political organisation. Following their success in the March 1990 local elections most of the 'democrats' lost interest in the workers' movement to concentrate on exploiting their new political positions in the apparatus, sometimes for political but too often for personal advantage.

The miners' strike of July 1989, which began in the Kuznetsk coal basin (Kuzbass) in Western Siberia and soon spread to the coalfields of Vorkuta, Donbas in Ukraine and Karaganda in Kazakhstan, fundamentally transformed the significance of the workers' movement in the political development of the Soviet Union. The Kuzbass miners established a regional workers' committee, with representatives of all the mining towns, while in Vorkuta and Donetsk workers' committees linking all the mines in the city were established.

Gorbachev used the 1989 strike wave as a lever against conservative resistance to reform, proclaiming the strikes to be a movement for 'perestroika from below' to be harnessed to further reform. The demands of the strikers were recognised as legitimate, only their methods being condemned, reflecting the failure of the Party and the miners' trade union to represent the miners' interests through constitutional channels. Thus, in the aftermath of the strike the local Party was encouraged to bring the strike leaders into its ranks and new trade union elections were held across the coal-mining regions in an abortive attempt to take the initiative back from the workers' committees, with the majority of incumbent trade union leaders being replaced by strike activists. At the same time a Law on Strikes was rushed through, which introduced a compulsory pre-strike conciliation and arbitration procedure and banned strikes in strategic sectors, although the Law proved completely ineffective in containing strikes.

In the wake of the strikes the Russian miners established connections with the reformist Inter-Regional Group of People's Deputies, and in particular with Boris Yeltsin. After consultation with Yeltsin, the Kuzbass miners called an anniversary strike in July 1990, on the eve of Yeltsin's dramatic resignation from the Communist Party, but that, and a political strike called in January 1991, proved dismal failures. However, a further miners' strike across the Soviet Union lasting from March to May 1991, which was again co-ordinated with Yeltsin and his supporters, marked the high point in the impact of the workers' movement. The 1991 strike also provided the opportunity to consolidate the Independent Miners' Union (NPG), with funding from Yeltsin, which had been established on the basis of the workers' committees in 1990 but had made little headway hitherto.

The strike waves of 1989 and 1991, which had seemed to have done so much to bring the soviet system crashing down, gave the impression of a powerful workers' movement, but they had spread so fast and had such a dramatic impact not because of the organisational capacity of the new workers' movement, but because the strikes had been harnessed by enterprise directors and regional political leaders in the bid to extract resources from the centre and, in 1991, by Yeltsin in his struggle with Gorbachev (Clarke, Fairbrother and Borisov 1995: chapters 2–4). In 1991 the final showdown between Yeltsin and Gorbachev made it clear that the miners' movement had been decisive not in its own right, but in a struggle for power between contending factions of the ruling stratum. The miners' strikes were not so much a cause as a consequence of the disintegration of the soviet system. But at the same time they showed that angry and frustrated workers could provide a dangerous political resource for opposition to the government and highlighted the need for institutions which could represent workers' grievances through appropriate institutional channels. It soon became clear that, as far as the new regime was concerned, such channels were best provided not by workers' committees and militant independent trade unions but by the traditional trade unions, appropriately reformed.

Following Yeltsin's counter-putsch and the collapse of the Soviet Union, the old apparatus gradually reconstituted itself in a new guise. The rhetoric of the transition to a market economy and a democratic polity concealed a shift in the balance of power from ministries to monopolistic enterprises and associations, from the Party to the executive branch of the state apparatus, and from the centre to the regions, all of which considerably weakened the political position of the workers' movement. Yeltsin felt that he had paid his debts to the miners with a tripling of their wages in May 1991, soon eroded by inflation, although the leaders of NPG remained faithful to Yeltsin until the spring of 1994.

The NPG leaders had banked on exploiting their political connections in Moscow, rather than building up their organisation on the ground, and the gamble had not come off. While the miners' leaders still had access to Yeltsin during 1992, his government moved progressively closer to the traditional FNPR, taming the traditional unions with implicit and explicit threats to remove their property and privileges. The government was still willing to sign agreements with the NPG leaders, but it was by no means as eager to implement them. But every time the NPG leaders prepared to call a strike, the political polarisation between Yeltsin and the Congress of People's Deputies forced them back into Yeltsin's arms. When the government invited the World Bank to collaborate with it in drawing up a programme for the decimation of the industry, the NPG leaders participated enthusiastically, in the naive belief that the jobs of the underground miners whom it represented would be preserved. Meanwhile,

NPG organisation in the workplace, which had never been strong, steadily declined as primary organisations, which included only underground miners, were unable to compete with the traditional miners' union, which represented all employees and was favoured by most employers. Having lost political favour and with little money coming in from membership dues, NPG became increasingly reliant on funding from the AFL-CIO-sponsored Russian-American Fund.

The same fate befell Sotsprof, the 'Association of Socialist [later Social] Trade Unions', established in Moscow in April 1989, and reconstituted in 1991 following an acrimonious split, which started off with no significant working-class base. However, Sotsprof had close connections with the small but influential Social Democratic Party, which gave it access to the Moscow city council (Mossoviet), which provided it with office facilities and with political, legal and administrative support, and then, following Yeltsin's counter-putsch, to the Ministry of Labour, which was initially a Social Democratic Party fiefdom and through which Sotsprof emerged as official representative of the independent workers' movement, with three seats on the Tripartite Commission for 1992. The Sotsprof leaders secured the legal obligation of management to negotiate a collective agreement with any established trade union in the 1992 Law on Collective Agreements, which they were then able to use to build up their organisation. However, Sotsprof's success was not to last as the government moved closer to the traditional unions, with the Sotsprof representatives being removed from the Tripartite Commission and the Ministry of Labour being taken away from the Social Democrats at the end of 1992. As Sotsprof lost its political influence, so its ability to defend its members was undermined and enterprise directors became more confident in resisting its demands. In the summer of 1993 its last prop was removed, when a government resolution effectively reversed the provisions of the Law on Collective Agreements. Sotsprof sustained itself by providing an umbrella under which small independent workplace trade unions could register legally as trade unions and concentrated increasingly on pursuing cases through the courts, primarily with regard to illegal dismissals, refusal to negotiate a collective agreement, and delays in the payment of wages. Sotsprof also sought to poach trade union organisations from the other alternative trade union federations, which exacerbated the tense relations between the alternative trade union leaders, and it was widely believed to retain informal support in the presidential administration, although it was never readmitted to the Tripartite Commission.

Meanwhile, strikes in other sectors and regions had been becoming more frequent, mostly involving specific professional groups of skilled workers, particularly in transport and engineering, who had a culture of professional solidarity and whose key positions gave them some industrial muscle. The traditional trade unions were particularly ill-adapted to represent the sectional interests of such workers, since the traditional unions were constituted on the branch principle, representing all the workers in an industry. The new alternative trade unions, on the other hand, were generally constituted on a professional basis, representing a particular occupational category, such as underground miners, bus drivers, train drivers, pilots or teachers. Striking workers would typically follow the miners' example and establish strike committees, which were courted by, and often subsequently affiliated to, one or another of the many newly established trade unions and worker organisations, but the latter had few members or resources and a very limited ability to do more than pass resolutions, hold token pickets and attempt to defend their own members against victimisation through the courts.

The most effective of the alternative trade unions was that of the air traffic controllers, the Federation of Air Traffic Controllers' Unions (FPAD), originally formed as a breakaway from the official union of aviation workers in October 1990 and on that basis organising the overwhelming majority of Russian air traffic controllers.[1] The FPAD was very successful in pressing the claims of its members against the Soviet government in 1991, and actively supported Yeltsin in his resistance to the August putsch. They were rewarded with a very favourable tariff agreement covering the profession, signed by the government in May 1992 following a strike threat. However, finding that the agreement was not being implemented on the ground, they issued another strike call for August 1992, but this was met by the government with threats of prosecution and the liquidation of their union. The strike collapsed in the midst of widespread intimidation and the subsequent history of the union has been one of intimidation and repression by government and employers.

Meanwhile, the collapse of the Soviet Union, the 'transition to a market economy' and mass privatisation demanded that the traditional unions adopt a new role for which they were unprepared, of defending the interests of their members in the face of a government and employers who had abrogated their former responsibility for their well-being. It is therefore no surprise that the trade unions approached the challenges of the transition to a market economy on the basis of their existing form. The first priority of the trade union apparatus was to retain intact the power, privileges and property of the trade unions, which meant that they had to find a new basis for their authority. While they might proclaim themselves the representatives of the interests of their members, the absence of commitment on the part of their members and the lack of any experience of collective organisation meant that such a claim was a very fragile basis on which to seek to retain their position. The strategy which came naturally to the leadership of the trade unions, and which was most realistic in the situation in which they found themselves, was to seek to survive as organisations by reconstituting and consolidating their relationship with those in power. This was not simply a matter of subordinating themselves to the new authorities, but much more of finding a new role for themselves by reconstituting

---

[1]   The pilots had broken away from the official union at the same time, but were effectively reabsorbed into the framework of the official union in 1992. The independent dockers' union was similarly formed by the breaking away of a professional group from the traditional union.

their traditional functions on new foundations. The traditional trade unions have therefore been not passive victims but active participants in the constitution of the structures of post-soviet power.

The destruction of the Party-state not only removed the external support for the authority of the trade unions, but also removed the support for their hierarchical internal structures. The abandonment of democratic centralism led to a radical decentralisation of the trade unions, which were reconstituted according to a federative structure in which each level of the organisation acted as an independent agent. This meant that the evolution of the trade unions in the wake of the collapse of the soviet system has not been a coherent and integrated process, but one in which each part of the organisation has tried to find its own way. At the federal level, the reconstituted Russian trade unions have sought an accommodation with the organs of Federal government, the Presidency and the Legislature. At the regional level, meanwhile, the trade unions have sought a role by reconstituting and consolidating their relations with the regional and municipal authorities. At the level of the enterprise, by contrast, the trade union organisation has sought to retain and build on its relations with enterprise management, securing its position by fulfilling its traditional social and welfare functions, institutionalising and developing its role in personnel management and even restoring some of its functions of encouraging the development of production, fostering the 'culture of labour' and strengthening labour discipline.

Following the collapse of the Soviet Union and Yeltsin's crash programme of price liberalisation and privatisation, the Russian economy went into free fall, with hyperinflation, large-scale lay-offs from state enterprises, the collapse of real wages and the escalating non-payment of wages by insolvent enterprises and organisations. Workers who protested were met with the common refrain, 'if you don't like it, you can leave' and activists were summarily dismissed, many vainly seeking reinstatement through the courts. In this context disgruntled workers had very few means and opportunities to take action on their own account.

Although the economic collapse did not provide fertile ground for worker activism, the catastrophic decline in living standards and the chronic non-payment of wages during the 1990s provided potential grounds for large-scale social unrest. Having initially courted the new workers' movement in the struggle for power, Yeltsin soon withdrew his support, as his priority having seized power became the consolidation of the authority of the state and the establishment of social peace. On these grounds Yeltsin sought an accommodation with the traditional unions. There were two fundamental reasons for this accommodation. On the one hand, it soon became apparent that the government needed the traditional trade unions to continue to carry out their traditional state functions of administering the social insurance system and monitoring health and safety at work. On the other hand, and more fundamentally, the government was very concerned to prevent the traditional unions from mobilising their considerable resources in support of the parliamentary opposition and, in particular, the Communist Party. When FNPR threw in its lot with the 'defenders of the White House' against Yeltsin's putsch in December 1993 the government moved swiftly, and the threat to confiscate the unions' considerable property and to remove them from the administration of the social insurance and health and safety systems brought them rapidly into line, with the conciliatory Mikhail Shmakov replacing Igor' Klochkov as FNPR President. In the event, FNPR retained its property, though it lost control of the social insurance fund and the monitoring of health and safety. Thereafter FNPR committed itself wholeheartedly to the principles of 'social partnership'.

Despite the unfavourable economic situation, strikes continued through the 1990s. However, the principal strike waves of the 1990s involved public-sector workers, primarily health and education workers, who were still paid from federal budget allocations on national pay scales, and coal-mining, which depended on massive state subsidies to maintain the high wages of the coal-miners, and were promoted as much by the employers as by the trade unions in the bid to extract money from the government. Once the coal mines were fully privatised, subsidies removed and sectoral bargaining replaced by enterprise bargaining, the coal-miners' unions lost their bargaining power and the occasional strikes were confined to single mines.[1] The actions of public-sector workers were similarly damped down by paying off wage arrears, providing for greater regional flexibility in wage-setting and, as in the coal mines, by taking tough disciplinary measures against managers who encouraged strike action, though the public-sector unions continued to organise annual 'days of action' involving pickets, protest meetings and occasional work stoppages until Putin introduced his 'National Projects' for health and education, which allocated federal funds for salary increases in priority areas, in 2005. Beyond these sectors, militant worker activism was largely confined to narrow strategically located professional groups, particularly in transport (pilots, air traffic controllers, dockers, bus and train drivers), pursuing their sectional interests through the alternative unions established to represent them on a professional basis (Clarke, Fairbrother and Borisov 1995: chapters 5–7), but faced with the concerted opposition of government and employers the alternative unions found themselves less and less able to have an impact. The most dramatic strikes of the 1990s, which occasionally involved armed confrontations, were associated with struggles for the control of privatised enterprises, with either the incumbent management or prospective new owners mobilising the workers in their support (Clarke and Kabalina 1995; Clarke and Pulaeva 2000).

---

[1]   The 'rail wars' of May 1998, when miners blocked Russia's strategic railway routes in protest at the chronic non-payment of wages, showed that the miners' mobilising capacity had not been completely contained. In the short term the protest secured the payment of wage arrears, but in the longer term mines which were unable to pay wages were closed and the miners lost their jobs.

By the end of the 1990s the traditional trade unions had consolidated their position in Russia, a consolidation which was affirmed by their affiliation to ICFTU in 2000 and sealed with the passage of the 2001 Labour Code, which was supported by FNPR, and which largely deprived the alternative trade unions of legal protection, bargaining rights and the right to strike. Personal rivalries and mutual suspicion of political and financial corruption had prevented the alternative trade unions from coming together in a single federation. Antipathy to Sotsprof and its leader, Sergei Khramov, had encouraged the fragmented alternative trade unions to come together to form a new trade union federation, with the encouragement of the AFL-CIO, in April 1995. However, conflict immediately broke out between the leaders of the alternative unions, particularly over the issue of the presidency of the new association, and the result was the creation of two competing organisations.

The Confederation of Labour of Russia (KTR) brought together the Federation of Air Traffic Controllers' Trade Unions (FPAD), the Russian Dockers Trade Union (RPD), the Russian Trade Union of Railway Locomotive Brigades (RPLBZh), the Russian Trade Union of Seamen (RPSM), the Association of Flying Crews (ALS), and also regional trade union associations – Spravedlivost' (Saint Petersburg) and the Yekaterinburg Association of Trade Unions. Later the Confederation of Labour of Saint Petersburg and Leningrad oblast', Confederation of Free Transport Trade Unions, the All-Russian Independent Trade Union of Service, Trade and Services Workers (ONP ROTU) and the Russian Confederation of Free Trade Unions (RKSP) also joined KTR. In 2006 RPLBZh left KTR and transferred to Sotsprof, alleging that the leadership of KTR was afraid to support radical actions, for fear of damaging its political contacts in the Government, the Duma and the Tripartite commission.

The All-Russia Confederation of Labour (VKT) was established in August 1995, though only registered in the spring of 1996, on the basis of the Independent Miners Union (NPG), whose chairman, Alexander Sergeev, was elected first President of VKT. Other founding affiliates were the Ural Trade Union Centre, the Inter-Regional Association of Trade Unions 'Solidarity', the Confederation of Labour of Kuzbass, the Russian Trade Union of Metalworkers, the Russian Trade Union of Public Service Workers, the Russian Trade Union of Engineers and Technical Workers, the Russian Trade Union of Medical Workers and the Trade Union of Drivers of City Passenger Transport. During 1996–7 the Russian Trade Union of Teachers and the Free Trade Union of Light Industry Workers were established within the framework of VKT, and regional associations were established in Rostov, Taimyr, Krasnoyarsk, Samara oblasts and the Komi Republic. Several of these trade unions had been affiliates of Sotsprof, but the metalworkers, public service workers, engineers and technical workers and city passenger transport drivers unions all left Sotsprof in 1998, while the health workers' union remained in Sotsprof but left VKT, although at regional level many of its branches retained their VKT affiliation, and the Moscow metro drivers' union left Sotsprof to join VKT. Also in 1998 the Russian Trade Union of Light Industry, the Trade Union of City Passenger Transport Drivers and the Trade union of Teachers of Russia decided to merge with the Russian Trade Union of Public Service Workers. Although VKT, like KTR, claimed an impressive membership, apart from NPG, itself in decline, most of these unions comprised little more than a handful of activists.

The VKT and KTR collaborated cautiously with FNPR in a joint campaign over the non-payment of wages sponsored by the ILO and ICFTU during 1997 and participated in joint trade union demonstrations at federal and regional levels. At the end of 1999 VKT and KTR were admitted alongside FNPR to the Russian Tripartite Commission, where the three federations collaborate. In 2000 VKT and KTR were admitted as affiliates by the ICFTU, alongside FNPR. However, relations with FNPR were severely strained by FNPR's support for the 2001 revision of the Labour Code, which undermined the position of the alternative trade unions. The KTR made a complaint to the ILO, which responded by reporting that a number of items in the new Labour Code, in particular the procedure for calling a strike, did not correspond to international standards, but the Russian government rejected the ILO ruling. In November 1999 VKT and KTR signed a co-operation agreement and in February 2000 established a Co-ordination Council with a view to a merging of the two organisations, but continuing rivalries meant that the merger was repeatedly postponed, most recently in fear that the merged organisation would be captured by the Kremlin, as had happened with Sotsprof, whose leader, Sergei Khramov, had been replaced by Sergei Vostretsov, a friend of President Medvedev from student days and reputedly a nominee of the Kremlin. The two organisations once again confirmed their intention to unite in December 2009, under an agreement signed in July 2009, but then found that to create a new merged organisation was both bureaucratically complicated and risked opening the door to a nominee of the Presidential administration. In order to avoid this, VKT decided on 7 April 2010 to affiliate to KTR with Boris Kravchenko, President of VKT, becoming the KTR General Secretary, and Igor Kovalchuk remaining the KTR President.

The Russian economy stabilised following the 1998 financial crisis and enjoyed a period of sustained growth for the following ten years, driven primarily by the export of primary products (oil, gas and metals) on booming world markets. Economic growth and the collapse of the system of industrial training in the previous decade strengthened the labour market position of skilled workers in strategic sectors, enabling traditional unions to sign collective agreements in those sectors which improved pay and conditions, though such improvements reflected management priorities in the face of labour market conditions rather than any increased activism on the part of the traditional unions. Nevertheless, in some cases the traditional workplace trade union did extract concessions from a reluctant management through threats of collective action, even if those threats were very rarely implemented.

An upsurge of foreign investment after the 1998 crisis, primarily in the production of consumer goods for the domestic market, also enhanced the opportunities for trade union activism. First, workers in foreign-owned plants had higher expectations than those in domestic industry, comparing their situation with that of workers in other plants of the same company abroad. Second, foreign-owned plants generally demanded much more intensive labour and higher standards of labour discipline than what was traditional in Russian enterprises. Third, the foreign owners lacked the local political connections that enabled domestic owners to mobilise the support of the police, courts, local authorities and media in the event of a dispute with their workers. As a result of these factors, the most effective and combative primary trade union organisations in Russia have been those in foreign-owned enterprises.

Table 3.1 Official statistics of strikes in Russia

Year	Number of enterprises in which strikes occurred	Number of workers involved		Number of working days lost to strikes		Average number of working days lost per strike participant
		Thousand	Average per enterprise	Thousand	Average per enterprise	
1990	260	99.5	383	207.7	799	2.1
1991	1 755	237.7	135	2 314.2	1 319	9.7
1992	6 273	357.6	57	1 893.3	302	5.3
1993	264	120.2	455	236.8	897	2.0
1994	514	155.3	302	755.1	1 469	4.9
1995	8 856	489.4	55	1 367.0	154	2.8
1996	8 278	663.9	80	4 009.4	484	6.0
1997	17 007	887.3	52	6 000.5	353	6.8
1998	11 162	530.8	48	2 881.5	258	5.4
1999	7 285	238.4	33	1 827.2	251	7.7
2000	817	31.0	38	236.4	289	7.6
2001	291	13.0	45	47.1	162	3.6
2002	80	3.9	48	29.1	364	7.5
2003	67	5.7	86	29.5	440	5.1
2004	5 993	195.5	33	210.9	36	1.1
2005	2 575	84.6	33	85.9	33	1.1
2006	8	1.2	149	9.8	1231	8.3
2007	7	2.9	413	20.5	2922	7.1
2008	4	1.9	480	29.1	7270	15.1

Overall, however, the first decade of the twenty-first century was marked by very low and declining levels of strike activity, as can be seen in Table 3.1, although the data refers only to officially notified strikes and excludes work stoppages which have not taken place in accordance with the strike legislation. Similarly, the state labour agency, Rostrud, reported that there were only 48 collective labour disputes in 2004, 41 in 2005, 18 in 2006 and nine in 2007. These figures are clearly grossly misleading. According to the data collected by the Centre for Social-Labour Rights, derived from press and other reports, there were 93 collective labour conflicts in 2008, 47 of which involved a stoppage of work, and 272 in 2009, 106 of which involved a work stoppage, while only one strike was officially recorded in 2009. The majority of these actions took place without any involvement of a primary trade union organisation. Those which did not involve a work stoppage generally took the form of meetings and pickets outside the limits of the enterprise. According to reports on their legal-protection activity by member organisations of FNPR, trade union lawyers were involved in 1101 collective labour disputes in 2007, including 14 strikes. Whereas earlier disputes were mostly about the non-payment of wages, FNPR reports that now they are mostly about pay and conditions (*Vesti FNPR*, 6, 2008: 79).

The strike wave in the mid-1990s mostly involved health and education workers and coal-miners striking over the non-payment of wages, often with the tacit support of the employers who hoped thereby to extract additional funds from the government. The upsurge in strikes in 2004–5 is largely accounted for by one-day strikes of teachers and health workers on 21 October 2004 and 12 October 2005 protesting at their low pay.

China

Unlike the Russian Revolution, which was centred on the industrial workers in large factories in the major cities, the Chinese Revolution was primarily a peasant revolution under the leadership of a Communist Party whose urban industrial roots had been severely weakened by its defeats by the Guomindang (GMD) in 1927.

The CPC had been instrumental in setting up China's first national trade union body in 1925. In the years that followed, both the GMD and the CPC struggled for supremacy of Chinese labour by setting up their own unions and occasionally working together or with the few relatively independent occupation-based unions and associations. In the climate of the time both parties followed Sun Yatsen's thinking that the presence of foreign imperialists on Chinese soil made it imperative that trade unions were part of a wider political struggle for liberation. In 1927, the right wing of the GMD seized power and immediately set about destroying communist influence in the increasingly militant labour movement. Guillermaz states that 13 000 trade unionists were executed and a further 25 000 died in the fighting (Guillermaz 1972: 226). This effectively ended collaboration between the CPC and GMD over labour issues at the national level as well as any systematic attempt by the CPC to rebuild effective trade unions on a national basis. This is not to say that communist organisers were entirely absent from the urban areas and indeed the ebb and flow of the urban labour movement between 1927 and 1949 broadly reflected the wider national picture and balance of class forces as a whole. Following the bloody events of 1927, labour organising entered what Perry calls a 'conservative interregnum' (Perry 1993: 88) that gave way to a 'radical resurgence' from 1937 up to liberation in 1949 (Perry 1993: 109) during which time labour protests became increasingly common and CPC influence grew accordingly. Nevertheless, the unions generally had a 'skimpy industrial spread and a limited "proletarian" base' (Ng and Warner 1998: 17) and this 'weakened their ability to make demands on the party' (Lee 1986: 30 cited in Ng and Warner 1998: 17). The ACFTU's Sixth Congress in 1948 reaffirmed democratic centralism as its organisational principle (Ng and Warner 1998: 17), perhaps wary that a less severe approach to internal trade union decision-making would lead to a repeat of past struggles and alliances with guilds and home-town organisations.

At the Congress the ACFTU decreed that workers would be organised on an industrial and geographical basis rather than along occupational lines. Ng and Warner find that the one-way nature of the trade union transmission belt that consequently developed between party and class in post-liberation China has its roots in pre-liberation conditions.

> The historical legacy of the pre-1949 period and the difficulties of organizing nationally led the CPC to use the ACFTU essentially as a one-way link between Party and 'masses'. (Ng and Warner 1998, 17)

Thus we can identify a tradition of CPC-affiliated organisers in China's working class but their strategy and tactics, especially with regard to workplace representation, was never far from national politics. As such there was no practice of effective representation and indeed this function of trade unions actually declined once the *danwei* system entrenched itself.

On coming to power in 1949 the Communist Party faced a severe economic crisis, with urban industry in decline and rising urban unemployment. This dictated a conciliatory attitude to capitalist employers, including the introduction of strict measures to control wages and secure labour discipline and the prohibition of strikes, with compulsory arbitration to resolve labour disputes. The Party-controlled trade union federation, ACFTU, was the instrument through which the Party-state tried to impose labour discipline, persuade workers to moderate their demands and resolve disputes bureaucratically. The subordination of the unions to the state was institutionalised in the simultaneous appointment of the ACFTU chairman, Li Lisan, as Minister of Labour. However, workers' unrest was not easily contained and the first two post-liberation years were marked by frequent strikes in both state and private enterprises, sometimes with the support of local union officials. The Party's response to the upsurge of labour unrest was to purge the ACFTU leadership of 'syndicalist' elements and to launch a series of campaigns that sought to institutionalise worker participation in management as a first step in the move to nationalisation, which it was hoped would remove the causes of worker unrest. The ACFTU was brought into line at its Seventh Congress in 1953, at which primary-level cadres who supported workers' demands were heavily criticised for 'economism' and ACFTU was committed to the implementation of the First Five Year Plan in the same year.

Nationalisation by no means removed the causes of worker unrest, as shown by the renewed strike wave in 1956–7, despite falling urban unemployment, rising wages and improved welfare benefits for industrial workers. With nationalisation complete, Mao famously declared that the era of class struggle was at an end, but 'non-antagonistic contradictions' remained, with 'bureaucratism' impeding the realisation of the workers' interests. In the Hundred Flowers Movement, against the background of the waves of strikes, the emergence of independent worker organisation and the Hungarian uprising in 1956, criticisms of bureaucratism flourished, but as the Movement threatened to get out of control a clampdown was launched with the 'Anti-Rightist' Campaign, in which ACFTU was purged once more and militant workers were sent to labour camps.

With the ACFTU under firm Party control and the working class cowed and exhausted, worker unrest declined through the disastrous Great Leap Forward and subsequent Three Years of Bitterness. No sooner than there were signs of economic recovery, Mao launched the Cultural Revolution as an attack on Party bureaucracy in 1965, of which ACFTU was a principal target, although Mao exhorted workers to stay at their posts and not to participate in the Cultural Revolution. Nevertheless, in January 1967 strikes spread through the major cities and brought much of industry to a standstill as workers exploited the chaos to press their economic demands. Then and in succeeding years the regime had to send the army in to the cities to pacify the workers.

Worker unrest, which was again brutally repressed, flared up once more in 1975–6, but Mao's death marked the end of ten years of chaos and opened the way to the new era of economic reform under Deng Xiaoping. The Democracy Wall Movement, which followed soon after Deng Xiaoping assumed power in 1978, provided workers with an opportunity to express their grievances and call for more democratic representation. The response of the new regime was to reconstitute the ACFTU, which had been dormant through the Cultural Revolution, and to emphasise the institutions provided for workers' participation, while proceeding cautiously with the reform of SOEs so as to avoid unrest. Although wages rose through the 1980s, inflation also escalated as price controls were removed from essential goods and there were scattered incidents of unrest among SOE workers, though not enough to constitute a significant challenge to the regime. This situation changed radically as students began to gather in increasing numbers in Beijing's Tiananmen Square to criticise corruption and demand more open government and to organise themselves independently of the official students' union. The Beijing Workers Autonomous Federation (BWAF) was established in solidarity with the students in April 1989 and had soon attracted 20 000 adherents. Similar organisations were established in other cities throughout China. The new workers' organisations pointed to growing inequality and falling workers' living standards alongside increasing cadre privileges, but most pertinently, criticised the ACFTU and began to demand workers' right to organise outside the ACFTU. The students were wary of worker participation in their movement, well aware of the likely consequences, and indeed as the presence of workers in the movement grew tension mounted rapidly, culminating in the move of the army into the Square and the brutal suppression of the demonstration. In the wake of the army occupation of Tiananmen hundreds of worker activists were imprisoned, an unknown number were killed, the Workers' Autonomous Federations (WAFs) were suppressed and ACFTU cadres who had supported the students were disciplined or purged. In order to contain further trouble, the regime put the brakes on the reform of SOEs and allowed SOE wages to rise in the years immediately after Tiananmen.

The Tiananmen incident led only to a temporary halt to reform, which was renewed with a vengeance following Deng's Southern tour in 1993. Foreign investment began to flow back into China, negotiations began for China to enter the WTO and in 1997 at the fifteenth Party Congress the radical reform of state enterprises was announced, 'holding on to the large and letting go of the small', alongside the rapid expansion of the private sector, employing a growing number of rural migrant workers.

During the 1980s and 1990s the main challenge of worker activism in China was posed by the reform of state enterprises, which provoked strikes and protest actions as large numbers of workers were laid off and state enterprises were unable or unwilling to meet social insurance and redundancy payments and even to pay wages. Privatisation only exacerbated these tensions as new owners asset-stripped state and former state enterprises, leaving the enterprise as a debt-burdened shell while they amassed profits elsewhere.

Protests by state enterprise workers were a particularly serious challenge because of their strategic location. On the one hand, the state enterprises facing large-scale redundancy and closure were concentrated in cities in the core industrial regions of the country. On the other hand, the workers being laid off and deprived of their birthright were the traditional core of the Chinese working class who were supposed to constitute the leading element in the country. Many of these workers, particularly in North-East China, appealed in their protests to traditional values of post-liberation China such as 'equality', 'honesty and 'selflessness'. As such their support for 'Chinese socialism' constituted a threat not so much to the rule of the Chinese Communist Party as to the current Party leadership, which had chosen the reform path away from those traditional values.

Over the course of the years of state-socialism SOE workers had acquired a relatively privileged economic position, at least in comparison with the mass of peasants who were excluded from the cities by the household registration system. The reform and eventual closure or privatisation of state enterprises threatened this position, undermining workers' traditional job security and eroding their social and welfare benefits even if it did not necessarily lead to a fall in real wages. In order to ameliorate the impact of reform the government introduced a comprehensive system of contributory social and health insurance; established re-employment centres within state enterprises to provide training and job placement, with the trade unions being assigned a significant role in administering these schemes; offered tax-breaks to enterprises which re-employed laid-off workers; offered early retirement packages to those approaching retirement age; and until 2005 provided for redundant workers to be kept on the books of their former employer (*xiagang*) and paid a modest fall-back wage for up to three years after being laid off, to give them time to find a job or open their own small business, during which time many took on other work. These measures seem to have been effective in averting and damping down protests associated with SOE lay-offs, which might otherwise have become explosive, but nevertheless the upsurge of protests temporarily slowed SOE reform at the end of the century.

Lay-off plans in Chinese SOEs have to be approved by the Staff and Workers' Congress, but this is usually a formality.[1] The trade union is likely to be consulted about the criteria for lay-offs, and may feed workers' opinions back to management, but it is not likely to have any influence over the scale of lay-offs. The trade union may monitor the process to ensure that legal restrictions on laying off more vulnerable categories of workers are observed and it may participate in selecting candidates for lay-off, with older and less skilled workers being the most likely to be selected.[2]

Although one aim of *xiagang* was to keep workers within the influence of both the enterprise and the trade union, once workers have been laid off they spend most of their time outside the work unit and so are much less subject to the influence of the trade union. Laid-off workers are also most likely to direct their demands directly to the government rather than to the management of the enterprise, which makes their protests potentially particularly dangerous for the authorities. The dangers were considerably increased if the local authorities used violence against the protesting workers.

Worker resistance to the reform of SOEs was considerably hampered by the insecurity and the divisions between workers opened up by reform. The immediate threat faced by the workers was that of being listed for redundancy and we would expect the response to that threat to be predominantly individualistic, as each worker sought to show his or her worth to the company and, often as important, sought the protection of the appropriate manager. Those who escaped the threat of redundancy could be expected above all to heave a sigh of relief, especially if the management

---

[1]   The focus of much working-class protest against lay-offs was the claim that the staff and workers' congress had either not approved the decision or that the meeting had been called out of town or that it had been so heavily policed that workers had been intimidated or had been unable to attend.

[2]   The selection of candidates for lay-off is a good indicator of the union's priorities, since management is likely to use economic criteria and prefer to lay off older, less skilled and less productive workers, while workers may tend to use social criteria and seek to protect their more vulnerable colleagues – older workers, the less skilled, those with dependents – from redundancy on the grounds that the best workers can most easily find new jobs.

could hold out the promise of increased pay and better conditions for those who remained. On the other hand, those listed for redundancy no longer had any leverage since they no longer had any opportunity to threaten the employer by withdrawing their labour and so would again be expected to look for individualistic solutions in the growing private sector.

The crackdown after Tiananmen and a significant rise in wages in SOEs in the early 1990s seem to have kept the lid on protest in SOEs in the first half of the 1990s,[1] but protest escalated from the middle of the decade as reform and associated lay-offs and non-payment of wages and benefits by insolvent enterprises moved beyond small to medium and large SOEs, particularly when there was suspicion of corruption and/or where bankruptcy meant the closure of the whole enterprise. Early protests seem to have taken the predominant form of pickets and petitions, but by the end of the century more radical forms of protest had become the norm, involving peaceful demonstrations, blocking roads or access to buildings and appealing to the local government to act to redress the workers' grievances. Protest by SOE workers was met locally by a mixture of repression and concession, the balance between the two depending on the character of the protest, the resources available to the local authorities and the political sympathies of the local state (Hurst 2004).

This wave of protests culminated in mass protests by laid-off oil workers in Daqing, laid-off metal workers in Liaoyang and laid-off or retired coal-miners in Fushun in spring 2002. Unlike earlier protests of SOE workers, which had been contained by detaining the presumed leaders and promising concessions to the workers, the mass protests of workers in the old industrial centres of the North were organised and lasted for weeks, with workers from other enterprises joining the protesters in solidarity. However, the authorities treated the protests with uncharacteristic caution and patience, no doubt having learned from the past that provoking a confrontation risked the protest spreading, and the protests eventually petered out. Many workers involved were temporarily detained by the police, but only two, who were deemed responsible for heading the protests in Liaoyang which involved workers from more than one factory, are known to have been arrested and sentenced to long prison terms. In general it appears that the scale and extent of repression has been in decline in recent years, perhaps because of the awareness of the government that repression can be counterproductive, and perhaps in part because of the large-scale international protests provoked by the Liaoyang events.

Protests by laid-off workers tend to constitute a one-off threat associated with the first stage of SOE reform, albeit one which is politically dangerous because large

---

[1] Citing Hussein and Zuang's research on taxation in China, Ng and Warner (2000: 106) argue that at this time the 'decentralization of wage determination with its attendant rise in bonuses... saw the onset of "wage bargaining" on a recognisable scale in Chinese enterprises', despite the prevailing repressive atmosphere. Although it is clear that the state had to make concessions to SOE workers, we do not know of any evidence that anything recognisable as bargaining was going on at this time.

numbers of workers take to the streets and can provide a nucleus for wider protest. However, the reform of SOEs also opens up new lines of conflict within the enterprise as those workers who remain in work face the erosion of their social and economic status within the enterprise and there are signs that workers employed in privatised SOEs are becoming more militant.

Despite the dramatic protests in Daqing, Liaoyang and Fushun, the reform of SOEs did not provoke sufficient unrest seriously to disturb the regime or to force a reconsideration of the role of ACFTU in SOEs, which continued to play the role assigned to it, of explaining to workers the necessity of reform and redundancy and of ameliorating the negative impact of reform on individual workers by assisting them in finding new jobs and providing charitable handouts to the needy.[1] On the other hand, the decline of the state-owned sector, and the parallel rise of the largely non-union private and foreign-owned sectors, had a more substantial impact on the ACFTU, severely weakening its claim to represent the working class as its membership declined by about 20 per cent over the 1990s, with a corresponding loss of income, capacity and legitimacy, as

> following the structural adjustments and the restructuring of SOEs and collectively-owned enterprises (COEs), a considerable number of trade union organisations [and branches] have been collapsed and their members washed away. (Wei 2000)

The pressure on ACFTU was not so much to change its practice in SOEs as to extend trade union membership and organisation to the new private and foreign-owned sectors, and to embrace the rural migrant workers, tens of millions of whom were finding work in these sectors. In 2003, the ACFTU's Fourteenth Congress officially acknowledged that migrant workers formed part of the working class and the following year ACFTU set a target of recruiting 6.6 million members per year over the period of 2004 to 2008, with migrant workers being a priority target. By 2006 the ACFTU was claiming almost 170 million members, including almost 41 million migrant workers (ACFTU 2007), and ACFTU claimed 212 million members in 2008.

The problem of finding jobs for displaced SOE workers has been exacerbated because the labour market has not only had to absorb the tens of millions of workers laid off by SOEs over the past two decades but also the tens of millions of peasants flooding in to the cities in search of work, so the first priority of ACFTU through the 1990s and the early 2000s was job placement and employment creation. The counterpart of the prioritisation of employment creation was that the trade unions

---

[1] The State Council released a number of documents addressing this issue, attempting to ensure that restructuring and its aftermath does not further increase industrial unrest. See for example, 'Notice on advancing the regulation of SOE restructuring. *Guanyu jin yi bu guifan guoyou qiye gaizhi gongzuo shishi yijian de tongzhi',* State Council, 19 December 2005.

were reluctant to take up issues of wages and working conditions for fear that higher wages, restriction of working hours and rigorous enforcement of health and safety regulations would weaken investment incentives and reduce employment growth (Pringle and Frost 2003). The neglect of the latter issues was, of course, reinforced by the dependence of the trade union on management in the workplace and by the desire of the local authorities to maximise economic growth (Howell 1998: 161). The single-minded pursuit of investment and economic growth, however, generated new sources of conflict as the profitability of new private and foreign-owned enterprises was achieved at the expense of the wages and working conditions of their predominantly rural migrant workers.

The rapid growth of the private and foreign-invested sectors from the 1990s was associated with the large-scale employment of rural migrant workers for long hours at minimal wages in often appalling conditions (Chen 2006). However, rural poverty and the massive rural labour surplus meant that migrant workers were initially ready to take jobs at almost any price. The household registration (*hukou*) system, originally introduced in 1958 to prevent peasants from moving to the cities, continued to provide an effective means of controlling rural migrant labour, since migrants had to secure a series of permits giving them temporary residence rights in order to work in an urban area and if they left one job they had only two months in which to find another without their permits lapsing. Nevertheless, protests and strikes by migrant workers in the coastal industrial zones have become increasingly frequent and well-organised, particularly as serious labour shortages began to emerge from 2004 so that the capacity of these migrant workers to strike has been considerably increased in recent years as labour shortages in the export-processing zones have meant that workers have had little fear of losing their jobs.

According to the available information, most strikes in China are organised by informal worker leaders, and strikes are often announced by distributing and posting leaflets around the factory. These leaders tend to be experienced workers, often holding supervisory positions, and usually rely on home-place networks in the organisation of strikes. The informal leaders sometimes use intimidation to encourage their colleagues to join the strike, but there is no evidence that such intimidation serves other than to encourage the strikers to overcome their fear of the employer and once they have joined the strike they are as enthusiastic as those who have not been subjected to such pressure.

While the Chinese government relied on severe repression of the supposed leaders, backed up by concessions to the workers, in dealing with the large-scale protests of laid-off state enterprise workers in Liaoning as recently as 2002 (Chen 2002), the balance between repression and concession has markedly shifted towards the latter in the last five years. The typical response of the authorities to strikes in the coastal regions today is to try to settle the dispute as quickly as possible and contain the strike before it spreads to neighbouring enterprises. It falls to the local administration to encourage the employer to make concessions and to the local trade union to persuade the workers to return to work, thus performing a mediating rather than a representative role. In China the policing of strikes, which are often associated with marches to the local government offices, can be aggressive and alleged strike leaders may be detained by the police for up to 15 days and subsequently dismissed and blacklisted by employers (or they may be bought off). Even quite naïve and innocent attempts of workers to create their own union organisation are blocked in favour of the establishment of an official union from the top down. Any attempts to organise workers independently which go beyond the boundaries of the enterprise are ruthlessly suppressed.

The local trade union office will frequently try to establish a trade union in non-union enterprises following a strike, and there have been cases in which striking workers have demanded the establishment of a trade union. However, such union organisations are generally established in the traditional way, by agreement with the management, and take the traditional form of a management union, so they have little capacity to prevent the recurrence of strikes and protests.

A good example of this phenomenon is that of a strike-hit joint-venture port in South China, where the crane operators' initial demand for a union representative paid for out of their own wages was deemed illegal by the chair of the city-level federation of trade unions. However, he supported the strikers' general demands on pay and a reduction of widening pay differentials, as well as the criticism of the 'mass advancement association' set up in place of a union by the Hong Kong managers of the port, which the port workers had condemned as a 'white collar club'. Promising to ensure that there would be no victimisation; the union leader mediated in negotiations and was instrumental in persuading workers to accept a management compromise offer of a 3 per cent pay rise plus a 500 Yuan subsidy for working at height. He also succeeded in getting both sides to accept the establishment of an official trade union at the port. However, the peace remained uneasy. Soon after agreement was reached, management made the height subsidy available to engineers, thus restoring the differentials. Moreover, workers rejected the official union's mainly white-collar and vetted candidates for the new union committee and voted for their own blue-collar representatives. A compromise was found via the installation of a 'capable' chairman leading the elected representatives but the issues at the heart of the dispute do not appear to have been completely resolved.

The strikes in the new booming capitalist industries in China have been steadily increasing in scale and extent, so that 'collective bargaining by riot' (Hobsbawm 1964: 6–7) has become the normal method by which migrant workers defend their rights and interests. The ebb and flow of this overall trend is also tied to the labour market. A shortfall in the numbers of skilled or experienced workers first emerged in South China in 2003 and led to intense competition among employers and more confidence among workers to take strike action. The shortages peaked in 2008, but re-emerged as China came out of the global recession in mid-2009 and appear to be having the same effect. Workers have developed a very good idea of what they can get away with and how far they can go, so that short sharp strikes and protests have become an extremely prompt and effective way of redressing their grievances (Chan 2008, 2009).

In March 2010, further evidence of migrant workers' capacity to exert pressure both on employers and the ACFTU emerged in dramatic fashion when up to 1,800 migrant workers organised a series of strikes at a Honda-owned parts factory in Foshan, Guangdong province. Many of the strikers were recent school-leavers or even school-students on work-experience schemes that Honda had taken advantage of in order to avoid the upward pressure on wages caused by the factors outlined above. The workers demands on Honda included an across-the-board wage rise of 800 Yuan and the reorganisation of trade union representation in the factory via democratic elections of worker representatives. After some prevarication, Honda's senior management in Guangdong was brought in to negotiate with the representatives, not least because at least four other Honda car plants in China were unable to continue production due to a shortage of parts. Most of the workers' demands were met and post-strike organisation in the factory remained strong enough for workers to issue an open letter of thanks to supporters worldwide. The letter drew attention to the conditions of delivery drivers at the plant who were not directly employed by Honda.

The strikes came at the same time as a spate of suicides among young workers at the massive Foxconn plant in nearby Shenzhen that had again brought sympathetic public attention to the plight of migrant workers – especially those employed in foreign enterprises. Fortunately, migrant workers in Guangdong province emulated their brothers and sisters at the Honda parts plant rather than the tragedy at Foxconn. The consequent strike wave not only brought significant wage hikes in enterprise-set wages and local government-set minimum wage levels, but also calls from China's leaders such as Hu Jintao for society to take better care of migrant workers. The Honda strikes in particular had produced a woeful response from the local trade union which dispatched officials – wearing yellow hats! – to persuade picketing workers to return to work. The incident ended in a brawl between angry strikers and union officials. Images of yellow-hatted trade union officials brawling with well-organised and disciplined young workers pursuing their legal rights against a Japanese multinational has increased pressure on the ACFTU to reform and induced damning criticism from senior ACFTU figures in Guangdong of its own local officials.

Vietnam

Labour conditions in Vietnam under French rule, particularly in the rubber plantations, were appalling and conditions deteriorated in the world economic crisis of the 1930s, with trade unions being illegal, strikes being brutally suppressed and activists repressed by the colonial power. The roots of Vietnamese trade unions lay in the experience of Vietnamese working in France, where they came into contact with French trade unions and the Communist Party and it was Communists who set up the first trade union federation, the Red Federation of Trade Unions, in 1929. From the start, trade union organisation was inseparable from the anti-colonial struggle against the French, the Japanese and finally the US and their puppet regimes, under the leadership of the Communist Party. In 1936, in accordance with Communist support for the Popular Front in France, the Federation was renamed the Brotherhood Trade Unions, but with the collapse of the Popular Front it was renamed the Anti-imperialist Workers' Association and, under Japanese occupation, the Workers' Association for National Salvation. Finally, in 1946, following the Viet Minh declaration of the independence of the Democratic Republic of Vietnam, Ho Chi Minh established the Vietnam General Confederation of Labour in Hanoi, on the model of the French CGT. (VGCL was renamed the Vietnam Federation of Trade Unions from 1961 to 1988.) Through all these changes the trade unions were essentially a wing of the Communist Party and trade union activity was subordinated to the anti-colonial and anti-imperialist struggles.

In 1948 a French colonial customs officer sought, on his personal initiative, to establish a Christian trade union federation to represent workers as a bulwark against Communism. Although still illegal, this trade union federation was tolerated by the French authorities. In 1952 the organisation was legalised and renamed the Vietnamese Confederation of Christian Workers (CVTC) and it expanded its membership rapidly. With the partition of Vietnam the CVTC was destroyed in the North and in the South fell into the arms of the CIA and became embroiled in the political intrigues in Saigon, though it continued to organise and mobilise workers, in competition with the Buddhists and the Communists, including calling and supporting strikes, mostly against foreign employers and in opposition to the anti-labour activity of successive governments, until the collapse of the Southern regime in 1974, when the CVTC leaders fled Vietnam and the organisation was destroyed (Wehrle 2008).

Labour militancy in Vietnam was reborn with the onset of reform and the influx of foreign investment. There were reportedly about 100 strikes in Vietnam between 1989 and 1994, most in foreign-owned non-union enterprises in the South of the country (Chan and Nørlund 1998:, 180–1). The 1994 Labour Code legalised strikes, but only under trade union leadership following an exhaustive procedure of mediation and arbitration. From 1995 to the end of the century there were about 60 officially recorded strikes a year and no doubt many more unrecorded strikes and work stoppages since, as a senior official of the employers' Vietnam Chamber of Commerce and Industry (VCCI) told us, 'the employers want to cover up the strike because they are usually at fault'. Since 2000 the number of recorded strikes has steadily increased, with massive strike waves of 387 recorded strikes in 2006, 540 in 2007 and 650 in 2008, the number of strikes falling by half in 2009 in the wake of the global financial crisis as workers were intimidated by lay-offs, plant closures and rising unemployment, although the number of strikes began to rise again in 2010, lasted longer and proved more difficult to settle. Not one of these strikes was led by the trade union and not one followed the legally prescribed procedure.

Table 3.2 Strikes in Vietnam by enterprise ownership

Year	Strikes	SOEs		FDI		Local private	
		No.	%	No.	%	No.	%
1995	60	11	18	28	47	21	35
1996	59	6	10	39	66	14	24
1997	59	10	17	35	59	14	24
1998	62	11	18	30	48	21	34
1999	67	4	6	42	63	21	31
2000	71	15	21	39	55	17	24
2001	89	9	10	54	61	26	29
2002	100	5	5	66	66	29	29
2003	139	3	2	101	73	35	25
2004	125	2	2	93	74	30	24
2005	147	8	6	100	68	39	27
2006	387	4	1	287	74	96	25
2007	541	1	1	405	72	135	27
2008	762	0	0	592	78	170	22
2009	310	4	1	239	77	67	22
Total	2978	93	3	2150	72	735	25

Source: Legal Department, VGCL.

Most strikes in Vietnam have been in non-unionised private and, increasingly, foreign-owned enterprises, which employ vast numbers of migrant workers in poor working conditions, forced to work long hours for minimal wages, while the number of strikes in SOEs has been in relative decline. It seems that the reform of state enterprises in the 1990s proceeded relatively peacefully, despite the massive scale of lay-offs, which mostly affected small SOEs. Most of the strikes in SOEs were around the non-payment of wages and lay-offs and redundancy compensation, which were particularly acute problems in the 1990s but which have declined in significance since then, so that there has been a marked fall in the incidence of strikes in SOEs since 2000. Moreover, the labour force in SOEs is more tightly monitored by the 'group of four' (Director, Communist Party cell, trade union and Youth League) than is the labour force in non-state enterprises so that discontent is more easily identified and mollified or snuffed out. The trade union is also probably more effective at monitoring management observance of the labour law and worker discontent in SOEs.

The Vietnamese Labour Code provides for redundancy compensation and, in the event of mass lay-offs, requires that the trade union should be consulted and the local labour bureau notified one month in advance. We know of only one case in which the union actively resisted redundancies. In an ABB joint-venture, the trade union protested proposed lay-offs in 1999 and the issue could not be resolved through conciliation and so was referred to MOLISA. Before the latter could respond, the trade union organised a demonstration on the company's premises, appealing to the Hanoi People's Committee for a solution, which passed the problem on to the Prime Minister's Office, whose inspection team over-ruled the closure and lay-off decision (Belser 2000: 25).[1]

The Vietnamese authorities have proceeded cautiously with SOE reform, rationalising predominantly through mergers and sustaining SOEs through credit from state banks, debt write-offs and tax remission. Corporatisation (equitisation) and privatisation since 1999 has mainly been directed at smaller and more competitive SOEs, so that the larger SOEs in 'strategic' sectors have mostly been untouched, though some have faced competition from new entrants (Klump and Bonschab 2004). This cautious approach to SOE reform in the context of rapid general economic growth has meant that employment in the state sector has increased steadily since the early 1990s and lay-offs have not been a major issue, while rising SOE wages seem to have smoothed over tensions that might be created by increasing pay differentials.

A very high proportion of strikes are in Ho Chi Minh City and the neighbouring provinces of Dong Nai and Binh Duong, which have the highest concentration of the foreign-invested enterprises (FIEs) that account for about two-thirds of all strikes. The vast majority of these strikes are in Korean and, particularly, Taiwanese-owned companies, often sub-contracting to global brands. This is partly because Korea and Taiwan are the largest investors in Vietnam, but also because Korean and Taiwanese investors have tended to use the authoritarian management methods inherited from the SMEs from which many of them have grown, but they are also working in very competitive, low-skilled, labour-intensive light industry where such management methods are common. The prevalence of strikes in FIEs in the mid-1990s was attributed to 'cultural differences' and some notorious strikes were provoked by such things as managers beating workers, but now strikes have a more straightforward economic foundation, primarily over wages, bonuses and working hours, the strike waves of 2005–8 being almost entirely around the issue of wages, with unpaid wages becoming a major issue from the end of 2008 as foreign investors fled leaving wages unpaid. The prevalence of strikes in FIEs is now explained by Vietnamese commentators by the fact that work is more intensive in foreign enterprises, that workers believe that foreign owners can afford to meet their demands and that they expect the state to support them against foreigners, an expectation that is not

---

[1] The provisions of the Labour Code effectively apply only to SOEs and joint-ventures. Most private and foreign-owned enterprises (and many SOEs) hire workers on short-term contracts, so can reduce the labour force without making redundancies by deciding not to renew contracts. Thus the state-owned coal company, Vinacoal, was able to lay off 16 000 contract workers without compensation, with the support of the trade union, in the face of an overproduction crisis in 1999 (Greenfield 1999: 18).

unfounded. It is normal practice, as soon as a strike occurs, for the local labour department officials to try to persuade the employer to meet the workers' demands so as to get them back to work as soon as possible, so that most strikes are settled rapidly, with the employer conceding the workers' main demands.

Strikes in Vietnam until the early 2000s were almost always wildcat strikes, in which one incident provokes a work stoppage which may lead to a walkout of a section and then of the whole factory. More recently it seems that strikes have become more organised, with informal workers' leaders circulating leaflets to announce the strike in advance. The workers usually assemble in front of the factory, often blocking the entrance and the road outside, but it is unlikely at this stage that they will have an articulated set of demands, as opposed to an accumulation of diverse grievances, although in some more recent strikes leaflets calling for the strike have included a list of specific demands. A representative from the local labour department, Department of Labour, Invalids and Social Affairs (DOLISA), usually accompanied by a trade union official, comes to the enterprise to investigate the dispute, having been alerted by a manager, a trade union officer in the enterprise, the local police or the local People's Committee.[1] The priority of the authorities is to get the workers back to work to preserve social peace and public order and to prevent the strike from spreading to neighbouring enterprises (a frequent event). To this end they hold a meeting with the strikers to hear their grievances and put together a list of demands which they can then take to the management. They will try to convince the workers to return to work immediately, on the grounds that their demands will be met, although the workers may refuse to return to work until they hear management's response. The officials will then investigate the case further and persuade the employer to meet what they judge to be the workers' legitimate demands, the resolution of the dispute being put in writing. The officials will also persuade the employer to pay workers for the days on strike and to guarantee no victimisation, so as not to exacerbate the situation. It is rare for the strikers themselves to play any part in the resolution of the dispute: negotiations take place behind closed doors between the employer, trade union and Labour Department officials. A district trade union official will formally represent the demands of the strikers and negotiate the resolution of the dispute, but this is just a means for VGCL to uphold its role where there is no workplace union or the workplace union is too weak and in reality it is the local Labour Department official who achieves the resolution of the dispute with the threat of legal and administrative sanctions. If there is no trade union in the enterprise, DOLISA will encourage the employer to set one up, on the grounds that a trade union is the best insurance against strikes – it is claimed that strikes are less likely to take place, or at least are more easily settled, in unionised than in non-union

---

[1]   Ho Chi Minh City, Binh Duong and Dong Nai People's Committees have formalised regular strike task forces comprising DOLISA, VGCL and VCCI staff as an alternative to the legal procedure for resolving disputes.

enterprises. In the longer term, VGCL and DOLISA may organise training in the labour law for the employer and employees.

A sharp distinction is made by the authorities between the 'legitimate' and the 'unreasonable' demands of workers, which corresponds to a distinction between strikes over rights and strikes over interests. Legitimate demands are those which arise from a violation of labour laws and regulations by the employer, while unreasonable demands are those which go beyond the assertion of workers' legal rights to an expression of their interests. 'There is no ground for workers to force employers to respond to demands that are higher than the legal provision', claimed a union official, member of the Ho Chi Minh City (HCMC) strike taskforce, in an interview in 2007. When a strike breaks out the authorities are able to press the employer to meet the 'legitimate' demands of the workers by pointing out the legal violations and threatening the employer with appropriate sanctions, but meeting demands for wages higher than those prescribed by the law is more problematic. This was shown particularly clearly in the strike waves of 2006 to 2008, which were motivated primarily by demands for higher wages to compensate for inflation.

A massive strike wave, with 150 strikes involving 140 000 workers, struck the South of Vietnam at the end of 2005 and beginning of 2006 which centred on demands for substantial wage increases to compensate for rampant inflation, stimulated by a (false) press report that the Labour Department had called on FIEs to increase their minimum wages by about 40 per cent and that the government was planning to increase the minimum wage, which had been unchanged for almost a decade, at the beginning of 2006, none of which materialised. Local officials pleaded urgently with the government, both directly and through VGCL, to announce an increase in the minimum wage and some employers insisted that they would not raise wages until the government announced a decision on the minimum wage,[1] but most employers met their workers' demands at once. On 6 January the Prime Minister issued Decree 03, which increased FIE minimum wages by about 40 per cent from 1 February 2006. However, as widely anticipated, the increase in the FIE minimum wage provoked a second wave of strikes as non-FIE workers walked out demanding wage increases.

The attempt to convert interest-based strikes into strikes over rights by increasing the legal minimum wage failed as a further wave of strikes erupted in the first quarter of 2007, particularly in March, with over 80 strikes, involving 100 000 workers, and in the first half of October, with 88 strikes involving over 100 000 workers.[2] An even larger strike wave broke out in the first quarter of 2008 and continued until July, with 649 strikes. Workers had learnt from the 2005–6 strike

---

[1]   Some reports suggested that employers were being encouraged by local officials to hold out until the government made a decision.

[2]   MOLISA report to the Prime Minister on strikes and labour disputes (March 2007); VGCL report to the Central Party Committee (October 2007).

wave that wildcat strikes were the fastest and most effective way to secure a wage increase. Employers had also learnt that a strike would draw attention to their violations of the labour law, so apart from illegal overtime working, which workers needed to make up their wages, it seems that the level of legal violations markedly reduced after the 2005–6 strikes. Nevertheless, the increase in the legal minimum wage and a higher degree of legal compliance by employers did nothing to reduce the incentive for workers to strike, as inflation ran ahead of pay increases. Fewer than 20 per cent of the demands put forward by strikers in 2007 were rights-based, and only 3 per cent of the 649 strikes in the first eight months of 2008 arose purely from rights-based disputes.[1] An experienced DOLISA official we interviewed in 2007 noted that 'even though the strike-affected companies comply with the labour law, the legal standards of working conditions are not sufficient for workers to subsist, especially when the inflation rate in industrialised regions has grown to 9 per cent in the last few months'. Marked features of the 2007 strike waves were the relatively large number of strikes in Japanese-owned companies, which had hitherto been noted as good employers who respected the law; the timing of the strikes, which occurred not before Tet, when new year bonuses are due, but after the Tet break, when labour shortages are most acute as workers change jobs or fail to return from their home villages; the location of the strikes, which erupted in Dong Nai and spread to Binh Duong provinces, where labour shortages are most acute, while there were fewer strikes in Ho Chi Minh City; the spread of strikes from textiles, garments and footwear to electronics, engineering and wood processing; the duration of the strikes, which lasted two or three times as long as the normal one to two days as the traditional approach to strike settlement, pressing the employer to respect the law, failed to work; and the marked reduction in violence and sabotage, with the strike becoming a peaceful method of bargaining. In one case, Harada Vietnam, a Japanese engineering company in Dong Nai IPZ, the management refused a visit of the strike taskforce because they wished to resolve the strike bilaterally between management and workers. 'We [the company] do not violate the law so this is just a problem between us and our workers. Let us solve it ourselves', the director of Harada said (Do 2007a: 9).

A witness told us about a strike in an IPZ in Ho Chi Minh City in October 2006:

I heard that leaflets were passed around one day before, calling for strikes. The next day, at exactly 7.30 am, all the workers gathered in front of the company's gate. They queued up in several orderly lines. No violence, no yelling. They all looked cheerful. A piece of paper containing workers' demands was given to the guard who passed it to the director. Security guards stood around the strikers but there was no tension. They even chatted and laughed loudly. One hour later, the director came out to talk to the strikers. He is Korean and cannot speak

[1] Report on 20 August 2008 of the National Labour Relations Committee.

Vietnamese; neither can workers speak Korean or English. Workers demanded an increase of 300 thousand dong by raising three fingers. The director shook his head and showed one finger. The silent bargaining continued until the director raised two fingers (VND 200 thousand) and workers applauded. They dispersed peacefully and returned to work the next day. (Do 2007b: 8)

Wildcat strikes have become institutionalised, at first as a form of 'collective bargaining by riot', but more recently as a form of peaceful collective bargaining. Both the 2005–6 and autumn 2007 strike waves were initiated by a strike in the same company, Freetrend, a Taiwanese footwear company in Linh Trung industrial park in Ho Chi Minh City. In the first seven months of 2008, 40 enterprises faced more than one strike. In two Korean companies in Long An, particularly, there were five strikes in 2008. Many companies experienced one strike each year in 2006–8.

Although Vietnamese strikes are wildcat strikes, they seem to be increasingly well-organised and disciplined, with workers displaying a high level of solidarity. The trade union and senior managers rarely have any advance knowledge of the strike, which suggests the complicity, at least, of line managers in the strike. Strikes nowadays will often be announced in advance by rumours and by the circulation and posting of anonymous leaflets, the style of which often suggests the involvement of educated white-collar workers. In several cases in 2007 strike organisers sent demands to the employer in advance and managed to control the strike to ensure that the strikers did not confront the police. In one case, a Taiwanese footwear company in Dong Nai, the strike organisers collected VND 1000 each from the 7000 strikers to finance a strike fund (Do 2007a: 9). Although the strike may initially involve a small group of workers, typically the entire labour force will stop work and assemble at the entrance to the factory. Once the workers have been persuaded to return to work they will usually resume work together, if not immediately then within a few days.

Strikes are organised on the basis of informal networks among the workers, often based on place-of-origin, and the strike leaders tend to be older, more experienced and generally male workers, often in skilled or supervisory positions. The informal leaders sometimes use intimidation to encourage their colleagues to join the strike but, as in China, there is no evidence that such intimidation serves other than to encourage the workers to overcome their fear and once they have joined the strike they are as enthusiastic as those who have not been subjected to such pressure. Officials from VGCL admit that there are 'informal leaders' behind the strikes: 'whenever there is a strike, there is always a leader. We [the strike taskforce which contains VGCL and DOLISA officers] have to approach these leaders and persuade them and then others will agree' a VGCL informant said. But they view these leaders as 'bad elements', 'black leaders', who incite workers to strike for their short-sighted, personal interests. As a provincial VGCL official stated: 'they think of the immediate interests of workers, they ignore workers' responsibility for the enterprise, they incite them to break the law, so we cannot accept them as standing committee members.'

This view was incorporated in the Amendments to the Labour Code that came into effect in July 2007 which imposed administrative and criminal sanctions against people who 'incite, embroil, or force' workers to strike.

However, these informal leaders are sometimes involved in negotiations to resolve the strikes. In December 2005, the Deputy Director of HCMC DOLISA was called by the owner of a Korean textile company located in Thu Duc district, asking for her help to settle a strike in his company. The strikers demanded higher wages and less overtime work. As soon as she arrived at the company, she proposed that the union represent the workers to negotiate with the employer about the strikers' demands. However, the Korean owner refused. He said: 'the strike is not led by the union. The union did not even know about the strike before it happened. So why should I negotiate with the union when they do not represent the strikers?' The DOLISA official, consequently, decided to allow the workers to select their own representatives to take part in the negotiation with the employer. Three representatives were swiftly 'elected' and the strike was settled. In a Japanese company in Hanoi, which faced a strike in 2004, the director gave those he suspected of being the strike leaders, who were good workers, good positions with allowances and selected them as representatives for the union standing committee, while keeping the HR manager as union chairman.

Sometimes the informal workers' leader and the trade union leader co-operate. In a Korean textile company in Binh Duong province, the union leader had been in post for five years, but he admitted that he dare not go against the employer as he was afraid of losing his job or being victimised. There had been two strikes in the previous two years in his company but neither was led by the union, though he had known when the strikes would happen. The real workers' leader was a thirty-year-old female blue-collar worker who had worked there for eight years and was well respected by other, younger, mostly women workers. Over the years she had set up her own 'underground union'. According to the trade union president, a representative is elected secretly in each section and these representatives report to the leader, who collects the workers' demands and then meets with the union leader who, as an intermediary, would take the message to the employer and report the response back to the informal leader. The two strikes had happened, he said, because the employer had refused the workers' demands. The union leader admitted that he supports the informal leader because she is only doing good for the workers – the task that he is not able to fulfil. Therefore, he would never tell the employer or anyone else who she is so as to protect her.

It is likely that such covert mediation between informal workers' leaders and management by trade union officers or line managers is not uncommon in FIEs. However, the recognition of the representative status of informal leaders is a very sensitive issue. In a strike in a Taiwanese company in July 2007 the Labour Department official rejected the suggestion from the regional VGCL officer that worker representatives be invited to negotiate with management on the grounds, as she later explained, that 'this is the most sensitive aspect of wildcat strikes. The strike was not organised by the union so if we invite workers' representatives into the room and let them negotiate with the employer, it means we acknowledge their role as representatives of workers while denying the role of municipal VGCL, District Eight Union, and the company union.'

Workers are very well-informed about the situation in neighbouring plants, so that if workers secure concessions through a strike in one plant, strikes almost immediately break out in neighbouring plants. The labour press, under official control but relatively independent, also played an increasing role in propagating information about industrial disputes until there was a clamp-down on press reporting of strikes in 2008, when the Party requested the labour press 'to cover objectively and honestly the implementation of the Party advocacy on international economic integration and FDI attraction and to avoid one-sided information that may create negative reactions in industrial relations and among the public' (Resolution 22 of the Party Central Committee, issued 5 June 2008, cited in Do 2008: 12).

The policing of strikes in Vietnam has been relatively benign. Strikers who gather outside the factory gates are not dispersed and action is rarely taken against strike leaders, although there have been reported cases of strike leaders who were prosecuted for disturbing public order or sabotaging companies' assets during strikes and of the arrest of workers who are suspected of being workers' leaders. The foreign investors also 'have a blacklist. They are not allowed to dismiss participants in a strike, but they can dismiss for attitude and discipline or not renew their contract', as a Zone official explained.

In Vietnam, workplace trade union organisations can only be established under the supervision and administration of the higher-level VGCL organisation, so that any other form of worker representation is illegal. Even the most innocent initiatives to create a trade union independent of VGCL can be met with a heavy hand. We talked to the deputy director of a Vietnamese private footwear company in Ho Chi Minh City in 2004, who had worked as a union leader in an SOE for over ten years and was now the trade union leader in his company. Believing in the benefit for the management of having a union, when the company was established he immediately thought about setting up a union-like organisation without any contact with or support from the provincial VGCL. 'My thought then was very simple', he said, 'I just wanted to have something similar to a union so that we, the management, know what the workers think about the company and how we can address their concerns. I thought if I did it internally it would be simpler than going through the higher level union.' He selected a workers' representative from each factory who would report to him the concerns and demands from workers. This informal union operated quite well for three months, as he recalled, until officials from the provincial VGCL and DOLISA visited the company. The *de facto* union was turned down as 'illegal'. But instead of recruiting the then-informal union into the VGCL, the officials asked the company to abolish the whole system and start the VGCL top-down unionisation procedure from the beginning.

The authorities take a much sterner view of any hints of independent labour organisation beyond the workplace, particularly when there is a suggestion of political motivation. Since unification, Vietnamese exiles have been active in opposition groups in the US but have had little penetration in Vietnam itself. In October 2006, the formation of two independent trade unions, the United Worker-Farmers Organisation of Vietnam, or UWFO (Hiep Hoi Doan Ket Cong Nong) and the Independent Workers' Union of Vietnam, or IWUV (Cong Doan Doc Lap), was announced, but all the known activists of both these organisations were soon arrested and jailed, while one disappeared, having fled to Cambodia (Human Rights Watch 2009) and there is no evidence that either organisation succeeded in establishing any workplace cells. After the first wave of strikes in early 2006, the Ministry of Public Security conducted an investigation and concluded that there was no political motivation behind the strikes, which only expressed the economic needs of workers. In general workers are well aware of the limits of the permissible and avoid getting involved in anything that might invoke punitive sanctions.

Labour activism is always closely related to the labour market situation, which has been changing rapidly in Vietnam as growing labour shortages emerge, even in the North, and was a major reason for the escalation in the number of strikes in 2006–8 and their damping down in 2009. The expansion of the foreign-invested sector has mopped up all of the available local workers in the cities around which the Industrial Zones and EPZs are located, so they have to rely increasingly on migrant workers from more distant rural areas. Labour shortages became increasingly acute with the surge of foreign investment following Vietnam's accession to the WTO in 2006. All of our informants noted that it was becoming increasingly difficult to attract rural workers to the cities because the high cost of living and low wages left them with little money to send back home, their main reason for coming to the city. Labour turnover has increased, and in some cases reached very high levels, but this is not so much because workers move to better-paid jobs elsewhere as because they return to their home villages. Employers are reluctant to respond to labour market pressures by raising the wages of production workers, particularly when they are competing for export contracts, and generally try to pay the going rate, which in labour-intensive sectors is the legal minimum wage. This means that there are fewer opportunities for workers to pursue an exit strategy and that they are more likely to seek higher wages through collective action. Once one group of workers successfully strikes for higher wages, others are likely to follow their example.

4

Traditional Trade Unions Adapting to New Conditions

In all three countries the traditional trade unions have sought to adapt to the radically changing industrial relations environment not by making fundamental changes in their structures and practices, but by modifying their traditional modes of operation to take account of the new circumstances.

In all three countries the transition to capitalist production relations has been associated with the introduction of a legal framework for the regulation of labour relations, which includes detailed regulation of such aspects as a minimum wage, maximum normal working hours, the legal limitation of overtime, enhanced rates of pay for overtime and night work, and extensive protective regulations for specific categories of employees, particularly women and young people. Alongside the legal regulation of the minimum terms and conditions of employment, all three countries have introduced collective bargaining procedures, bureaucratic-legal systems for the mediation and arbitration of individual and collective labour disputes, and systems of tripartite consultation at national and regional levels. However, without any fundamental changes in their structures and practices, these new institutional forms merely replicate the traditional close collaboration between trade unions and government, on the one hand, and trade unions and management, on the other, so that the trade unions are not able effectively to represent the grievances and aspirations of their members. At the same time, the legal and institutional changes, on the one hand, and the pressure of worker activism, on the other, create the space in which enterprising and energetic trade union officers are able to undertake more positive initiatives and to create the possibility of more effective trade unionism.

The pressure of worker activism and the union response has been rather different in each country, partly reflecting the different economic trajectory and political circumstances of each. Russia experienced a catastrophic economic decline through the 1990s, with some stabilisation and uneven recovery following the 1998 financial crisis, driven primarily by the export of fuel and raw materials. China and Vietnam experienced equally dramatic economic growth over the same period, with the rural surplus population providing a cheap labour force for export-driven growth of manufacturing, with high levels of foreign investment focused on the coastal regions of China and the south of Vietnam.

Worker unrest in Russia through the 1990s primarily took the form of increasingly desperate protests of workers who had not been paid their wages for months or even years on end, with much less frequent strikes and protests over the erosion of wages

76

by inflation or the failure of employers to meet their statutory obligations or to implement the collective agreement. While the traditional unions responded to worker unrest primarily by lobbying state bodies and organising symbolic protests, the alternative unions were more active pursuing their demands through the courts and encouraging more militant action in the workplace. With the stabilisation of the economy at the turn of the century, the pressure of worker activism declined, but this equally meant that the leverage of the traditional trade unions declined and lobbying and protests had a steadily diminishing effect. At the same time, the traditional unions faced some competition from the alternative unions. If they were to retain members, they had to show that they could deliver something to their members within the framework of 'social partnership' to which they were committed. Hence FNPR has put steadily increasing emphasis on the negotiation of federal and regional tripartite agreements, branch tariff agreements and collective agreements at the level of the enterprise and has encouraged its member organisations to seek to use such negotiations at least to maintain existing standards of pay, health and safety and social and welfare provision, and if possible to improve the terms of successive agreements. The FNPR and its member organisations have also sought to provide services to individual members, to augment the traditional social and welfare benefits administered by the union, following the lead of the alternative unions in expanding their legal apparatus in order to provide legal advice and representation for union members, but FNPR has not until recently shown much interest in organising, being more concerned to hold on to existing members than to recruit new ones.

China has a relatively long history of worker unrest that has punctuated the whole state-socialist period and has always been associated with episodes of political instability. China has faced two phases of worker unrest in the reform period, the first in the 1990s dominated by unrest among traditional SOE workers facing large-scale lay-offs and the loss of their former status and privileges, which created problems of public order but did not pose a serious challenge to the trade union. The priority of ACFTU was to consolidate its position in state enterprises by signing collective agreements and to contribute to the maintenance of social peace by administering job placement and job creation programmes.

Since the turn of the century there has been a rapid increase in strikes and protests, predominantly of rural migrant workers, in ununionised private and foreign-owned enterprises, which have become progressively better organised and more effective as migrant workers have gained more experience and as labour shortages have strengthened their bargaining position. The response of the Party and ACFTU was to seek to extend trade union organisation to the new private and foreign-owned sectors and to bring employment relations in these sectors into the framework of regulation by collective agreements, although there was little sign that ACFTU expected to do any more than extend its traditional trade union model to the private sector, the new workplace trade unions being intended to serve more as an arm of Party-state control than as a body representative of the workers (Gallagher 2005). Moreover, the regime's fear of the political implications of unemployment has meant that ACFTU has been encouraged to give priority to employment creation over increasing pay, making it very difficult for ACFTU to endorse demands for pay increases to compensate for inflation on the part of their members.

Whereas the Russian trade unions have been under pressure to reform as a result of their loss of membership, competition from alternative trade unions and the need to legitimate their representative claims in the face of the state, ACFTU has been under more direct pressure to reform from the Party-state, but at the same time the Party-state has set the limits to reform by insisting that social harmony is the absolute priority of the trade unions. This means that in China, as in Russia, there is both the space and the incentive to undertake local reform initiatives, but in China such initiatives are more likely to be neutralised or, if the reforms are generalised, bureaucratised, for fear that they will provoke the conflict that they are supposed to constrain.

Vietnam has a much shorter history of worker activism than Russia or China, with lay-offs from SOEs having apparently proceeded fairly smoothly as they were largely compensated by the growth of employment in both private and public sectors. Serious pressure for union reform only mounted as strikes began to break out in private and foreign-owned enterprises in the South. The immediate response of VGCL was to increase union membership and extend union organisation to Privately Owned Enterprises (POEs) and FIEs, in the expectation that strikes would be less likely to occur in unionised enterprises, while leaving primary responsibility for strike resolution to MOLISA. More broadly, VGCL remains committed to its traditional model of trade unionism, relying on state regulation and state power, and in the Vietnamese political system it has the power to press its own priorities. Thus, VGCL has sought to push responsibility for the increasing number of strikes onto the state and its reform proposals have centred on legislative and administrative intervention, for example through minimum wage adjustment, the state regulation of wages through the compulsory registration of wage tables and administrative intervention to resolve disputes. VGCL recognises the weakness of its primary organisations in the private and foreign-owned sectors, but rather than seeking to strengthen its primary organisations it is proposing to displace them by giving increased power and responsibility to higher-level trade union organisations.

Although there is some scope for more active workplace unionism in Vietnam, because primary organisations are largely left to their own devices, overall trade union reform has progressed much less far in Vietnam than in Russia or China. Nevertheless, some directions of activity are common to all three countries. First, the trade unions have made the signing of a collective agreement the principal indicator of an active primary organisation and have launched campaigns to extend the coverage, if not always the quality, of collective agreements. Second, the trade unions maintain their traditional close collaboration with state bodies in the formulation and implementation of labour and social policy, for example in setting a minimum wage and in collaboration with state inspectorates. Third, the trade unions have made some efforts to provide legal advice and to represent their members in individual and collective labour disputes. Fourth, the trade unions have made some efforts to strengthen their primary organisations. Finally, the trade unions have all sought to expand their membership and extend trade union organisation to the new private sector.

In this chapter we will review the general directions and overall limitations of trade union reform in these areas in all three countries. In the next chapter we will look at examples of trade union best practice, concentrating primarily on the example of Russia, in order to identify the possibilities of further progress in trade union reform.

Collective agreements

In all three countries, the state determination of the terms and conditions of labour has been replaced by their determination on the basis of legally prescribed minima, supplemented by collective agreements between employers and employees. We have already seen the significant role played by trade unions in lobbying the government over legal regulation of the terms and conditions of labour, but legal regulation can only set the minimum standards, so the trade unions in all three countries have put steadily increasing emphasis on the negotiation of collective agreements, in the first instance at the enterprise level, supplemented by higher-level sectoral agreements and tripartite municipal, regional and national agreements.

Collective agreements in principle make it possible to determine terms and conditions of employment which are acceptable both to the employer and to the employees. The coverage of collective agreements has become a formal indicator of the effectiveness of regional and local trade union organisations in all three countries. Higher-level trade unions therefore encourage their primary organisations to sign collective agreements, with very little attention being paid to the quality of those agreements.

Russia

Collective agreements were established in the Soviet Union under Stalin and from 1929–34 the unions attempted to use collective agreements as an instrument for increasing productivity (Ruble 1981: 17), but this attempt proved ineffective. Collective agreements were abolished in 1934 and were not formally reintroduced until 1947. In 1957 the collective agreement, which had the force of law, was defined by a resolution of the Central Committee of the Communist Party as the juridical foundation for all trade union activity at the enterprise level. Nevertheless, promoting production remained the unions' primary formal obligation, and their relationship with the Communist Party was not altered by the resolution (Ruble 1981: 33–4). The 'central task' of the unions, defined in the Preamble to their constitution, was unambiguous and unchanged from that defined by Lenin: 'to mobilise the masses for the attainment of our principal economic goal – the creation of the material and technical basis of communism, for the further strengthening of the Soviet Union's economic and defence power, for ensuring a steady rise in the people's material and cultural standards' (Godson 1981: 113).

Since wages, working hours and other terms and conditions of employment were determined centrally, there was little to negotiate over in the collective agreement, which typically included the administration's responsibility to realise the 'social development plan' of the enterprise and the trade union's responsibility to ensure that the workers realised the enterprise's production plan. The centrality of the production plan to the collective agreement is exemplified by the fact that collective agreements were not signed in the 'non-productive sphere', such as public administration, health and education.

The move towards 'self-management' of enterprises in the late Brezhnev era was reflected in the 1984 Law on Collective Agreements, which ensured that the increased discretion in managerial decision-making associated with the development of self-management did not exceed the bounds of party policy by prescribing the format of the collective agreement in detail. Inscribed within this law were all the customary assumptions regarding the role of trade unions under communism. The model agreement began with a formal undertaking of the labour collective to fulfil the plan and their socialist obligations, so that 'planning targets for the enterprise become part of each worker's individual responsibility' (Butler 1988: 226). The employees similarly committed themselves to engagement in socialist competition and the development of a communist attitude to labour, to take the initiative in making inventions and introducing technological innovations. This was followed by provisions regarding pay, which implemented the centrally determined tariff scales and norms, and the right (and duty) of workers to participate in production conferences, where they were supposed to put forward suggestions for increasing productivity and improving conditions. The typical agreement specified the extent of training and re-training to be provided, and resolved to improve labour discipline. The only real scope for modification of the standard terms of the collective agreement lay in the final section which dealt with health, housing, social and welfare provision, spelling out the details of the enterprise's social development plan, which could include the provision of facilities out of the enterprise's own funds, and this was usually the only section in the formulation of which the trade union played any role.

The second half of the 1980s saw a steady increase in the role of collective agreements, particularly following the 1987 Law on State Enterprise, which considerably increased the scope for discretion of enterprise management in determining wages and employment, but the 1984 Law was not replaced until the collapse of the administrative-command system in 1992, which immediately implied that wages and working conditions would be determined independently by the enterprise. Ambiguities in the 1992 Law on Collective Bargaining and Agreements provided space for alternative trade unions by providing bargaining rights to any properly constituted trade union and allowing for multiple collective agreements, each covering the members of the trade union with which it was signed. These ambiguities, which led to chaos in the bargaining process, were ironed out in the 1995 revision of the Law and the 2002 Labour Code, which considerably strengthened the traditional unions by prescribing that only one collective agreement, which would apply to all employees, would be signed in each enterprise or organisation and giving bargaining rights to the majority trade union (generally the traditional union or, where no union has a majority, a 'yellow' union sponsored by the employer).

The Law locates collective agreements within the framework of a system of social partnership and allows for a range of agreements, from collective agreements between employees and employers through various kinds of higher-level agreements: general, regional, branch (inter-branch) tariff, territorial and other. Higher-level agreements are only binding on those employers who are signatory to them, and the low level of employers' organisation means that they serve as little more than a reference point for primary trade union organisations negotiating collective agreements. Although higher-level trade union bodies encourage their primary organisations to incorporate the terms of branch and regional agreements into their own collective agreements, there is little or nothing that the trade unions can do to force a reluctant employer to agree to such terms.

The collective agreements still tend to be formal documents. The draft of the collective agreement will typically be prepared by the various management departments and the trade union on the basis of the previous agreement. Although shops may be asked to submit proposals for inclusion in the collective agreement, and the draft may be circulated for comment, negotiation of the agreement is usually a bureaucratic process that does not involve any mobilisation of the membership. The director will usually decide unilaterally whether or not to accept trade union proposals and the union will rarely contest the director's decision, although a memorandum of disagreement may be prepared as an appendix to the collective agreement. The FNPR report on the 1999–2000 collective agreement campaign noted that FNPR did not know of a single case in which a primary trade union organisation had taken any kind of action in support of its demands (FNPR 2001: 12).

The FNPR has made the signing of collective agreements, as the cornerstone of the system of social partnership, a major priority and regional trade union organisations are judged by the extent to which they manage to persuade their primary organisations to do so. The preparation and signing of the collective agreement was a well-established ritual in the industrial sector in the soviet period, but in public services it is a more recent innovation. This is the principal explanation for the fact that the number of collective agreements signed each year increased steadily through the 1990s. According to the Ministry of Labour's figures, 68 800 collective agreements were signed in 1993 and 144 600 in 1999. These figures are substantially lower than those issued by FNPR, a difference that is largely explained by the fact that the majority of collective agreements are signed for a period of two or three years and many are not registered with the Ministry of Labour. According to FNPR, in 1999 a collective agreement was in force in 72 per cent of reporting enterprises, a big increase on the 60 per cent of the previous year (FNPR 2001). By 2008 FNPR reported that 56 branch tariff agreements, 77 regional agreements, 6461 territorial agreements and 169 307 collective agreements were in operation, the latter covering 89.51 per cent of establishments which had an FNPR primary organisation, although some of these agreements represented only a prolongation of a previous agreement (*Vesti FNPR*, 6, 2009: 134). This was a small increase in the coverage, though a decline in the number, of collective agreements compared to the previous year, because of the decline in the number of trade union organisations. Of course, trade union penetration of the new private sector is minimal,[1] so the latter figure considerably overstates the coverage of collective agreements. In 2008 the coal-miners' trade union, once one of the strongest and most militant of the FNPR unions, had managed to sign collective agreements in only 65 per cent of the enterprises in which it had a primary organisation (*Vesti FNPR*, 6, 2008: 63), although it increased this to almost 80 per cent in 2009 (*Vesti FNPR*, 6, 2009: 179). In the wake of the 2008 global financial crisis, up to a quarter of employers refused to sign or prolong collective agreements (*Vesti FNPR*, 6, 2009: 135).

The FNPR conducted a survey of collective agreements signed in 2000 which found the usual violations of labour legislation regarding such matters as the regularity of payment and inadequate payment for stoppages and administrative leave. In Tomsk, some collective agreements even gave the employer the right to cut wages in the event of financial difficulties (*Vesti FNPR*, 1–2, 2001: 48).

Most enterprise collective agreements retain the traditional form, detailing management's plans for the next year in the spheres of the development of production, improvements in health and safety, training and upgrading of skills and the provision of social and welfare benefits, usually now with additional sections covering wages and employment, which were formerly the preserve of higher authorities. Although most agreements have been simplified in recent years, removing all of the rhetoric related to the building of socialism, socialist competition and much of the detail concerning changes in the production process, the installation of plant and equipment and so on, the tendency is still to take the previous year's

---

[1]   Some employees of new private enterprises are enrolled in organisations which call themselves trade unions but which are in fact insurance companies. These are a means of providing tax-exempt bonuses to employees. In a household survey conducted by ISITO in Moscow, Samara, Kemerovo and Syktyvkar in May 1998, 10 per cent of those working in new private enterprises said that their enterprise had a trade union organisation, against 85 per cent in state enterprises, 80 per cent in budget organisations and 75 per cent in privatised enterprises. In the 1999 CLMS survey, 6 per cent of private-sector employers said that they had a trade union organisation, against 70 per cent of privatised and 83 per cent of state enterprises, although 12 per cent of private employers said that they had a collective agreement, half of which must be with non-union bodies.

agreement and insert new figures, usually with disclaimers, such as 'within the limits of financial possibilities', to cover contingencies.

In May 2001 we conducted a survey with our Russian colleagues of 1454 presidents of trade union primary organisations in nine Russian regions (data is available at go.warwick.ac.uk/russia/trade#Survey). Fifteen per cent of trade union presidents in the survey reported that they had not concluded a collective agreement. About a third of these regarded a collective agreement as unnecessary, the majority of whom had complete confidence in their administration, but a quarter did not conclude a collective agreement because the administration refused to negotiate or the two sides were unable to agree, despite the fact that according to the law the administration is obliged to negotiate and to conclude an agreement if the trade union proposes to do so. In over three-quarters of the enterprises with a collective agreement the draft agreement was drawn up in the traditional way, by a joint commission of management and the trade union. In a quarter of enterprises the trade union president reported that there had been no disputes or conflicts during the negotiation of the collective agreement and in three-quarters of the cases where there was a disagreement it was resolved by compromise, in 10 per cent of cases it was resolved in favour of management and in only 4 per cent was it resolved in favour of the union. In one hospital the trade union president confessed to a researcher that she had signed an agreement prepared by the chief doctor but did not know what it contained as she had not read it.

Trade union presidents were asked how much influence they had over the employer in a number of spheres. Almost three-quarters of respondents felt that they had no influence at all on the level of pay. Trade union presidents thought that they had more influence in their traditional spheres of activity of working conditions and the provision of social and welfare benefits, but a third of the presidents felt that they did not even influence the resolution of social welfare questions. We can conclude that close collaborative relations between the trade union president and management do not guarantee that the trade union will have a substantial influence on the living and working conditions of its members. Nevertheless, the pay-off from collaboration is suggested by the fact that presidents who characterised their relations as more or less conflictual were significantly *less* likely to have influence in the traditional areas of social welfare and working conditions while they were no more likely to have influence in relation to the level or regularity of payment of wages.

Collective agreements have generally continued to be negotiated between the employer and the enterprise trade union as the social and welfare branch of the administration, rather than as representative of the workers in opposition to the employer, although in the best of cases there will be consultation with the employees, with the draft collective agreement being circulated throughout the organisation and discussed at a general or delegate trade union meeting. Nevertheless, even in these cases, improvements in the terms and conditions of employment depend primarily on the labour market situation and the employers' considerations of labour motivation, rather than on the organised strength of employees. At the same time, the trade union is under pressure from the higher levels of the trade union and is constrained in negotiation by the expectations of its members so that since the beginning of economic recovery in 1998 there has probably been a tendency for the quality of collective agreements to improve over time. Whereas in the 1990s collective agreements rarely included any binding commitment on wages and rarely provided any significant improvement on the terms and conditions prescribed by the Labour Code, today it is far more common for the collective agreement to include provision for expansion of the range of benefits and increases in pay, within the limits of the financial capabilities of the enterprise. Genuine pay bargaining, backed up by threats of collective action, can be found in rare cases, particularly in the booming sectors of oil and gas and metallurgy.

The weakness of primary trade union organisations and the limited leverage over them of higher trade union bodies led the traditional Russian trade unions to put a considerable emphasis on the negotiation of higher-level agreements from an early stage in the transition. An increasing number of sectoral (branch tariff) agreements have been signed between the branch trade union and relevant employers' association. These agreements generally lay down the minimum wage and minimum social and welfare provision for the branch and may also include clauses on pay differentials and on the mechanisms for providing pay increases to compensate for inflation. The principal barrier to the development of effective sectoral agreements in the past was the absence or weakness of employers' organisations. In many cases sectoral employers' associations were established on the initiative of the trade unions, to provide them with an interlocutor, and often developed out of former state bodies responsible for the relevant industry. The coverage of sectoral agreements is often very limited as they apply only to employers who are signatory to them. However, the FNPR unions attach considerable importance to these branch tariff agreements because they provide a reference point for the negotiation of collective agreements at the enterprise level. By 2007 FNPR-affiliated and cooperating trade unions had signed 62 branch tariff agreements, the only branch unions not to have at least one such agreement being those in the military, the security industry and the physical culture, sport and tourism trade union, although many of these agreements cover only small sections of the industry and many major sectors have no coverage at all. In some industries FNPR claimed that the branch agreement had achieved a remarkably high level of coverage, one hundred per cent in coal-mining and the construction and construction materials industry, 92.9 per cent in the mining-metallurgical industry, and 85 per cent in textiles and light industry (of course this is the percentage of establishments with an FNPR trade union organisation that are covered by the branch agreement, not the percentage of all establishments). It is striking that in all these cases, except for the mining-metallurgical industry, the claimed coverage of the branch agreement is substantially higher than the percentage of enterprises signing a collective agreement.

Very few of these branch agreements had met the key tasks set for them by FNPR. For example, only three of the 29 agreements in the private sector (oil, chemicals and construction) provided for a minimum wage equal to the subsistence minimum; nine included recommendations on pay differentials and eight on the average wage in the industry. Fifteen fixed the proportion of basic pay in the wage, but only four achieved the FNPR goal of setting this at 70 per cent of pay (*Vesti FNPR*, 6, 2008: 25, 61–71). The global financial crisis made the negotiation of new tariff agreements in 2009 very difficult. Seventeen new agreements were signed, but four of those expiring were merely extended and some simply lapsed. Inflation meant that in 6 of 29 private-sector agreements the specified minimum wage had fallen below the legal minimum. In some cases, such as the oil industry, major employers refused to sign the tariff agreement (*Vesti FNPR*, 6, 2009: 139–40, 182).

Regional agreements are also signed in almost every region between the regional trade union organisation, the regional administration and the regional employers' organisation or, in the absence of such an organisation, by an *ad hoc* collection of the largest employers. In 2008 regional agreements were signed in five Federal Districts and in all but two regions, Ingushetiya and Tyva (*Vesti FNPR*, 6, 2008: 142). Regional agreements essentially delineate the social and labour policy of the regional administration, sometimes including commitments regarding the financing of public-sector organisations, most notably health and education, and wages in those sectors, and regarding the cost of housing and public services. The participation of the trade unions in the regional tripartite commissions that draw up such agreements is very reminiscent of the participation of trade unions in the drawing up of regional social and labour plans in soviet times, although today trade union lobbying is much more public. The public-sector unions are particularly active in lobbying to secure a regional agreement which provides more favourable pay and conditions, with corresponding financial allocations, for the public sector. As a result of the decentralisation of state power and public finances, from 2004 to 2009 there was also a rapid growth in the signing of territorial agreements at sub-regional levels.

China

Individual labour contracts between the enterprise and its employees, in place of guaranteed state employment for life, had first been introduced on an experimental basis in the early 1980s, and from 1983 a series of 'temporary regulations' established contractual hiring as the norm for all new employees, but state enterprises were slow to transfer existing employees onto individual contracts (Warner 1995). The 1994 Labour Law formalised the contractual regulation of labour relations. Following the enactment of the Law, individual contracts became the norm for all employees and, by the end of 2001, 120 million employees had signed such contracts. However, it was not until the Labour Contract Law that came into force in 2008 that written contracts became mandatory, so many workers, particularly in the private sector, were employed without any contracts. In addition to the Labour Law, employment conditions were regulated by national laws and regulations which set the minimum labour standards, supplemented by or implemented through provincial and municipal regulations appropriate to local conditions.

The growing incidence of open conflict accompanying the abandonment of the administrative regulation of labour relations raised the question of the form of regulation appropriate to the emerging market economy and, in particular, the balance between the legal regulation of individual labour contracts, which was initially the preference of the Ministry of Labour (MOLSS from March 1998), and the regulation of labour relations on the basis of collective contracts negotiated between employers and trade unions, which was the preference of the ACFTU.

The trade union was empowered to sign labour contracts on behalf of individual workers in joint-ventures under regulations issued by the State Council in 1980 and 1983. Warner and Ng (1999: 303), referring to Shen 1990, characterise these as 'collective agreements' although, at least juridically, they remained individual labour contracts.) Legislative foundations for the application of collective contracts were first laid down in the 1992 Trade Union Law, which specified that 'trade unions may, on behalf of the workers and staff members, sign collective contracts with the management of enterprises or institutions. The draft collective contracts shall be submitted to the congresses of workers and staff members for deliberation and approval' (article 18). The 1994 Labour Law provided more detailed specification of the character of such collective contracts, noting that the collective contract could cover such matters as 'labour remuneration, working hours, rest and vacations, occupational safety and health, and insurance and welfare'. Where there is no trade union, the collective contract can be concluded by elected representatives of the staff and workers (article 33). The collective contract has to be submitted to the labour administrative department for approval (article 34), which also mediates in the event of a dispute, and the collective contract has 'binding force' on both parties and sets minimum standards for individual contracts (article 35). The Law was supplemented by the 'Provisions on Collective Contracts' issued by the Ministry of Labour on 5 December 1994, which stressed that the collective contract should be concluded on the basis of 'equality and unanimity through consultation' (cited in Ng and Warner 2000: 105). These regulations were updated in January 2004 on the basis of consultation between MOLSS, the ACFTU and the two employers' organisations, but China still has no distinct law on collective agreements, despite constant lobbying by ACFTU for such a law.

Although the Ministry of Labour experimented with the collective contract system in 350 enterprises, it had no plans for its comprehensive implementation. Zhu Jiazhen, the then Vice-Minister of Labour, emphasised the subordinate character of collective contracts: 'the labour contract system defines a legal labour relationship, to establish a labour relationship between two parties, and so it is at the first place. The collective contract system is to adjust labour relations on the basis of the labour contract. Therefore, it is at the second place' (Zhu, Y. 1996). The ACFTU, on the other hand, saw collective contracts as an extension of the system of 'democratic participation in management' and the principal means of regulating labour relations in the emerging market economy. ACFTU President, Wei Jianxing, described the implementation of the collective contract system as 'the crux of implementing the Labour Law' (*Workers' Daily* 13 December 1994). The December 1994 meeting of the ACFTU Executive declared the implementation of collective contracts as one of the focal points of trade union work and it became the first priority in the ACFTU work schedules for the next three years (Li 2000: 208).

The principal purpose of the collective contract was to install a collective institutional framework for 'harmonious labour relations' following the erosion of the direct control of the terms and conditions of labour by the Party-state. The trade union had a dual role in regulating labour relations, of representing their members and preserving social stability. In December 1992, at the Fifth Meeting of the Eleventh Executive Committee of the ACFTU, Hu Jintao, the member of the CCP Politburo who was in charge of the trade union at the time, made the Party's priority clear:

> The trade unions at all levels should assist the Party organs and government to mediate these conflicts. On the one hand, they should actively reflect the opinions of workers and staff members, promoting the improvement of reform measures; on the other hand, they should enhance workers' and staff members' awareness of the overall interest, adopting a correct attitude towards the conflicts and difficulties in the course of reform, ... the trade unions should strive to maintain national and social stability, guaranteeing the smooth progress of reform. (China Institute of Labour Movement 1993: 598–607)

A series of laws and circulars emphasised that the negotiation of collective contracts should be consensual, not conflictual, a process of 'collective consultation' rather than 'collective bargaining' (Warner and Ng 1999: 303–4) and that disagreements should not provide the pretext for any disruption of production (Li 2000: 224). Where there is disagreement over the conclusion or implementation of a collective contract, it should be referred to the local tripartite Labour Arbitration Committee, chaired by the labour administration, and if arbitration fails, to the People's Court (1994 Labour Law, article 84).

The ACFTU initially launched a campaign to encourage primary trade union organisations to sign collective contracts on its own initiative, with little reference to the government, but progress was slow because enterprises were reluctant to sign collective contracts without authorisation from their superior state bodies, forcing the ACFTU to enlist the support of the Party and state administration at local level. The ACFTU established a target of signing collective contracts in 30 per cent of SOEs and 30 per cent of FIEs and closely monitored progress towards the attainment of these targets, but the campaign only really gained momentum when it finally secured the endorsement of the Party-state. On 17 May 1996, a joint circular endorsing the implementation of collective consultation and the contract system was issued by the Ministry of Labour, ACFTU, the State Trade and Economic Commission (STEC, the body responsible for SOEs), and the China Enterprise Management Association (CEMA), the official employers' organisation, in which these four bodies required their own subordinates at all levels to follow the united leadership of local governments and Party committees, closely co-ordinating and jointly ensuring the implementation of the collective contract system. The collective contract campaign would now be a joint effort of Party, government and trade unions, under the name of the unions but backed by the authority of the Party and government, with a uniform model of application. The ACFTU issued model contracts to enterprises through the local unions and put intense pressure on its lower-level organisations to achieve their targets (Li 2000: 212–17).

According to the ACFTU, while only 48 000 enterprises had signed collective contracts by the end of 1995, 135 386 enterprises had signed collective contracts by the end of 1996, although the targets for foreign-funded enterprises were missed (fewer than 10 per cent were covered at the end of 1995) and the campaign had little impact in non-state enterprises (Warner and Ng 1999: 297). After the initial burst of activity, the pace of the campaign slowed and, by the end of 1999, the number of enterprises signing collective contracts had only increased to 146 655, covering 46 million employees. According to the ACFTU figures, the number of enterprises signing collective agreements leapt to 332 233 in 2000, but while the number of enterprise agreements had doubled, the number of workers covered only increased by 30 per cent, to 60 million in 2000, so it is likely that the statistical increase is largely accounted for by the addition of regional and local agreements covering a large number of small enterprises (all data from annual *Zhongguo gonghui nianjian* (Chinese trade union yearbooks)). According to MOLSS figures, in 2001 there were 270 000 collective contracts registered at the local labour bureaux, covering 400 000 enterprises and 76 million workers.[1] The collective agreement campaign gained a further boost at the end of 2001 with the passage of a new trade union law, a joint conference of the MOLSS and ACFTU in Nanjing and the introduction of a national system of tripartite consultation, which made promoting the collective agreement system one of its main priorities for 2002 (Clarke and Lee 2002). However, while the number of agreements almost doubled again, to 629 000 in 2004, the number of

---

[1]   ACFTU claimed that in October 2001, 510 000 enterprises had concluded collective contracts, covering 75.7 million employees (*renmin ribao* 20 November 2001: 1) and in March the figure had reached 592 000 enterprises (*ACFTU Bulletin*, 7, 2002). The ACFTU tends to report a larger number of collective contracts than the Ministry of Labour and Social Security for several reasons: first, because a significant number of contracts are denied registration because they provide conditions inferior to those already specified by law; second, because ACFTU reports the number of enterprises covered, rather than the number of contracts signed; third, there may well be over-reporting because the number of collective contracts signed is a key performance indicator for local and regional ACFTU organisations.

employees covered increased by only 15 per cent, to just fewer than 70 million workers. By the end of 2006, ACFTU reported a further substantial increase in coverage, with a total of 862 000 collective contracts having been signed, covering 1.538 million enterprises and 112.5 million workers or 59 per cent of all enterprise workers in China. Sixty-six thousand regional collective contracts, covering 753 000 enterprises and 29.6 million workers and 19 000 industry-specific collective contracts, covering 172 000 enterprises and 12.9 million workers were also reported to have been signed across the country (ACFTU 2007).

The establishment of tripartite consultative committees (TCC) at national, provincial and municipal levels deserves special attention, as it represents ACFTU's effort to strengthen its influence on social and labour policy formulation, and further to promote collective consultation and agreements at the enterprise level through tripartite intervention.

The new Chinese Labour Contract Law, which came into force at the beginning of 2008, specifies that where there is no trade union, workers may elect their own representatives to negotiate a collective contract with management, something that was already permitted under the 1994 *Regulations on Collective Contracts*. In the final version of the law the qualification was introduced that they can only do this under the 'guidance' (*zhidao*) of the next highest level of the ACFTU, to ensure that this provision would not open the door to the establishment of independent trade unions (or, in a more optimistic reading, to preclude the formation of 'yellow' unions).

The rapid introduction of collective contracts on the basis of a bureaucratic campaign organised from the centre, employing the authority of the Party-state to provide model contracts and to induce enterprises to sign collective contracts, made its mark on the character of the collective contract in the first stage of its implementation. Warner and Ng surveyed the incidence and content of collective contracts in 62 medium and large SOEs and JVs. They found that, at least in Shenzhen, most firms closely followed the model supplied to them, making only minor modifications, and that collective bargaining in China 'betrays a meticulous degree of state intervention and control' (Warner and Ng 1999: 305). On the basis of his more detailed case studies, Li (2000) also emphasised the continuing role of the Party-state in regulating labour relations and found a very high degree of formalism in the signing of collective contracts in order to achieve the targets set by the ACFTU. He found that the collective contract was widely regarded as a requirement imposed from above and that higher trade union bodies and the Party organisation played the dominant role in their initial introduction.[1] Negotiation was dominated by

---

[1] Ding, Goodall and Warner (2002: 444) reported that the collective contract was said by union officers in a number of SOEs to be 'just a formality required by the superior'. One Shanghai SOE reported that the collective contract was not really relevant to SOEs because the Party, management, the trade union and the Youth League are on the same 'battle line'.

management and the Party, with the trade union role being primarily to propagandise the agreement among the workforce.

Such formalism is to be expected of a system introduced on the basis of directives from above and in accordance with the strategy described by Wei Jianxing at the December 1995 ACFTU Executive Committee meeting as 'instituting the system firstly and improving it secondly' (*Workers' Daily*, 20 December 1995: 1). While the emphasis was on unanimity and conflict avoidance, with the bureaucratic reconciliation of any differences, the intention was still that the trade unions should represent the interests of their members. The revised Trade Union Law, adopted in October 2001, enjoined ACFTU to 'take economic development as the central task', but also emphasised that 'the basic duties and functions of trade unions are to safeguard the legitimate rights and interests of workers and staff members'. It was to be expected that the emphasis in the first stage of the introduction of the system would be on the preservation of social stability.

The Chinese preference for the term 'collective consultation' over the term 'collective bargaining' is not merely an ideological obfuscation; it is an accurate description of the process, although the increasing use of the term 'bargaining' in the Chinese press and academic discourse may be indicative of more recent qualified progress towards more authentic bargaining (Brown 2006). 'Collective consultation' does not represent the negotiated settlement of conflicts of interest between employers and employees. The introduction of employment contracts, in place of the lifetime state employment guarantees, transformed the relationship between the enterprise and its labour force into one between employer and employees. However, neither the enterprise director nor the trade union in SOEs was free to represent the interests of employer and employees in contract negotiations. Both continued to be subject to the direction of the Party, directly and through higher trade union and state bodies. The Chairman of the ACFTU, Wei Jianxing, emphasised the need for the trade union to develop its own constituency, noting that 'if the union only clings onto the Party and the state, it has no reason to exist' (Chan 2000b), and under his leadership the ACFTU made a series of efforts to strengthen the status of trade unions and to protect workers' interests. However, following his retirement in 2003, a new and more conservative leadership was installed in ACFTU, committed primarily to maintaining social harmony rather than more effectively representing workers' interests.

The trade union in China continues, in the words of the ACFTU constitution, to be 'a bridge and a bond linking the Party and the masses of the workers and staff members, an important social pillar of the state power of the country'. Wage and employment decisions of enterprise management continue to be constrained by guidelines issued by local government and Party authorities. Although the powers of the enterprise Party organisation to intervene in management have been curtailed, it remains in place to monitor the performance of trade union and management in SOEs and, on a less formal basis, in joint-ventures, but in private and foreign-owned enterprises there is rarely a Party organisation to monitor management or, where it exists, the trade union.

The principal limitation on the quality of collective agreements in China is not the subordination of the trade union to the Party, but the continued dependence of the workplace trade union on management, so that the trade union still functions as a branch of the administration responsible for personnel management rather than as a body representative of the employees. In SOEs the process of collective consultation was integrated into the traditional system of consultation, formalising elements of the existing 'democratic participation of staff and workers in the management of the enterprise' on the basis of the supposed identity of interests of management and employees. Although the draft of the collective contract is usually drawn up by the trade union, on the basis of the previous contract or a model agreement provided by the higher trade union body, the terms of the collective agreement are almost universally dictated by management. On the basis of self-censorship, the trade union only makes proposals which it regards as acceptable to management and, if management does not accept those proposals, the trade union defers to management's judgement in the name of the interests of the enterprise. In some enterprises senior members of management actually participate in the negotiations on the trade union side (Clarke, Lee and Li 2004: 264). At the same time, the trade union President, as a member of the Board of Directors or Supervisory Board, often participates in the formulation of management's response to the trade union proposals for the collective contract. This is an indication of the extent to which neither the trade union nor the employer distinguish the trade union's role as representative of the employees from its role as representative of the enterprise. In the best of cases, mostly in SOEs and former SOEs, the trade union will circulate the draft collective agreement to get feedback from employees, will report any additional proposals from employees to management that the trade union judges to be 'reasonable' and will advise the management of any of its proposals which are likely to provoke unrest. Management may amend the collective agreement in the light of such discussions, but in the final analysis decisions about the content of the collective agreement are taken unilaterally by management. In the majority of cases the adoption of the collective agreement is a formality. If the workplace trade union should choose to put pressure on the management, this would always be in the traditional way, by appealing for the intervention of superior administrative agencies, but never by initiating any form of collective representation or collective action of the labour force.

The collective contract does not usually include any detailed specification of the terms and conditions of labour. In most cases the collective contract merely sets the minimum standards for individual labour contracts and so it rarely includes any more than the minimum legal provisions, and some of the collective agreements concluded fall short even of this minimum standard. In addition the collective contract may specify some of the social and welfare benefits provided by the enterprise, but often does not include reference to many of the benefits which are in fact provided by the enterprise. The fact that these are not included in the collective contract considerably reduces the effectiveness of the collective contract as a means of regulating labour relations because it means that these benefits can be withdrawn at the discretion of management without consultation.

In China wage consultation was instituted separately from the collective agreement. The coverage of wage agreements has extended over the last few years, so that by the end of 2006, more than 300 000 wage agreements had been signed, covering 37.2 million workers with a further 8.2 million workers covered by regional wage contracts (*China Labour Bulletin* 2007: 9–10), but wage agreements are generally only over the minimum wage and the size of the total wage bill and rarely specify wage rates for specific posts or occupations, which is the most sensitive issue because of the tendency to increase pay differentials in the market economy. Unlike the collective contract, the lead in wage negotiations is generally taken by management, usually following the guidelines of the local Labour Bureau and, in SOEs, regulations that restrict the rate of increase of wages to the rate of increase of productivity. Management proposals are submitted to the trade union for consultation and the trade union reports the employees' response back to management, which may take account of such responses in formulating its final proposals, particularly where proposals to increase differentials threaten to provoke employee discontent by leading to a reduction in the wages of rank-and-file workers (Clarke, Lee and Li 2004: 247). Pressure to increase wages generally comes not from the trade union, but from the Personnel Department, in response to problems of recruitment and retention, particularly of more highly skilled employees.

The collective contract system was at first largely confined to SOEs and joint-ventures and made only limited progress in foreign-invested, township and village (TVEs) and private enterprises, where trade union penetration was very low. The ACFTU has placed increasing importance on organising workers and protecting workers' rights and interests in FIEs but the priority of the Party-state is not so much to protect workers' rights as for the unions to provide a channel for conflict resolution (Lau 2001: 617).

Although trade union membership in FIEs is nominally quite high, very few have an effective trade union organisation and the trade union is not able to control those employers who exploit their favourable labour market situation to impose low wages, long working hours and punitive disciplinary systems on their employees, often in violation of the relevant laws (Chan 2001; Chan 2000a: 45–6; Chan 1998; Chang and Zhao 1995; Chiu and Frenkel 2000: 37–42).[1] Although labour relations in such enterprises are unambiguously capitalist, local government, and correspondingly the local trade union organisation, has generally been reluctant to intervene in such cases

---

[1]   In reality, trade union density in FIEs is probably only about 10 per cent, but the trade union president is usually a manager filling the post on a part-time basis and many employers do not pay their 2 per cent levy to the union (Chan 1998: 140; Chiu and Frenkel 2000:. 38–9).

for fear of frightening off foreign investors and losing jobs (Howell 1998), despite the fact that such employers tend to be oriented to short-term profit, generate serious social tension and make little contribution to the long-term development of the productive and human resource potential of the host economy. On the other hand, municipal and provincial union cadres, faced with outright violations of workers' legitimate rights, say that they want to protect workers' legitimate rights and interests, but at the same time do not want to frighten off foreign investors. Nevertheless, it seems unlikely that the low incidence of the signing of collective contracts is an indicator of a reluctance of foreign employers to submit themselves to the power they give to the trade union, as Warner and Ng imply (Warner and Ng 1999: 311), so much as of the fact that they see it as irrelevant, while the labour administration and the Party do not have the leverage that they have over SOEs and joint-ventures to induce them to sign agreements.

Trade union membership is much lower in private enterprises, particularly in the smaller private enterprises that have grown very rapidly over the last few years, and in township and village enterprises, many of which have now been privatised. Many of these enterprises have very poor wages and working conditions, often do not provide their employees with labour contracts and frequently violate other aspects of labour legislation (Chan 2000a: 45–8). While they may provide employment for laid-off workers and new entrants to the labour force, they act as a drag on economic development by providing stiff competition for those more progressive enterprises, usually using more advanced technologies and human resource management policies, which do not violate the legitimate rights and interests of their employees, and their widespread violation of labour legislation brings the law into disrepute.

Genuine negotiation between the trade union and employer does occasionally take place, particularly in joint-ventures which have inherited the trade union from the former SOE partner, where the role of the trade union is to monitor the foreign partner on behalf of the state (Zhang 2009: 207), although success in such cases seems to rely heavily on the character and influence of the trade union president rather than any advance in the system of representation or mobilisation of the labour force (Clarke, Lee and Li 2004: 248). For example, the enterprise union in an electronics joint-venture in Hangzhou had negotiated successive annual wage increases via collective consultation that had departed from the benchmarks set in laws and regulatory guidelines. This was achieved even though the company itself was not posting large profits and three-quarters of the workforce was made up of migrant workers whose pay has been traditionally limited to the local minimum wage or less. The enterprise union had taken part in 15 collective negotiations with the company that mostly centred on upholding labour standards – especially special protection for women workers – and labour relations issues such as the collective contract, job deposits, punishments and fines, and resignation procedures. Management had also agreed to consult the union before dismissing non-union, that is temporary workers, as well as union members. The success of the negotiations has been criticised by some observers as relying too heavily on the performance of the trade union chair, who was also a senior figure in the almost entirely Japanese-managed company.[1] Others pointed to the fact that the lack of direct participation from the workforce placed the consultation outside the spirit and letter of the law. On the other hand, trade union researchers in Hangzhou argued that the process had gained approval of the workforce by winning tangible material benefits such as reduced working hours and improved pay and that this was more important than strict adherence to inappropriate legal guidelines.

Because of the difficulties of establishing trade union organisations in small private enterprises, ACFTU has sought to establish local trade union organisations covering all of the private enterprises in one district or one industrial sector, which then sign collective contracts with employers' associations at the industrial or local level (Chan 2000a: 49).[2] Two main forms have emerged: primary-level trade union federations (*jiceng gonghui lianhehui*) and federated primary-level trade unions (*lianhe jiceng gonghui*). The difference is that trade unions in the former category are independent in their own right whilst the latter is made up of trade union small groups (*xiaozu*) or branches (*fen hui*) where there are insufficient numbers to establish a separate trade union (Li J.P. 2005). These have proved effective in areas dominated by one type of production often with lots of smaller enterprises employing migrant workers on a seasonal basis.

It might be expected that such an approach would be formalistic, providing a substitute for the recruitment of members and the formation of trade union organisations at the enterprise level and with no means of enforcing the agreements reached, since the signatories on behalf of the employers are usually enterprise associations established under the relevant government departments rather than being genuine employers' organisations. However, in 2002 Clarke and Lee were informed by the ACFTU in Chengdu, where a Sichuan provincial law makes these agreements enforceable on all employers in the relevant locality or sector and about 30 such agreements had been signed, that the signing of these agreements had been followed by an increase in membership of the private enterprise trade union and that workers had been taking cases to the City Arbitration Committee when employers failed to abide by the agreement. The Committee had initially refused to hear their complaints on the grounds that they did not have labour contracts, but the city ACFTU successfully argued that the collective contract, which provided for a negotiated minimum wage slightly above the official minimum, constituted a basis on which their cases should be heard. Such initiatives have inherent flaws and are not sustainable, though they may be instrumental in protecting workers' interests in the short term. Their limitation is that they are agreements between the trade unions and

---

[1]   The management board was dominated by Japanese managers with a ratio of 7:2.
[2]   The possibility of establishing such district or sectoral unions was prescribed in a document jointly issued by the Ministry of Labour, ACFTU, STEC and CEDA in May 1996.

the local authority responsible for supervising local private business, not between the trade unions and employers (Clarke, Lee and Li 2004: 249).

This is by no means an isolated example. Indeed, a sectoral agreement originally drawn up on an experimental basis in Xinhe, a town in Zhejiang Province, has been hailed by MOLSS and ACFTU as a model for the country as a whole. Well-organised strikes and disciplined demonstrations in Xinhe, led by experienced skilled workers, persuaded the local town-level trade union chair to 'trail blaze' (*chuangxin*) new practices in collective consultation by setting up a local sectoral union. The agreement to enter into negotiations with the trade union over a sectoral agreement was led by a minority of larger factories, employing between 50 and 200 workers. Their willingness encouraged the majority of much smaller family-run enterprises to take part (Pringle 2010).

A sector-wide piece-rate wage table and collective contract was agreed following genuine bargaining, despite the fact that most of the workers' representatives were employer-recommended. Given that the town was dominated by small-scale enterprises running seasonal production of woollen sweaters and employing 12 000 migrant workers, the agreement constituted an unprecedented breakthrough in the private sector. When worker representatives put forward rates for middle of the range sweaters that were higher than the market rate, some employers wanted to abandon the whole process of consultation, believing they could get a better price by risking further strikes and sticking to individual agreements. At this point the union sought and received government help in order to keep the employers at the table.

> Resistance from the bosses was very strong...and many of them wanted to abandon it. We had no choice but to get the government leaders involved. We could only continue with the bosses' agreement – even if it was reluctantly given. (Yu 2004)

The process involved six rounds of consultation, overcoming fierce employer opposition, to ensure that rates could only go up in subsequent negotiations, as indeed has been the case. The experiment, which has since been tested in other sectors, was certainly a breakthrough in that it implicitly recognised that enterprise-based unions obscured the opposition of interests between employers and employees and that existing union law and practice was incapable of producing industrial peace in this instance. But at the same time, it suffered from a lack of autonomous worker participation. Promises by the chair of the newly established sector trade union for woollen workers in the town to organise elections have not so far been met. Nevertheless the case demonstrates that in certain conditions, a higher trade union body can directly assist, and in this case actually reorganise, primary trade unions to take a more effective approach to collective agreements. The experiment has since been identified as an example for possible future legal/institutional development and the local trade union press has reported similar exercises in the nearby towns. For example, the Zeguo Town Pump Makers Union was established in late 2004 and has since carried out three rounds of collective consultations (Liu 2007; Xia 2005). The model is also being applied and adapted in other parts of China. Sector-level trade unions have been established in the single industry towns of Laomiao (producing fireworks) and Gongli (building materials). Agreements were concluded in late 2007 at Ducun (glass containers) and Meiyuan (building materials) in Shaanxi's Fuping County (Yi 2007). As news of the Xinhe experiment has spread, approval from senior trade union officials and other government departments followed and article 53 of the new Labour Contract Law makes legal provision for sector- and district-level collective contracts. However, the success of the Xinhe experiment depended heavily on the background of high levels of overt conflict, including strikes and protests, which preoccupied the local authorities, and high labour turnover, which concerned the employers, enabling the local authorities to orchestrate a negotiated agreement which benefitted all parties. Whether such a model can be implemented in less favourable circumstances must be open to serious doubt.

The wave of disputes in 2010 sparked by economic recovery and, in particular, the strikes at the Honda plant in Guangdong province during March 2010 appear to have strengthened the hand of reformers in union and government circles who wish to see a more international and recognisable approach to collective negotiations. The Guangdong provincial government is currently debating the latest draft of its 'Regulations on the Democratic Management of Enterprises' and some labour activists have heralded the regulations as an historic opportunity that could open the way to 'genuine bargaining' (CLB 2010 http://www.clb.org.hk/en/node/100838). The draft regulations currently state that if 20 per cent of the workforce demand wage negotiations, the union is legally obliged to organise the democratic election of worker representatives to take part in subsequent negotiations. The strikes have also led to calls in the mainstream non-union media for collective contracts 'to play a greater role in labour relations' and dispute resolution (Yi and Yue 2010).

Vietnam

The 2002 Vietnamese Labour Code provides for the signing of a collective agreement between the employer and the representative of the employees, which must be 'the executive committee of the trade union of the enterprise or a temporary trade union organisation'. The collective agreement must be approved by more than 50 per cent of the members of the labour collective and its provisions cannot be inferior to the provisions of the relevant laws nor can the terms of an individual labour contract be inferior to those of the collective agreement. The principal provisions of the collective agreement should cover 'employment and guarantee of employment; working hours and rest breaks; salaries, bonuses, and allowances; work limits; occupational safety and hygiene; and social insurance for the employees'. Under the 1994 Labour Code, the government stipulated the wage scale and wage tables for all enterprises. Under the 2002 amendment it still does so for SOEs, but only stipulates the general principles of their formation for other employers, in consultation with VGCL and the employers, although this latter provision has not been implemented. However, the employer is required to consult with the trade union in formulating its wage scales, regardless of whether there is a collective agreement, and register them with the local labour administration.

There is no centralised system of reporting the number of collective agreements, so there are no consolidated figures. In 2000, VGCL reported to the ILO that there were collective agreements in 56 per cent of SOEs, 36 per cent of FIEs and 20 per cent of Domestic Private Enterprises (DPEs) (Fair Labor Association 2004). A national VGCL official told us in 2004 that there were collective agreements in 70 per cent of unionised SOEs, under 50 per cent of unionised FIEs, and 20 per cent of unionised enterprises in the private sector, although VGCL in HCMC claimed that 100 per cent of state and equitised state enterprises, about 60 per cent of FIEs (although only 30 per cent of enterprises in EPZs) and 65 per cent of unionised private-sector enterprises had collective agreements. According to research carried out by MOLISA in 2006, only 20 per cent of enterprises had collective agreements, with collective agreements in 73.3 per cent in SOEs, 21 per cent of FIEs, but only 4.9 per cent of Vietnamese private companies. Many collective agreements are initiated not by the union but by the management, sometimes under pressure from Corporate Social Responsibility (CSR) organisations. The absence of collective agreements in unionised enterprises was explained by a number of factors: the weakness of the trade union organisation, the reluctance of the employer to undertake obligations which he could not be confident that he could fulfil and the perceived pointlessness of signing a collective agreement which contained no provisions higher than the minimum legal standards. By June 2009, VGCL reported that 65.22 per cent of unionised enterprises were covered by collective agreements, 96.33 per cent in the state sector, 64.57 per cent in the foreign-owned sector and 59.21 per cent in the private sector, although VGCL admitted that half of these collective agreements did not provide any benefits higher than those prescribed by the law (VGCL Resolution on Collective Bargaining, 18 June 2009, cited in Do 2010, chapter Eight).

In most enterprises in Vietnam collective bargaining is a formality, the content of the collective agreement being dictated by management, usually modelled on the template provided by MOLISA and VGCL, based on that attached to the Labour Code. There may be some consultation with workers about the content of the collective agreement, though in one Japanese company wage 'negotiations' are held in secret: the HR manager puts forward proposals for new wage rates to the union board, but workers are not informed: 'we have to do this [wage negotiation] secretly because if we announce to workers, they may have unexpected reaction or misunderstanding', the union chairman explained. The chairman had some reason to fear the workers' reaction. In 2008 the HR department presented a draft collective agreement to the union board, but the union board was not satisfied with the agreement because it was 'too general and provided for no better benefits for workers'. Nevertheless, under pressure from the management the union chair had to sign the draft. However, when workers heard about the draft they rejected it, apparently on the instigation of their team leaders, since it provided no additional benefits, so the collective agreement was put on hold. Similarly, in March 2008, when management proposed a below-inflation pay rise, workers, again instigated by their team leaders, who were the informal workers' leaders (six of whom sit on the union board), threatened to strike. When management received written complaints from 1200 individual workers overnight, they conceded and increased the proposed pay rise.

According to MOLISA in 2006, over 90 per cent of collective agreements merely repeat the minimum legal provisions regarding the core terms and conditions of employment (MOLISA Employment Policy Department Report, October 2007), and indeed one local DOLISA official in Hanoi reported that 30 per cent even fall short of this. Management is reluctant to include anything above the bare minimum in the collective agreement since the agreement is legally binding. However, many collective agreements include some additional provisions, most typically wedding and funeral benefits. Sometimes there are also meal and transport allowances, picnics and excursions and bonuses to be paid at Tet and for various holidays, which may be at the discretion of management. The collective agreement may also include trade union promises to organise emulation campaigns and to admonish or discipline workers who perform badly. The collective agreement should include agreed wage and bonus scales, but these might be set at the minimum level so that the employer can minimise social insurance payments, severance pay and so on. Sometimes in such cases there will be a separate wage agreement, or the company may simply pay higher rates at its discretion.

The VGCL did not attach a great deal of significance to collective bargaining until the waves of wildcat strikes from 2006. There was no significant discussion of collective agreements at the VGCL conference in 2003 and VGCL still does not have a collective agreement or industrial relations department. Until the end of 2008, the Socio-Economic Policy Department of VGCL was in charge of collective bargaining, while the Legal Department took care of labour disputes. The two Departments were merged into the Policy-Legal Affairs Department after the tenth National Congress. Nevertheless, as in China, the enterprise union in SOEs can be an effective instrument of employer paternalism and in some joint-ventures, where the enterprise trade union president has Party backing, genuine collective bargaining with the foreign partner can be seen. In all three joint-ventures visited by Do, Clarke, and Lee in 2004 regular negotiation over the collective agreement was a trade union initiative, the draft was circulated to all employees for suggestions and there was real bargaining with the employer, including bargaining over wages and bonuses. The employer in each case refused to meet the full demands of the union and the union compromised on the basis of the financial position of the company. Trade union members did not seem to play a very active role in the bargaining process, with few suggestions coming from workers, perhaps because they had confidence in their leadership. In a domestic private company the only request that had come from workers in the last bargaining round was that one woman wanted to be allowed to wear her shirt outside her trousers, but management refused because it would look untidy. In one of the joint-ventures workers asked for higher allowances for working in harmful conditions, but the union considered the allowances to be sufficient and did not put the demand forward. In another joint-venture annual wage increases were negotiated and incorporated in the collective agreement. In the previous negotiation the union had asked for a 10 per cent pay rise and a reduction of the working week from 46 to 44 hours. The management agreed a 5 per cent increase and the hours reduction. There have been repeated arguments in this company over the size of bonuses, the determination of which the foreign director insists is a management prerogative (he told us that he introduced the question of bonuses into the collective agreement to make it clear that their payment was non-negotiable, at management's discretion). None of the three enterprises has had a strike, but the union is able to play on management's fear of strikes in their negotiations. In the last case, the trade union president reported that the union leaders had to go to the shops on occasion to dissuade workers from stopping work to allow the union to pursue grievances through dialogue.

In response to lobbying from VGCL, the government now requires all enterprises to develop wage tables based on the state wage table format and register these wage tables with the local labour administration. The labour authority also provides specific criteria for a wage table, including the minimum increment between wage steps and the minimum wage disparity between unskilled and skilled workers. In order to by-pass the new regulations many enterprises now maintain two wage systems: one is the real wage table that is applied in the enterprise; the other is the wage table registered at the local labour administration. Workers receive wages defined by the first wage table while the company pays social insurance contributions on the basis of the second wage table.

Apart from providing enterprise trade unions with a model collective agreement, the higher trade union and labour administration bodies provide very little support to enterprise trade unions in their collective bargaining. A senior VGCL officer commented complacently that 'actually there is no wage negotiation, the union monitors individual labour contracts to make sure that they are not worse than the collective agreement. ... If they really negotiated, the higher union would have to hire consultants', but a DOLISA officer argued that

> in practice DOLISA makes a greater contribution to collective agreements than VGCL: we check it when we receive it from the enterprise to see if it is legal. We can make suggestions to both sides about the level of mutual agreement. Before the 2002 amendment of the labour code DOLISA played a major role. Since then,

we still review and evaluate collective agreements. Enterprises prefer to ask for advice from DOLISA rather than VGCL because we are the specialists ... . We suggest that they can negotiate higher than the minimum standards, for example free lunch or wedding and funeral benefits ... [because] it brings benefits for both sides – this advice should be provided by VGCL, but we review the collective agreements.

The power of a workplace trade union is very limited when there is no freedom of association and no effective right to strike. There is little doubt, however, that, even confined to its role as a branch of the management apparatus, the trade union can serve to ameliorate social tensions in the workplace if it carries out its consultative role effectively and if management is responsive to its suggestions, in which case it functions more as a progressive human resource department than as a body representative of its members. However, such cases are the exception rather than the rule, particularly in the private and foreign-invested sectors where trade unions are set up on the initiative of management, usually headed by a senior manager (most often the HR director), and there is no Party organisation to monitor the performance of the trade union. The weakness of workplace trade unions, even in their minimal role as consultative bodies, is shown by the extent to which management uses other channels, such as surveys and internet sites, to tap the views of the labour force in both China and Vietnam (Zhang 2009: 208).

Following the wave of wildcat strikes in 2006, VGCL came under increasing pressure to ensure that its workplace organisations would be more responsive to workers' grievances and aspirations. In an attempt to strengthen the role of the trade union in collective bargaining, VGCL issued Directive One in October 2006 regarding the criteria for union evaluation, in which the most important condition for a primary union to receive the 'Strong Union Award' – the most prestigious annual award by the VGCL for the best workplace unions – is to negotiate and sign a collective agreement with better-than-minimum benefits for workers. To assist the primary unions in collective bargaining, the VGCL also required the higher-level unions to provide support before and during the bargaining process and to explore the possibility of negotiating above-workplace agreements with groups of employers.

In order to promote collective bargaining, VGCL in HCMC organised a Spring Collective Bargaining Campaign from January to April, starting in 2007. The district and EPZ unions were required to propose specific targets for the number of enterprises with collective agreements. The higher-level unions had to visit enterprises to support workplace unions in preparing for negotiation of the collective agreements as well as to persuade the employers to initiate the bargaining process. After almost one year, the outcome of the campaign fell short of expectation. The first reason was limited human resources of the unions at the intermediary level. On average, each district union has two to three officers and they have a lot of work to do,[1] so they have little time to devote to supporting collective bargaining and only a small number of workplace unions receive such support from higher-level unions. Second, despite the support of the higher-level unions, the negotiation at the workplace was carried out between the enterprise union and the management, without any direct involvement of the higher-level union organisation.

In early 2007, MOLISA and VGCL signed an annual co-operation work plan, in which the two parties agreed to raise the percentage of enterprises covered by collective agreements to 60 per cent and the Tenth VGCL Congress in December 2008 proposed that by the end of 2013, over 70 per cent of enterprise unions should have concluded collective agreements that provide better working conditions for workers. There have been also proposals within the VGCL and governmental circles about setting up a collective bargaining department in the union system and an industrial relations unit in MOLISA. An Industrial Relations Promotion Centre was eventually established in MOLISA by a decision of the Prime Minister in February 2009.

Sectoral bargaining was provided for by the 1995 Labour Code (chapter 5) but was largely ignored until the annual meeting between the Prime Minister and VGCL in March 2007, during which an experiment in sector bargaining was proposed by VGCL as a way to overcome the ineffectiveness of collective bargaining at the enterprise level. With the approval of the Prime Minister and the support of MOLISA, VGCL organised a number of seminars and workshops to discuss the possibility of sectoral bargaining. Two industries were selected for the experiment: garments and coal-mining. Garments is one of the leading export industries and also suffers most from labour conflicts. Coal-mining, on the other hand, has to face an increasing number of work accidents. The initial idea is that the sector agreement should provide a framework of minimum labour standards, based on which member enterprises will negotiate their own collective agreements. Sectoral bargaining called for a major reform in the organisation of sectoral unions, since sectoral unions have traditionally only included workers in state-owned enterprises, so VGCL plans to extend membership of sectoral unions to non-public enterprises in the same industry, starting with an experiment in the garment and textile industry. Similarly, some sectoral unions will be split into industrial unions. For instance, in 2007, the coal and mineral industry union and the garment and textile union were separated from the industrial union and the ship-building industry union was also split from the transportation union. However, the experiment in sectoral bargaining has stagnated due to disagreement between MOLISA and VGCL about the coverage of sectoral agreements. While VGCL insisted that they should cover all enterprises in one industry, MOLISA held that it is impossible to persuade the whole industry to participate; instead, a group of willing companies is enough.

---

[1] According to the VGCL statistics, by the end of 2007, there were 1791 higher-level unions (district, EPZ, local industrial unions) with 4771 full-time officers.

Eventually, the experiment in sectoral bargaining was abandoned in coal-mining and in garments covered only HCMC, Hanoi, Dong Nai and Binh Duong, instead of the whole country. The target was to negotiate with non-state employers to pay workers at least 5 per cent more than the minimum wage, with a differential between wage grades of at least 10 per cent, but this discouraged non-state employers from joining the agreement and at the end of 2009 the sectoral agreement had still not been concluded, with only a handful of state-owned companies having agreed to participate in negotiations.

Conclusion

In all three countries the trade unions have made great efforts to extend the scope of collective bargaining, but the weakness of workplace trade unions has meant that collective agreements only very rarely provide for anything significantly better than the statutory minimum terms and conditions of employment. In attempts to overcome this limitation the trade unions in all three countries have sought to develop sectoral agreements, but without strong workplace organisations the trade unions have little leverage to exert on the employers. In such circumstances, sectoral agreements tend to reflect the priorities of government and of the more prosperous employers to regulate wages and working conditions to reduce levels of conflict, to reduce labour turnover and to discipline backward employers who can only compete by intensifying the exploitation of the labour force.

The limited capacity of the trade unions to achieve any improvement in wages and working conditions through collective agreements has led them to continue to rely most heavily on their traditional collaboration with government bodies and with administrative intervention.

Collaboration with state bodies

State-socialist trade unions were thoroughly integrated into the administrative apparatuses of the Party-state, participating at all levels in the formation and implementation of policy. With the transition to a capitalist market economy these administrative apparatuses have lost a great deal of their power and influence, but they continue to have regulatory functions even where they do not have a directive role. In addition, new state apparatuses have developed to administer and regulate the new labour market, health and social insurance institutions. The trade unions retain considerable leverage over the state apparatus through their participation in state bodies.

In Russia, under the 1996 Trade Union Law, the trade unions have the right to participate in the management of the state funds of social insurance, employment, medical insurance, pension and other funds formed from insurance payments, and also have the right to trade-union monitoring of the use of the resources of these funds. The Law also stipulates that the opinion of corresponding trade unions should be taken into account in consideration of drafts of legislative and other normative-legal acts affecting the social-labour rights of workers, and also the right of trade unions to propose adoption of those or other acts and to participate in their consideration. Under the revised Labour Code the trade unions have the right to monitor the observance of labour legislation by employers and their representatives and the Labour Code provides a legislative basis for the collaboration of the state labour inspectorate with the trade unions. The branch trade unions also collaborate closely with the relevant ministries. All these forms of collaboration are institutionalised at federal and regional levels through participation in the federal and regional Tripartite Commissions, the regular exchange of information with the relevant government departments, trade union participation in government commissions responsible for the formulation and implementation of policy and legislation, and the organisation of joint action with the various government inspectorates. Until 1993 the trade unions had the right of legislative initiative, which meant that they could propose legislation, and they have restored this right in some Russian regions, such as Samara, but more generally they organise lobbying of legislative bodies and attempt to form sympathetic factions of deputies in the State Duma and in regional legislatures.

The limitations of the regulation of the terms and conditions of labour on the basis of collective agreements when the enterprise trade union is so dependent on management has led the trade unions in all three countries to attach primary importance to legislative and administrative measures, through which the state rather than the trade union takes responsibility for the protection of the rights of labour. The trade unions devote considerable resources to lobbying within the political system for the passage of favourable legislation regarding wages and working conditions and on pressing the authorities to enforce such legislation through the state systems of labour and health and safety inspection. This leads to a certain degree of ambiguity as to the relevant responsibilities of the trade union, on the one hand, and the Ministry of Labour, on the other. In Russia, FNPR and the Ministry of Labour worked closely together through the 1990s, but the withdrawal of the state from its responsibilities in the field of labour culminated in the abolition of the Ministry of Labour in 2004, handing full responsibility to the trade unions. At the other extreme, in Vietnam MOLISA regards itself rather than VGCL as the effective protector of the rights of labour, while in China ACFTU and the Ministry of Labour each try to pass responsibility to the other, although the Ministry of Labour in both countries is politically much weaker than are the trade unions and so is unable on its own to force the trade unions to take up their responsibilities.

In Russia the trade unions have to lobby from outside the state and political apparatus, primarily through their participation in tripartite structures at federal and regional levels, supported by representation on public management bodies, lobbying of federal and regional legislatures and public demonstrations. In China and Vietnam the trade unions are an integral part of the Party-state and are able to press their interests within Party structures, although dedicated tripartite structures formally institutionalise the rights of trade unions to consultation. It also suits the government to move such lobbying outside the state apparatus, where trade union pressure can be counterbalanced by employer representation, so there have been attempts to develop mechanisms of tripartite consultation in those countries too. In all three countries a major barrier to the development of effective systems of tripartite negotiation has been the weakness or absence of employer organisations.

In Russia, tripartite structures were established at the Federal level by Presidential Decree in 1991 and soon extended to the regional level, providing a forum within which trade unions could lobby government, and government could consult the trade unions on social and labour issues, with employer representation playing a subordinate but increasing role as employers have gradually organised themselves. Tripartite Commissions at Federal and regional levels draw up the annual General and Regional Agreements, nominally between government, employers and trade unions, which are more an expression of hopes and aspirations than of any binding commitments on the part of government or employers. The trade unions have lacked the political strength and public support that would be necessary for them to force the government to engage in serious consultation, to say nothing of negotiation, so most commentators agree that the trade unions have achieved little if anything for their members from their participation in tripartite structures (Ashwin 2004; Ashwin and Clarke 2002: chapter Six).

In China provision for tripartite consultation was made in article 34 of the 2001 Trade Union Law, although tripartite structures had existed prior to this. The National Tripartite Consultative Committee (NTCC) was established in August 2001 and instructions were sent to all provincial governments to establish their own TCCs by the end of 2002. The second meeting of the NTCC in February 2002 decided to extend tripartism to municipalities and townships across the country. By the end of 2001 there were already 15 provincial TCCs and by June 2002 their coverage extended to 20 out of 31 regions. The scope of tripartite consultation in China is limited by the fact that it was designed primarily as a fall-back mechanism of dispute resolution and only covers issues that fall within the competence and authority of the Ministry of Labour, all other issues being dealt with on the basis of direct interaction between trade unions and government. However, the main limitation of tripartism in China is that the participants do not act as independent representatives of the three parties, which is the precondition for any system of tripartite consultation. The MOLSS does not have the authority to represent the government as a whole, China Enterprise Confederation (CEC) does not effectively represent the interests of employers, nor does ACFTU effectively represent the interests of employees. On the one hand, the base of both organisations is in the SOEs and they have little penetration of the private or foreign-invested sectors. In particular, foreign employers do not belong to CEC and do not participate in tripartite structures, instead undermining employers' organisation by lobbying government directly through their

Chambers of Commerce. On the other hand, both organisations are more strongly influenced by the Party and the government than they are by their own membership (Clarke and Lee 2002).

The Vietnamese government is also attempting to strengthen its co-operation with the unions and employers' organisations by developing channels for tripartite negotiations. Decree 145 issued in 2004 formalised the tripartite consultation mechanism at national level. Decree 145 allows the nationally recognised social partners (the Vietnam General Confederation of Labour, Vietnam Chamber of Commerce and Industry and Vietnam Cooperative Alliance (VCA)) to be consulted by the Government on the formulation of labour-related policies and laws. Until now, however, this Decree has yielded few meaningful impacts on Vietnam's industrial relations system. A tripartite National Labour Relations Committee was established in 2007 to serve as a forum for tripartite consultation and negotiation and to advise the Prime Minister on labour relations issues, but most of the time the social partners are consulted on a case-by-case basis only. At provincial level, as VCCI has only 7 branches with limited capacity and VCA represents only the cooperatives rather than companies, tripartism remains infeasible. In bigger provinces and cities where VCCI and VCA set up permanent branches, although they participate in provincial tripartite labour arbitration councils together with VGCL and the local labour administration, this mechanism has been largely ineffective. As in China, foreign employers do not participate in VCCI, but lobby the government directly through their Chambers of Commerce, although VCCI reports that a number of foreign investors in HCMC, including European and American companies, have joined VCCI since 2006.

The trade unions in all three countries have largely succeeded in retaining the legal protection of minimum labour standards, although such protection is always under threat from neo-liberal reformers who claim that such protection destroys jobs. The most important policy areas in which the trade unions of all three countries have been active in relation to the representation of their members have been the determination of the legal minimum wage, on the one hand, and collaboration with the state labour and health and safety inspectorates, on the other.

The minimum wage

The most contentious and significant area of legislation is the statutory minimum wage. Although the statutory minimum wage is supposed to define the bare subsistence minimum below which wages should not fall, in Russia the minimum wage was eroded by inflation during the 1990s to be a small fraction of the subsistence minimum, while in both China and Vietnam the statutory minimum wage generally serves as the guideline for the basic wages of workers in new private and foreign-owned enterprises, with many enterprises illegally paying below the minimum. The minimum wage is differentiated according to the geographical location in all three countries, with the provincial and in some cases the local government having discretion in setting the minimum wage in China and regional governments setting their regional minimum wage alongside the federal minimum in Russia.

In Russia the attempt to increase the minimum wage to the level of the subsistence minimum has been a central focus of the campaigning of FNPR at Federal and regional levels. The trade unions secured an apparent victory with the passage of the new Labour Code in 2001, which specified that the minimum wage should be no less than the adult subsistence minimum, at a time when 40 per cent of employees earned less than the subsistence minimum. However, the clause also specified that the method and period of introduction of such a minimum wage would be established by a Federal Law. President Putin immediately responded by insisting that such a law would impose on the President's prerogative and that the minimum wage would be set as part of the budgetary process in accordance with financial possibilities. The FNPR has accordingly waged a long-drawn-out campaign to secure a commitment on the part of the Federal government to increase the minimum wage to the level of the subsistence minimum, and its regional organisations have lobbied regional governments similarly to set the regional minimum wage at the subsistence minimum. The FNPR has made the inclusion of such a clause in its regional agreements a major priority. In 2008, 32 of 77 regional agreements set an obligatory legal minimum wage and 18 included a recommended minimum, 21 also providing for the obligatory indexation of wages and five specifying the minimum basic wage as a proportion of earnings (*Vesti FNPR*, 6, 2009: 187–8). However, these agreements have a primarily symbolic significance because in many cases both their coverage and the means of their enforcement is very limited.

In China, ACFTU has not been so enthusiastic about increasing the minimum wage, for fear of eroding competitiveness and inhibiting the growth of employment. Nevertheless, local government has increased the minimum wage in direct response to strike waves, apparently without any pressure from ACFTU (Chan 2008).

The situation in Vietnam is a little more complicated because there are two minimum wages, one for domestic and the other for foreign-owned enterprises, the former being much lower than the latter. This does not mean that wages in foreign-owned enterprises are higher than in domestic enterprises, because domestic enterprises, particularly state and former state enterprises, generally pay substantially more than the minimum. However, the domestic minimum wage serves as the reference point for public-sector pay scales, as well as for many benefits and charges, so the government is very reluctant to increase the domestic minimum wage because of the knock-on effects of such an increase. Moreover, following Vietnam's entry to the WTO, the government is obliged progressively to remove the differential between domestic and foreign wage minima so as to eliminate the differential by 2012. It is not feasible to reduce the minimum wage for foreign-owned enterprises, so convergence will entail disengaging public-sector pay scales, benefits and charges from the domestic minimum wage and progressively increasing the domestic minimum wage until it matches the foreign-owned minimum. This provides good reason for the government to try to restrain growth of the foreign-owned minimum wage.

The minimum wage in Vietnam remained unchanged in the face of rapidly increasing inflation from 1999 to 2005 and many workers in the private and FIE sectors had had no pay increase during that period. The VGCL had been half-heartedly lobbying the government to increase the minimum wage for some time, but in the wake of the strikes that broke out at the end of 2005, VGCL came to see increasing the minimum wage as a primary means of heading off strikes. Law-abiding employers will increase wage rates in response to an increase in the legal minimum, while the authorities will be able to use the legal increase as a lever to compel employers faced with strikes to increase wages. The VGCL began to put pressure on the government to increase the minimum wage through tripartite meetings, by waging a media campaign and lobbying at the National Assembly and Party committees. However, there are two dangers in such a course of action. The economic danger is that raising wages generally will reduce the competitiveness of the locality (or country) as an investment location. The political danger is that raising the statutory minimum wage in direct response to workers' protest is likely to politicise the latter, so that workers in future come to address their wage demands directly to the state.

We can illustrate the politics of the minimum wage by briefly comparing cases from China and Vietnam. In Shenzhen in South China the minimum wage had been increased a little year by year by the city government, but the rate of increase slowed markedly in 2004 and 2005, to less than half the 4–5 per cent per annum rate of previous years. Following a wave of strikes in 2004 and 2005 the city authorities increased the minimum wage dramatically in July 2005 and July 2006, by one-third over the two years for those employed inside the Special Economic Zone (SEZ) and 46 per cent for those employed outside the SEZ, and this seemed to have damped down the strike waves in Shenzhen. However, the large increases in 2005 and 2006 had aroused the workers' expectations, so that when the city government failed to increase the minimum wage in July 2007 a new round of strikes erupted (Chan 2008, 2009), forcing the hand of the city government .

In Vietnam, towards the end of 2005 there was a growing number of strikes in the South in which workers held out for wages above the statutory minimum and employers were persuaded by the local authorities to meet their demands. There were widespread press reports in the autumn of 2005 that the government intended to increase the minimum wage from January 2006, raising workers' expectations, but in the event no announcement of an increase was forthcoming. The issue came to a head at the end of 2005, when 18 000 workers walked out at Freetrend, a Taiwanese footwear company, on 28 December 2005. As soon as the strike began, officials from the Zone trade union arrived and persuaded management to raise wages. Freetrend's human resources manager was reported as saying that 'the current salary is a temporary measure to calm workers' minds while waiting for an official decision on minimum salary adjustments from the government' (*VietnamNet*, 05/01/06).

However, the following day, workers at six neighbouring enterprises went on strike, demanding pay increases of 30–36 per cent, and over the next two weeks there was a total of 69 recorded strikes, most at FIEs, with demands for higher pay, social and health insurance payments and shorter working hours, in many of which workers were reported to have broken windows and smashed up offices and equipment. Although some employers insisted that they would not raise wages until the government announced a decision on the minimum wage, most employers met their workers' demands at once. On 6 January the Prime Minister issued Decree 03, which increased FDI minimum wages by about 40 per cent from 1 February 2006, with an additional 7 per cent premium for skilled workers, and the strikes stopped. However, as widely anticipated, the increase in the FDI minimum wage provoked a second wave of strikes as non-FDI workers walked out demanding wage increases, with about 20 such strikes in February. However, the government was reluctant to increase the minimum wage for domestic employers because this would not only increase the wage bill for one million public employees, but also the payments to six million pensioners, veterans and other recipients of social benefits.

The strikes provoked an intense post-mortem, which sharpened positions in the long-running debate about the causes of and appropriate response to wildcat strikes. Some VGCL officers insisted that the government was to blame for the strikes. The union had long been pressing for an increase in the legal minimum wage, a proposal which had been endorsed by MOLISA in September 2005, provoking many complaints from foreign investors (*Vietnam News* 29 September 2005), but the government had prevaricated, first deciding to increase the FDI minimum wage from 1 January, and then postponing the proposed increase to 1 April in response to an appeal from foreign investors to delay the increase until after the Tet holiday bonuses had been paid. According to VGCL officers it was this confusion that provoked the strikes. By contrast, on 5 January, Pham Minh Huan, Director of MOLISA's Wage and Salary Department, in an interview with *VnExpress*, stated that the conflict was not about where the government had set the minimum wage, but about the actual salary that companies are paying workers. He emphasised that it is the responsibility of the trade union to negotiate wage increases with employers and the government would respect their decision. He also warned that the minimum wage for FDI enterprises would in future rise more slowly than the lower minimum wage for domestic private enterprises because WTO entry would mean that Vietnam would have to phase out discrimination against foreign employers, reinforcing the argument that in future wage increases would have to be negotiated in the workplace (Clarke 2006: 356). Nevertheless, the minimum wage was increased again in January 2008 and in May 2009 as inflation persisted.

The VGCL in Vietnam attaches much more importance to regular increases in the minimum wage than does ACFTU in China, and regularly lobbies the government for such increases, while ACFTU puts much more emphasis on the development of collective bargaining and wage negotiations as the means of increasing wages. This is a symptom of the fact that VGCL has progressed far more slowly in developing representative trade union functions and is much more inclined to leave the regulation of industrial relations to the Ministry of Labour than is ACFTU, but it is also a result of ACFTU's primary commitment to increasing employment rather than increasing wages as the means of maintaining social stability. It may also be that ACFTU is more sensitive to the concerns of local government that increases in the minimum wage will discourage investment, so that it is better to make piecemeal concessions to the most aggrieved workers rather than legislate for a general wage increase, whereas in Vietnam the minimum wage, although geographically differentiated, is set centrally, while wages are substantially lower than in China and modest wage increases do not threaten Vietnam's competitive advantage.

Labour inspection

Cases which reach the courts are only the tip of the iceberg of legal violation by employers – it is only because employers normally expect to get away with gross and persistent legal violations that they persist in them, despite the expectation that they will lose in the event of a court action. In most strikes and protests in China and Vietnam it turns out that the employer has been violating labour legislation in paying wages below the legal minimum, in failing to pay wages due, in working excessive hours, in failing to pay for overtime and night work at the prescribed rates, in failing to make prescribed health and social insurance contributions or in failing to meet statutory standards of health and safety at work. The implication is that the effective enforcement of labour legislation in the workplace would make a considerable contribution to reducing the incidence of strikes and protests.

In all three countries violation of labour, social insurance and health and safety legislation is endemic. In principle the trade unions, with their extensive network of members and voluntary trade union officers, should be in the best position to monitor the enforcement of such legislation and indeed, in the state-socialist period, this was in principle the responsibility of the trade union, which had an army of voluntary inspectors assigned to the task, although the priority of production meant that infringements were often tolerated by the union.

The increased subordination of the trade union to management and the proliferation of non-union workplaces in the new capitalist economy have meant that the trade unions are even less able to monitor and remedy legislative violations than they were in the state-socialist period. On the other hand, the relevant state inspectorates do not have the staff or the political weight to inspect workplaces or enforce the legislation. Once they have carried out their statutory duties to investigate accidents and to carry out routine certification of premises, the inspectors have very little time to devote to routine inspection. Moreover, even leaving aside the inevitable corruption of labour inspectors, they are understandably reluctant to visit premises which violate the law, which substantially increases their workload, so they prefer to visit establishments which they are confident will reveal few violations, unless they are forced to investigate an enterprise in response to a strike or protest.

In this context the trade unions press for an increased role for state inspectorates and look towards collaboration between higher-level union bodies and state inspectorates as the means of overcoming the weakness of workplace trade unions and the conservatism of the inspectorates. The principle underlying such collaboration is that trade union representatives in the workplace should identify legislative violations and bring them to the attention of the relevant inspectorate, which would then use administrative and judicial means to secure the enforcement of legislation. Higher-level trade union organisations will meanwhile organise joint inspection teams with state inspectors to investigate enterprises under their jurisdiction, either on their own initiative or at the request of a primary union organisation.

In many cases low-paid workers are only able to earn a living wage by working excessively long hours and/or working in harmful working conditions. These cases pose a dilemma for the trade union, since enforcement of the law would entail a reduction in workers' wages. Such a dilemma can only be resolved through negotiation of the trade union with the employer, through which the trade union can secure a wage increase to compensate for the loss of earnings as a result of the reduction in hours or improvement of working conditions, but without the capacity for such negotiation the trade union has little choice but to continue to tolerate such illegal conditions.

In Russia, responsibility for health and safety was taken away from FNPR following its confrontation with Yeltsin in December 1993 and the establishment of a State Labour Inspectorate, which was staffed by transferring 90 per cent of labour inspectors from the trade unions (FNPR 1996: 56), although trade unions are still permitted to employ their own labour inspectors, who have the right of access to any establishment in which the trade union has members. The FNPR has placed increasing emphasis on collaboration with the state labour inspectorate, with which it signed a collaboration agreement in 2006, in the inspection of premises, but staff shortages on both sides mean that such inspection is bound to be inadequate, so the initiative in the identification of violations of labour and health and safety legislation has to lie with the primary trade union organisations.

In 2007 FNPR employed 537 technical labour inspectors, an increase of 57 from the previous year, and had 299 064 voluntary health and safety inspectors in workplaces, a slight decline from the previous year. The full-time inspectors carried out 13 688 health and safety inspections, 4914 jointly with local bodies of the Federal Labour Inspectorate, 596 jointly with the public prosecutor and 5808 jointly with other inspectorates. These inspections identified a total of 159 387 violations. In addition, voluntary inspectors identified a further 201 335 violations. The inspectors also investigated 10 201 industrial accidents, 2919 of which had a fatal outcome (*Vesti FNPR*, 4, 2008: 73–5). In addition, in 2007 the FNPR carried out 4473 labour inspections jointly with the Federal Labour Inspectorate. On the basis of material provided to the Inspectorate in 2007, administrative sanctions were imposed on 886 managers and officials, an increase of 80 per cent over 2006 (*Vesti FNPR*, 5, 2008: 15).

The identification of violations is only one aspect of the attempt to secure the implementation of labour and health and safety violations, and is insufficient if such identification does not lead to the remedying of the situation. For example, in Perm' krai in 2006 the health workers' trade union initiated a programme of health and safety inspection which found a multitude of violations, but also found that spending on health and safety fell far short of the budgeted expenditure because of financial shortfalls, so decided not to expand the programme of inspection, which would merely compound the problem by leading to larger financial penalties being imposed on violating institutions. Instead, the regional trade union organisation decided to appeal to the governor and deputies of the Legislative assembly with the demand to assign funds for the improvement of working conditions and health and safety in the regional budget for 2007 and to develop a regional targeted programme 'Safe work in budgetary organisations' to plan concrete actions directed at support, and particularly financing, for the protection and improvement of working conditions. In parallel, the FNPR and health workers' regional committees appealed to the Office of the Public Prosecutor of Perm' krai concerning the infringement of the Labour Code regarding assignment of funds for health and safety. These actions had some effect, with modest allocations for health and safety being included in the regional budget for 2007.

China's Law on Safety in Production was introduced in 2001 and stipulated 14 basic systems and/or measures which, on paper, are relatively strict, but implementation is constrained by a weak labour inspectorate and poor trade union participation (Pringle and Frost 2003: 315). Article 46 stipulates the rights and responsibilities of employees pertaining to occupational safety. They are built around six core rights (Pringle and Frost 2003: 311): to safety information and training on prevention; to safety equipment that conforms to national standards; to criticise and make suggestions; to refuse to carry out instructions from management that violate laws or regulations; to stop work in life-threatening situations; and to receive compensation following an accident at work.

The Law on the Prevention and Cure of Occupational Diseases came into force on 1 May 2002 and stated the responsibilities of enterprises with regard to safe working conditions, industrial accident insurance, measures to prevent occupational disease, and the provision of information to workers.

Writing in 2003, Pringle and Frost found in these laws potential opportunities to improve China's record on occupational safety and health, but pinpointed union weakness as a key constraint to improved implementation of labour legislation in general and occupational health and safety law in particular.

The new laws and standards provide a legal framework that could, if utilised, force enterprises to comply with adequate standards. There is more than adequate information available ... The problems lie in the lack of confidence and experience among younger workers and managers. Workers are in general ignorant of the laws and the vast body of expertise on OHS, while younger managers often feel compelled to manage facilities more in line with profit than fairness. (Pringle and Frost 2003: 315)

To date, workplace inspections have not matched the levels of industrial development that economic reform has induced. There are more than 3000 labour inspection agencies in China and around 40 000 inspectors (Cooney 2007: 607), but the inspectorates are dependent on local government for their financing and are managed by the local labour bureaux. As such, they are not inclined to offend powerful local interests, and they have very limited powers of enforcement. Article 7 of the State Regulations on Labour Inspection obliges these agencies to solicit the views of trade unions and other 'relevant departments' (State Council 2004). The ACFTU has its own network of labour supervision and inspection committees at various levels. It claims that almost a quarter of all enterprises and organisations had 'labour protection supervision and examination committees', with 1.621 million labour protection inspectors in 2006, covering over 40 per cent of the workforce, while a third of higher-level trade union organisations also had 'labour protection supervision and examination organisations'. Overall, the trade unions at all levels participated in 2.301 million safety production inspections in 2006 (ACFTU 2007). In practice, these committees have no power over working conditions unless they have the backing of government departments.

In Vietnam, responsibility for monitoring the enforcement of labour legislation is divided between the Ministry of Labour, Invalids and Social Affairs (MOLISA) and VGCL, but even senior VGCL officials recognise that the priorities of increasing investment and employment inhibit such enforcement. On the government side, all the functions of labour inspection have been the responsibility of MOLISA since 2002, when the Hygiene Inspectorate, which used to be part of the Ministry of Health, was merged into the Labour Inspectorate. Under the 1990 trade union law monitoring of labour and health and safety legislation is also a responsibility of VGCL, though until recently the union has done little to put this into effect outside the state sector.

According to Government Decree 61/1998/ND-CP of 15 August 1998 every enterprise should be inspected at least once a year, but in 2004 MOLISA had only 350 inspectors and VGCL had 100 inspectors to check on nearly 100 000 enterprises (though VGCL claimed to have examined 13 000 enterprises in 2003). In 2004 in Hanoi there were 11 inspectors responsible for 700 state enterprises, 600 foreign-invested enterprises and over 20 000 private enterprises. The HCMC had five inspectors for more than 30 000 enterprises (Clarke, Lee and Do 2007: 550). By 2008 the total number of inspectors was unchanged, with 50 based at MOLISA and 300 allocated to 64 provinces, though there were now 33 inspectors in HCMC. When the press pointed to weak enforcement as a major cause of pervasive violations of labour rights by employers, the Government approved a long-standing proposal of MOLISA to increase the number of labour inspectors by 70, but MOLISA complained that they could not recruit more inspectors due to the low salary and in fact, at the beginning of 2009, the number of inspectors in MOLISA had fallen to 43, with 326 in local offices, sufficient to inspect each enterprise every 150 years (*Vietnamnet* 07/01/2009 http://english.vietnamnet.vn/social/2009/01/822636/).

There are no statistics on the number of legal violations uncovered by the labour inspectors, but it is unlikely, even with increased numbers, that the inspectors will have time to make many routine inspections, once they have dealt with cases of industrial accidents and complaints which have given rise to work stoppages. This means that responsibility for monitoring the enforcement of labour legislation, as for the negotiation and enforcement of collective agreements, in practice falls to the enterprise- and district-level trade union organisations.

Penalties for violation of labour legislation are derisory, but DOLISA or VGCL can threaten to refer an employer to the People's Committee or the relevant Ministry and the latter can make life very difficult for an employer, in the last resort even revoking their investment licences, and this threat is much more effective than the threat of judicial sanctions. However, the main emphasis is on training and educating employers, especially foreign employers, in their legal obligations, and using persuasion in the event of violations, so that it is very rare for sanctions to be imposed on employers who violate the law.

To improve the role of the union in monitoring compliance on 31 December 2007, the VGCL issued Decision No. 1693 to strengthen the inspection and monitoring mandate of primary and higher-level unions. The Decision requires the primary and higher-level unions to prepare annual plans for inspection of employers' compliance with labour and union legislation. The unions can carry out inspection themselves or in collaboration with the authorities. Apart from regular inspection visits, the unions have the right to carry out irregular inspections, without giving prior notice, if necessary. After each inspection visit, a written record with recommendations for improvement will be made. If the employer fails to follow the recommendations, the union has the right to inform the relevant authority to allow it to take further action.

A major issue in Vietnam has been the failure of employers to pay social insurance contributions for their employees. In Vietnam the social insurance contribution is now 21 per cent of the basic salary of workers, with 16 per cent paid by the employer and 5 per cent by the employee. Many employers only sign temporary contracts with their workers, particularly in industries such as construction, since temporary workers have to pay social and health insurance contribution for themselves and only receive compensation from the employer for industrial injury if they can prove that the injury was the fault of the employer. According to Vietnam Social Insurance (VSI), 44 per cent of employed workers are not covered by social insurance, only 10 per cent of non-public enterprises pay social insurance contributions for their workers and only 50 per cent of the workers employed by these enterprises receive social insurance benefits. In the first attempt to tighten the enforcement of the SI legislation, in early 2008, VSI of Ho Chi Minh city sued two Korean companies for evading SI obligations for five years while still deducting workers' salaries for SI contributions. The VSI won the case and the court allowed automatic deduction of the fines and compensation from the two companies' bank accounts.

Employment creation

The ACFTU has long been preoccupied with the problems of employment creation both to reduce the social tensions generated by massive lay-offs from state enterprises and those arising from the growing number of young people flocking to the cities in search of work. Up until 2003, the main thrust of ACFTU's basic work was outside the actual workplace and focused on the establishment of support centres for 'workers' communities in need' (*kunnan zhigong qunti*). These centres were called Workers' Support Centres (*kunnan zhigong bangfu zhongxin*) and targeted laid-off or unemployed workers whose basic livelihood needs were not being met. According to the *Workers' Daily*, many of those who received assistance were facing severe difficulties in finding re-employment, were owed considerable amounts of money in unpaid wages and medical costs from bankrupted SOEs (Zhou 2002). Most of the Workers' Support Centres (WSC) were established between 2002 and 2003 following the Ninth Presidium Meeting (expanded) of the ACFTU Thirteenth Congress in September 2002, which included a discussion of the experience of WSCs in the city of Tianjin (interview, labour researcher, Beijing, 12 February 2006). The conference ended with a call to set up 200 such centres within three years, a call that was quickly upgraded to an opinion when the union released the 'ACFTU Opinion on the establishment of Workers' Support Centres' in January 2003 (Beijing Federation of Trade Unions 2003).[1] By November 2005, the union had established WSCs in ten provinces, 329 cities and more than 1600 counties. By June 2005, city-level WSCs had issued just under 1.5 billion Yuan to workers (Pan 2005). In 2005, the *Workers' Daily* summed up the main tasks of the centres, some of which directly replaced the Re-employment Centres (*zai jiuye zhongxin*) that SOEs were in theory meant to provide for laid-off workers, although in practice many of these centres were 'ghost towns'. First of all, the WSCs provided employment introductions and retraining and were an integral part of the union's 'three-year-three one and a half million' (*san nian san ge 150 wan*) employment project that aimed to provide training to 1.5 million laid-off or unemployed workers, employment introductions to another 1.5 million and re-employment to a further 1.5 million (Qiao 2005). Second, the centres were to provide livelihood assistance, including medical costs and children's education costs. Third, was the provision of advice and direct assistance to workers who had found

---

[1]   '*Zhonghua zong gonghui guanyu jianli kunnan zhigong bangfu zhongxin de yijian*'.

work and came to the centres petitioning the union for help following rights violations. The response included sending teams to relevant work units (*danwei*) or government departments to negotiate a satisfactory outcome. Finally, the WSCs were to provide legal assistance and/or advice to workers who were pursuing claims through legal channels.

The ACFTU's own statistics suggest that the WSCs had an impact, although as always caution is required when reviewing union statistics pertaining to the meeting of quotas. The *Workers' Daily* reported that by September 2004, the union at all levels had organised over 11.4 million job introductions; provided over two million training sessions to laid-off or unemployed workers; and helped to find work for just over two million workers (Qiao 2005). In 2004, the union issued over four billion Yuan to over 3.5 million cases involving hardship, an increase of 36 per cent on 2003 (ACFTU 2005).

The trade union and labour disputes

A fundamental duty of a trade union in a capitalist market economy is to represent its members in the event of an individual or collective labour dispute. This is an idea that is completely alien to the conception of a state-socialist trade union, one of whose primary responsibilities is to maintain labour discipline so that, far from representing members who are disciplined by management, a state-socialist trade union typically endorses such disciplinary measures. Of course, where a dispute arises out of a management failing, for example a violation of labour or health and safety legislation, even a state-socialist trade union has a responsibility to intercede on behalf of the worker, although where such violations have been necessitated by the need to achieve the production plan the trade union would be likely to overlook management's failing. This conception carries over into the approach of post-socialist trade unions to labour disputes, which is, in general, to pursue such disputes on behalf of members only when the dispute arises out of a clear violation of the law on the part of the employer. This is expressed in the distinction frequently made by trade union officers in all three countries between the 'reasonable' and 'unreasonable' demands of workers, with the trade union only being prepared to pursue the former.

The prescribed procedure for the resolution of labour disputes in all three countries involves mediation and arbitration. If mediation and arbitration fails then recourse is provided to the judicial resolution of the dispute through the courts. The contractual regulation of labour relations on the basis of individual labour contracts means that labour disputes are *prima facie* disputes between an individual worker or workers and the employer. In both Russia and Vietnam a collective labour dispute is defined as a dispute over the negotiation or enforcement of the collective agreement and a strike is only permitted in pursuit of the resolution of such a collective dispute once the procedures for mediation and arbitration have been exhausted. This means that in practice a collective labour dispute can only be initiated by the trade union. In China there is no distinction between the procedures for the resolution of individual and collective disputes, since there is no legal provision for collective action in pursuit of a dispute. For judicial and statistical purposes, a collective labour dispute is defined in China as any dispute involving three or more workers.

In all three countries, the close integration of the trade union into the structure of management, and the traditional identification of trade union officers with the priorities of management, underlies a tendency for the trade union to seek to reconcile any differences of interest between employees and management within its own structures and so guarantee that its negotiations with management will be consensual. When employees appeal to the trade union or make suggestions through the consultation process, the trade union officers themselves decide whether or not to respond to the complaint or suggestion depending on whether or not they regard it as 'reasonable', that is, likely to be acceptable to management. To this extent the trade union could be said to 'mediate' between workers and management (Li 2000: chapter 6; Zhang 1997), but this mediation does nothing to challenge the asymmetrical power relationship between the two parties. It should not be surprising, therefore, that workers in all three countries are more inclined to take their problems to their line managers than to their trade union representatives.[1]

Most individual labour disputes are resolved informally, with or without the mediation of the trade union, by negotiation with the relevant management departments. The most contentious individual disputes are usually those regarding punitive measures, including dismissal. In such cases the aggrieved worker can in principle contest the legality of the measures, usually on procedural grounds, but in practice few workers have a sufficiently detailed knowledge of the law or the resources to take their case through the legal system. This is the point at which a worker is most likely to look to the trade union for support. A central aspect of the trade union's responsibility to represent the rights and interests of its members is its provision of legal advice and representation in judicial proceedings.

Legal action to resolve collective labour disputes has severe limitations. On the one hand, legal action individualises and fragments the dispute because there is no provision for collective or 'class actions', except in Russia and Vietnam in the case of a formally declared collective labour dispute. On the other hand, legal action is a very long-drawn-out process, generally involving endlessly deferred hearings and repeated appeals to higher-level courts.

---

[1]   Twice as many of the workers interviewed by Qi Li would appeal to their manager if they had a dispute over pay or dismissals as would appeal to the trade union (Li 2000: 198). In Russia, the 1999 CLMS survey found that only 11 per cent of employees in unionised enterprises would turn to the trade union for help, almost four times as many turning to the employer.

Russia

The Russian Labour Code retains much of the protective apparatus of its Soviet predecessor but, as in soviet times, it is systematically flouted by management, violations traditionally being met 'with understanding' by the trade union. Legal action to secure the implementation of labour legislation was pioneered by the alternative unions, which generally lacked the collective strength to negotiate directly with management, and this was one of the main recruiting tools of these unions, which could offer protection to their members. The alternative unions protected their members against victimisation and illegal dismissal, often for their trade union activity, but also sought compensation in cases of industrial injury and, by the middle of the 1990s, were very active in pursuing the non-payment of wages through the courts. Faced with the challenge of the alternative unions, these initiatives were taken up by the traditional unions, which saw in legal action a means of defending their members without having to engage in collective action or direct confrontation with management. Today legal action, or the threat of legal action, over violations of the labour law or the collective agreement has become the preferred means by which the traditional unions seek to defend the interests of their members and has become thoroughly integrated into the structure and practice of the best of the regional and enterprise trade union organisations, which have hired lawyers and opened legal advice centres to service their members and member organisations.

In Russia, the provision of legal advice is one of the most time-consuming activities of the regional trade union organisations and provides virtually their only contact with ordinary members. The legal department is usually the largest department in the regional trade union apparatus, and is accorded a much higher priority than any other department.

In the soviet period workers could turn to the enterprise lawyer for legal advice, but today this channel has been closed off, while very few primary trade union organisations have their own legal specialist, although developing the legal competence of primary trade union leaders is a priority aim of trade union training. In principle union members should appeal in the first instance to their own trade union committee, but in many cases they go directly to the regional offices of their branch union or the federation or even to FNPR in Moscow. Many trade union lawyers think that the preoccupation with individual cases is a distraction from what should be their main task of defending the collective interests of the workers, but the weakness of primary trade union organisations and their reluctance to engage in collective action reinforces the continued individualisation of the regulation of labour disputes. Moreover, the regional trade union leadership tends to see this work as very important for the public image of the trade unions as organisations to which those in trouble (and not only union members) can turn. The provision of legal advice is generally seen very much within the framework of the traditional view of the trade union as a welfare agency solving individual problems, so many of the problems addressed are not in any way work-related.

The FNPR reported in 2008 that the number of lawyers employed by its member organisations had almost doubled from 768 in 2003 to 1337 in 2007. The number of labour inspections and violations of labour legislation identified had correspondingly almost doubled, from 22 092 and 67 298 in 2003 to 43 004 and 160 510 in 2007 respectively. The proportion of violations which were remedied also increased from 82 per cent to 91 per cent over the same period. As a result of investigations member trade unions managed to get 1719 employees restored to their jobs in 2007, 1148 managers and officials were disciplined, of whom 62 were dismissed. Member unions also referred 1503 cases to the public prosecutor, of which 1067 received a positive response, 15 of which led to criminal proceedings. Trade union lawyers assisted in the preparation of documentation for 69 330 cases which went to a Labour Disputes Commission and 24 487 court cases. Lawyers represented union members in 15 792 court cases, 97 per cent of which were settled wholly or partially in favour of the worker, which may suggest that, as in China, trade union lawyers only provide support in open and shut cases. Trade union lawyers provided assistance in 1101 collective labour disputes, of which 14 involved strike action. Although the trade union was successful in the vast majority of these disputes, including half of the strikes, it appears that these were the disputes involving only a small number of workers (on average only three workers were involved in each of the 988 disputes that was resolved successfully, as against an average of almost 400 in each of the remaining 113 disputes). Trade union lawyers received 84 381 written requests for help and 591 288 through personal consultations (*Vesti FNPR*, 5, 2008: 45–7; the data for 2008 is not directly comparable, *Vesti FNPR*, 3, 2009: 41–3).

The traditional trade unions in the best of cases will go through the procedure to declare a collective labour dispute, in principle as a preliminary to strike action but in practice as a bargaining tactic, since very few collective labour disputes culminate in a strike. On the rare occasions in which collective unrest erupts into strike action in Russia this has most often been taken despite the traditional trade union and often in face of the overt opposition of the trade union, which, if it does not ignore the dispute, seeks to confine it within 'constitutional' judicial channels. Even where the enterprise trade union has itself initiated or supported a strike, it often finds its call opposed by higher trade union bodies, whose collaboration with the state apparatus is conditional on their ability to maintain social peace.

A not untypical example of this is the strike that took place in Esaul'skaya Mine in Kuzbass in 2007. The mine was one of the most productive mines in Kuzbass, with a strong trade union committee which had secured high wages and good social benefits in the collective agreement and which had long been in dispute with the higher levels of the trade union over what were seen as the conciliatory positions of the latter. The dispute arose when a new management came into the coal concern, which was determined to show the trade union at Esaul'skaya who was the boss. Esaul'skaya, like a number of other mines, had always worked eight-hour shifts, which suited the workers because the mine was a long way from the city where the workers lived, although according to the Labour Code coal-miners should only work six-hour shifts. Following a number of fatal accidents, the local prosecutor had got a court order instructing the concern to move all its mines to the six-hour shift regime. The new management accordingly declared the change in the work regime, but was unwilling to negotiate an increase in pay to compensate for what was effectively an increase in working hours. The workers were incensed, but the mine trade union committee held them back from a wildcat strike, warning them of the dire consequences of such an illegal action, while it went through all the procedures required to initiate a collective labour dispute and to call a strike. However, a series of attempts was made to declare the strike illegal through the courts, on the grounds that the dispute sought to challenge the law, which could not be the subject of a collective labour dispute and that an agreed schedule of work to preserve the mine during a work stoppage had not been drawn up. Workers and members of the trade union committee were threatened with dismissal, the union was denied premises to hold meetings and all manner of threats and barriers were raised. Above all, both the regional and central committees of the miners' union not only failed to support the mine trade union, but publicly condemned it. Faced with the concerted opposition of the management, the courts and the regional administration the workers went on strike with little hope of success. On the first day of the strike the management locked the workers out and after a few days the mine began to work a six-hour shift. The trade union president resigned and five activists were dismissed.

The result of the opposition to strikes of the traditional trade unions is that strikes are much more likely to be spontaneous, usually without going through the prescribed legal procedures, and organised, and more rarely initiated, by alternative trade unions. Where supported by the workplace trade union against the advice of the higher-level union organisation, a dispute may result in the workplace union disaffiliating from its higher trade union organisation and reconstituting itself as an independent trade union, which subsequently may affiliate to one of the alternative union federations. This has most typically happened in municipal transport, the health service and education, where alternative unions have cells in individual bus parks, schools and medical establishments.

Most alternative trade unions in Russia have been born in the heat of such struggles, organising workers who have been disillusioned by the passivity of the traditional union, particularly small groups of workers in relatively privileged occupations who have some bargaining power. However, once the moment of struggle has passed it proves extremely difficult to sustain such an alternative trade union in opposition to management and to the traditional union. The result is that most alternative unions either fade away to a small nucleus of embattled militants, or find an accommodation with management and degenerate into a 'yellow' company union. In Russia today the alternative trade union movement finds itself at an extremely low ebb. The Independent Miners' Union, which was the heart of the movement, has virtually disintegrated. The trade unions of dockers and of air traffic controllers, originally formed as breakaways from the traditional sectoral unions, are engaged in a possibly terminal struggle for survival. The independent trade union of Ford workers in Vsevolozhsk, Leningrad region, is the only success story on which the alternative unions can pin their hopes, but attempts to build out from this example have so far had very limited success. Nevertheless, the alternative trade unions have acted as a spur to the traditional trade unions in harnessing worker activism. As Mikhail Shmakov, FNPR President, has acknowledged, 'in general the existence of the alternative trade unions is even helpful. Competition does not allow us to stagnate' (*Vesti FNPR*, 1–2, 1999: 60).

China

The 2001 Trade Union Law requires the trade union to provide 'support and assistance' to an employee who 'believes that the enterprise infringes upon his labour rights and interests' if the employee applies to labour arbitration or the courts (article 21), but the role of the trade union in the prescribed procedures for mediation of disputes within the enterprise is to chair the mediation committee, rather than to serve as the employee's representative. In practice, it appears to be very rare for the trade union to provide advice or representation for employees, either in the informal resolution of grievances or in formal dispute procedures, and it is most likely that trade union cadres will try to resolve disputes and grievances either by persuading workers of the necessity of the management decision or, at best, by playing the role of mediator between the management and workers. In the reports of strikes and social protests publicised by monitoring organisations like China Labour Bulletin and China Labor Watch, it is generally the case that the grievance has been festering for a number of years, suggesting that the enterprise trade union has turned a blind eye to blatant violations of the rights and interests of employees, perhaps hoping to resolve the problem, or more likely to contain the complaints, within the enterprise.[1]

In China juridical procedures have become the principal means for the resolution of labour disputes. The pivot of the system is the process of arbitration because, while an appellant can by-pass the stage of mediation, it is only possible to take a case to court by appealing against an arbitration decision. Mediation takes place within the enterprise and is supervised by the trade union, which chairs the mediation committee. This can work in the case of trivial disputes (Taylor, Chang and Li 2003: 167–8), but in any more serious dispute the trade union is very unlikely to support the worker against the management, and there have been plenty of cases of victimisation of enterprise trade union leaders who have been so rash as to do so (Chen 2003:

---

[1]   The 2001 Trade Union Law, while not endorsing a right to strike, provides for the trade union not only to mediate in the event of a work stoppage, but even to 'reflect the views and demands of the workers' (article 27) in seeking to resolve the dispute and restore production.

1017). The weakness of the system of mediation as a means of redressing workers' more serious grievances is indicated by the fact that, while the number of recorded disputes has escalated, the number of cases going to mediation has declined rapidly and the proportion of appeals against mediation decisions has increased, so that the burden of resolution of labour disputes has fallen on the local arbitration committees and the courts (Cheng 2004: 278–9). Between 1987 and the end of 2005 1.72 million labour disputes went to arbitration, involving 5.32 million employees, more than half of whom were involved in collective disputes, with a growth rate of 27.3 per cent per year (*China Daily*, 27 August 2007). In 1995, China's courts handled 28 285 labour disputes but by 2004 that number had increased fourfold to 114 997 (Shen Jie 2006: 130). In 2006 there were 13 977 registered collective labour disputes, involving a total of 348 714 workers, and 301 233 individual cases. The statistics show that the combination of the new Labour Contract Law (making it harder for employers to lay workers off), the new Labour Mediation and Arbitration Law (making it easier and cheaper for workers to pursue claims) and the global financial crisis already had a dramatic impact in 2008. For example in Dongguan, a key manufacturing town in the Pearl River Delta, the courts dealt with a total of 23 044 cases in 2008, an increase of 159 per cent over 2007! When a journalist from the respected *Caijing* (*Finance and Economics*) magazine asked the Dongguan Labour Bureau for figures on arbitration, he was informed that at present these statistics were 'too sensitive' and remained secret (*baomi*). The last available statistics from the Shenzhen Labour Arbitration Court reported an increase in arbitrated cases in the first quarter of 2008 of 277 per cent, with arbitration committees in manufacturing areas of the city such as Bao'an and Longgang posting increases of 392 per cent and 360 per cent respectively (Zhou 2009)!

The majority of arbitration cases are resolved at least partially in favour of the worker. In 2006, workers won 47 per cent of cases heard by an arbitration committee, with employers winning just 12 per cent and the remainder partially won by both parties (China Statistics Publishing House 2007: 516–17). These settlement ratios have been fairly constant over the last decade, with the number of cases partially won by both parties gradually creeping up over the years, although there appears to be wide regional variation in the results of labour cases dealt with by the courts and in some cities worker victories have been very high: 90 per cent in Ningbo in Zhejiang and Zhongshan in Guangdong (Shen 2006: 130).

In order to strengthen the union's role in supporting workers in legal disputes ACFTU issued 'Trial Methods on Unions' Participation in Labour Disputes Settlements' in 1995, which emphasised that unions should provide legal assistance to workers and should set up their own legal agencies to represent such workers. The ACFTU established legal departments at national, provincial and local levels and set up local legal advice centres to provide advice and legal representation for workers in arbitration and court proceedings (for details of a pioneering legal advice centre, see Pringle 2010). The Shanghai provincial ACFTU organisation also established a network of 'Labour Law Surveillance Committees' under its district and county trade unions and 'labour law surveillance points' in enterprises (Shen 2006: 361), which are essentially early warning and basic advice centres also found in other provinces. By the end of 2004, the ACFTU had set up 2990 legal assistance services staffed by a total of 9976 people, 766 of whom were qualified lawyers (ACFTU 2005). However, in general there are quite strict limits as to which cases ACFTU lawyers will take on. On the one hand, they will only provide support in cases where there has been a flagrant legal violation, so that they can guarantee to win. On the other hand, they are much more reluctant to provide support in the case of collective disputes and will almost never provide legal support for workers who have been involved in collective action (Chen 2003: 1014–16). For this reason, in South and East China there has been a mushrooming of legal advice centres run by NGOs, which help workers to file and pursue the kinds of cases in court that ACFTU steers clear of. Recently ACFTU in Guangzhou has sought to encourage such legal NGOs to collaborate with its own apparatus, on condition that they break off their links with foreign partners (Chan and Pringle 2008).

A pioneering trade union-run rights centre at city (county) level in Zhejiang claims to take on all cases, regardless of the difficulties involved. Its establishment was a contentious process that involved overcoming sustained opposition from government and legal departments as well as employers over turf, interests and politics. Final approval was only won after the trade union chair used leverage derived from his position as a member of the local People's Congress in a complex lobbying process. As with the placement of financially independent trade union staffers in three enterprises in Guangdong, one of the important factors in this case is that the centre concerned has not recruited staff for the centre from the traditional union networks but from 'society' in general.

The striking feature of ACFTU's extensive legal apparatus is that the provision of legal advice and the monitoring of legal violations by employers is undertaken almost exclusively at the level of city, county, municipal and provincial trade unions, and barely if at all within the workplace by the enterprise trade union. The escalation in the number of cases proceeding to arbitration and judicial resolution is an indicator not of the success but of the failure to develop effective trade unions and adequate industrial relations institutions. On the one hand, the majority of cases turn out to involve a patent violation of the law on the part of the employer, often going back for years, which the workplace trade union has failed to address or resolve. On the other hand, judicial procedures for dispute resolution exacerbate social unrest as much as they contain it. The procedures are time-consuming, expensive and strongly biased against the worker. The result is that the process is very long-drawn-out and frustrating for the workers, with the original grievance being compounded by a growing sense of injustice, provoking street protests and demonstrations outside arbitration tribunals and local authority buildings.

The more than 400 workers poisoned by cadmium dust while producing batteries in factories owned by the Asian TNC Gold Peak fought a four-year campaign for compensation. Their struggle involved two separate processes of arbitration and court appeals. Looking back at their attempts to go through formal channels of dispute resolution one Gold Peak worker explained how perceived bias on the part of the judge aggravated the situation:

> At both the arbitration and appeal courts we were frequently told our evidence was not allowed. For example, we made a DVD of conditions in the factory but the judge said this was impermissible evidence. This made us both angry and more determined to fight for justice from the Gold Peak bosses. (Pringle, interview with Liu XX, Hong Kong, 12 December 2005)

In her comparison of labour protests in the public and private sectors, Lee (2007: 188) found that

> Radicalisation of conflict may occur in any stage of the arbitration-litigation process. When workers with standing grievances find legal grounds for their case, they expect official attention. But bureaucratic red tape and political pressure from the big companies or state firms may affect whether workers may even lodge a complaint.

Vietnam

In Vietnam, according to article 163 of the amended Labour Code, all enterprises which have a trade union are required to set up a conciliation council with an equal number of representatives of employer and employees (in the 1994 Labour Code this did not apply to foreign-owned enterprises or those with fewer than ten employees). If there is no conciliation council, or if agreement cannot be reached, an individual dispute can be referred to the district conciliator in the local DOLISA office or to the labour court. A collective dispute is referred upwards to the regional Arbitration Council. If the trade union is not satisfied with the result of arbitration it can refer the case to court or, with the support of a majority vote of the labour force, it can legally call a strike.

Workers do not have confidence in the neutrality of the conciliation council – employee representatives are often managers and are unlikely to rule against the employer – so very few cases are referred to enterprise conciliation councils and many enterprises have not even bothered to set them up. All ten enterprises visited by Do, Clarke and Lee had a conciliation council, but not one had ever heard a single case. The HCMC Arbitration Council conducted a survey of conciliation at the enterprise and district level (covering 24 districts), which identified 84 collective cases and 1118 individual cases which had been to conciliation since 1995, of which

823 had been successfully resolved. The conciliator in District One of HCMC provided conciliation in about 100 cases in 2003, mostly in SMEs, particularly Taiwanese and Korean, in which the main issues were wages, social insurance, maternity benefits and the illegal termination of contract. However, many of these cases had not been referred directly by the complainant. As the labour department representative explained, they don't wait for a request, they just go down to the enterprise as soon as they hear about a problem, usually when the HR Department or a foreman phones DOLISA and asks for help. This kind of fire-fighting is not officially a function of DOLISA, but they have been asked to take it on by the local People's Committee – 'we don't call it strike resolution, we call it initial resolution to ensure social stability in the district'.

The VGCL attaches considerable significance to legal advice and legal education because it sees lack of knowledge of the law, on the part of both employers and workers, as one of the main causes of strikes. The ninth National Congress of VGCL in 2003 acknowledged members' right to request free legal advice from the union regarding labour and trade union legislation. To implement this policy, VGCL issued Decision 785 in 2004 to set up counselling centres and offices in each provincial and sectoral union. At the district level, a legal advice group was to be established and at the workplace at least one member of the union executive board should be assigned to provide legal advice to workers in the enterprise. The Decision also required the higher-level union to support primary unions in legal counselling. By 2008, 16 centres, 32 offices and 332 counselling groups had been set up. Seventy-two professional union counsellors had been trained and certified by the provincial departments of justice. Union libraries have also been set up in many provinces.

Apart from the labour law and union law, the union legal counsellors also support workers and primary union leaders in enterprise law, social insurance regulations, anti-corruption law, and HIV/AIDs Prevention. At each union above primary level, at least one union official is appointed as the focal point for legal advice and education. The legal counsellors not only answer questions that workers and primary union leaders bring to them, but also approach workplaces through the loudspeaker system, meetings, and contests on labour and union legislation. In the three years 2005–7, the unions reported that they had organised 230 788 seminars and meetings on labour and union legislation for 10.1 million people, issued 2.1 million publications, trained 500 primary union leaders on legal counselling skills, and provided legal advice to 15.5 thousand workers. Provincial and city unions also held dialogue with local employers to persuade them to create favourable conditions for workers to take part in law-education events.

However, legal advice centres are usually established within the regional trade union offices, which are protected by security and so are not very welcoming to workers. Hai Duong union has overcome this difficulty by moving the legal advice office out of its official building, close to the main road, so that the office is much more easily accessible for workers and union leaders. Apart from that, Hai Duong union has put up a lot of advertisements close to industrial zones and on the main streets in the province about the legal advice of the union. Hanoi federation of labour provided free legal counselling services to workers and enterprises after the wave of strikes at the North Thang Long IPZ. However, this initiative did not have any recognisable success.

Collective labour disputes in Vietnam should be referred to the regional Arbitration Council when they cannot be resolved by the enterprise conciliation council. However, because the conciliation council does not work almost no disputes go to arbitration. By 2004, the Hanoi Arbitration Council had had two cases since it was set up in 1997. One was a dispute about working hours at the Maxim restaurant in 1998, and this was resolved by the Council. The second was at ABB, but the case was broken down into individual cases which went to the labour court. Two members of the HCMC Arbitration Council told us independently that it had had only one case since it was set up in 1998, though neither could remember the details. Overall, only about one case a year in the whole country is resolved through the prescribed conciliation and arbitration procedure. The law provides for a strike as the ultimate means of resolution of a collective labour dispute, once the possibilities of mediation and arbitration are exhausted, but since the strike has to be called by the trade union and the trade union is dependent on management, not one of more than 2500 officially recorded strikes that have occurred since the law was introduced in 1994 has been in accordance with the law.

The official view of strikes in Vietnam is that they are primarily provoked by legal violations by employers, indicating the absence of effective trade union monitoring of working conditions, because of the absence or ineffectiveness of a trade union organisation, so that it is hoped that the more effective trade union monitoring of the enforcement of the Labour Code and the implementation of collective agreements will remove the primary cause of strikes, while the simplification of the disputes procedure will ensure that workers are able peacefully to achieve their legitimate demands.

The VGCL has tended to see strikes not as a reflection of its own failings, but of the failure of government to respond adequately to VGCL's labour and social policy proposals, including the provision of low-cost accommodation for migrant workers and the timely adjustment of the minimum wage;[1] its failure adequately to monitor

---

[1] The high cost of housing is a major problem for migrant workers, who constitute over 60 per cent of the labour force in industrial regions. Unlike China, there is very little provision of dormitory accommodation either by employers or by local authorities. The lack of dormitories is attributed partly to the Government's failure to allocate land for the development of dormitories and partly to the preference of workers, who do not like living in a dormitory where they continue to be under control of the management. In response to representations from VGCL, the Prime Minister agreed in early 2007 to create more incentives for companies to build dormitories for their workers. This initiative, however, made little progress due to delays in land-clearance.

the enforcement of labour legislation through the system of labour inspection; and its failure to provide sufficient legal protection for trade union officers in private enterprises. Some unionists have even blamed the local authorities for embracing foreign investment at the expense of workers: 'some provincial authorities are laying a red carpet on the back of workers to welcome foreign investors.'[1] The VGCL has accordingly tended to see the solution not as lying in changing its traditional practice of trade unionism, because strikes are, after all, increasingly rare in SOEs, but in extending its traditional model to the private and foreign-owned sectors, even proposing that the state-determined wage tables, which still apply to SOEs, should be extended to the private sector.

Nevertheless, VGCL recognises that it should be playing a more active role in the resolution of disputes. Resolution 5a/NQ-BCH issued in July 2005 by the VGCL urges unions at all levels to 'actively develop and implement initiatives to prevent illegal strikes and labour disputes at enterprises; practise the function of organising and leading strikes as prescribed by the law; settle strikes and labour disputes quickly to stabilise production; protect the legitimate rights and interests of workers. When a dispute fails to be resolved by conciliation, the unions must support the workers to bring the case to Court and provide any assistance required to assist them during procedural process.' On a visit to the South after the strike wave, the VGCL chairwoman, Cu Thi Hau, emphasised that protection of workers' interests had to be the top priority of the union:

> In a globalising market economy, protection of workers' interests must be regarded as the top priority of the union so that workers will place their confidence in us. Only in so doing, the trade union becomes strong and sustainable... Trade unions at all levels should focus on protection of workers' rights and interests: at the macro level, the union should take part in the making of legislation on wage, social insurance, and labour dispute settlement. At the local level, the unions have to develop capable and devoted union officers who can negotiate with employers, organise and lead strikes as well as monitor management's compliance with the law. (*Nguoi Lao Dong*, 20 February 2006)

While there is a recognition that the failure of VGCL to monitor the enforcement of labour law and to represent its members is a major cause of illegal strikes, the attention of the Party-state initially focused on the reform of the dispute resolution procedure, on the grounds that illegal strikes occur because the existing procedure is too complicated and long-drawn-out. After long debates, the amendment of chapter 14 of the Labour Code was passed by the National Assembly on 29 November 2006 to come into force on 1st July 2007. The amendment made a radical distinction

---

[1]   Mai Duc Chinh from central VGCL in a tripartite roundtable meeting on dispute resolution held by the ILO in March 2006.

between rights-based and interest-based conflicts. Conflicts over the implementation of legal rights should be settled by the Chairman of the district People's Committee. Only if the latter fails to resolve the dispute within five days do workers have the right to start procedures for a strike in such conflicts. The amendment was also supposed to clarify and simplify the procedure for calling a legal strike (and for declaring a strike illegal), shortening the period required for mediation and arbitration, but also requiring that a strike call should be backed by 75 per cent of employers at larger enterprises (more than 300 employees) and 50 per cent at smaller enterprises. Perhaps most significantly the amendment also provided for workers in non-unionised companies to elect a representative group of three members who are allowed to negotiate with the employers and even organise strikes on the workers' behalf. This last amendment was reportedly pushed by MOLISA and the National Assembly and at first vigorously opposed by VGCL, but the latter finally traded its agreement for concessions elsewhere.[1] Despite the hopes of its proponents, the amendment of the Labour Code proved completely ineffective as a new wave of strikes broke out in the South in October 2007, the majority of which were in unionised companies, none of which was legal and in none of which were workers' representatives elected. The MOLISA has therefore gone back to the drawing board to consider further amendments to the Labour Code.

The fundamental problem is that Vietnam has sought to transplant a bureaucratic rights-based system for the regulation of industrial relations, embodied in government laws and decrees and Party instructions and enforced by the subordination of employers and trade unions to the Party-state apparatus, into the emerging capitalist economy, without having any adequate mechanism to ensure that those laws, decrees and instructions are respected by employers. The failure of the system is not a failure of understanding on the part of the workers, but the failure of MOLISA and VGCL to monitor the behaviour of the employers. Workers are not interested in engaging in long-drawn-out bureaucratic procedures to secure their legal rights, they are interested in securing what they regard as their legitimate rights and interests by the most effective means at their disposal, and the most effective means has proved to be the wildcat strike. Having learnt that they can defend their legal rights by a short, sharp strike, workers since 2005 have increasingly used the wildcat strike as a means of pursuing their interests and securing pay rises.

The VGCL recognises that the dependence of primary organisations on management is a major barrier to the unions' effective protection of workers' interests, but has been trying to address this problem not so much by strengthening its

---

[1] The debate around the revision of chapter 14 was noteworthy for the very active, and largely successful, lobbying of VGCL in opposition of some of the proposals of MOLISA. The VGCL launched a major consultation exercise, used the labour press to push its arguments, and invited key members of the National Assembly to union conferences.

primary organisations as by by-passing them, transferring responsibility for the protective functions of the union from primary organisations to higher union bodies.

The activity of higher-level unions in seeking to by-pass weak and ineffective workplace unions is closely co-ordinated with the local authorities, on whose authority they largely rely. In order to resolve strikes quickly and to prevent them from spreading, strike taskforces were set up, initially on an experimental basis, in seven industrialised provinces and cities: HCMC, Binh Duong, Dong Nai, Da Nang, Hai Phong, Hai Duong, and Hanoi, institutionalising the previously *ad hoc* method of strike resolution. The taskforces consist of Labour Department and union representatives of the appropriate level and they play the leading role in negotiating with the employers on strikers' behalf, although representatives of the employers' organisations are not included. The establishment of strike taskforces was formalised in the 2006 revision of chapter 14 of the Labour Code.

Because of the failure of enterprise unions to take up grievances, or in the absence of an enterprise union, a considerable number of grievances are submitted directly to the higher-level unions. For instance, the Binh Duong IPZ union receives 50 written grievances a day. When it receives notice of a grievance, the IPZ union calls the enterprise union leader, if there is one, to investigate the case. Then a union official will visit and talk to the employer to address the problem. If the employer refuses to co-operate, the union would inform the labour authority, who issues a warning to the employer. The final measure is to send labour inspectors to the enterprise, but only a very few cases have resulted in labour inspection.

District-level union organisations in the most strike-prone regions began to play a more active role in attempting to prevent strikes after the 2006 strike wave, sending staff to the most vulnerable enterprises and advise them to remove legal violations or adjust working conditions so as to prevent strikes. In anticipation of strikes at sensitive times, such as following an increase in the minimum wage, before Tet (when the failure to pay Tet bonuses may easily lead to strikes) or after Tet (when companies run into labour shortages as a high proportion of migrant workers do not return to their jobs and workers may demand higher wages) or after a burst of inflation, the district unions make a list of the most strike-prone enterprises. 'The date for minimum wage adjustment is yet to come but we have listed 20 "hot spots" – these are enterprises that do not have regular orders and workers do not have enough work. We monitor these companies closely to have a quick reaction if strikes happen', said a district chairman. The unions also send officials to the high-risk areas to support the workplace unions in addressing complaints of workers. The vice chairman of another district union told us: 'after Tet, we were worried that strikes would happen. We sent the most experienced officials down to hot spots. For example, when the union of PH Shoes informed us that workers there were complaining about salaries and there was a high risk of a strike, we sent a union official there. He discussed with the company union and agreed a salary increase of ten per cent and attendance allowance to VND 80 000 with the employer. They avoided a strike.' 'We often say to employers that our principle is to help companies resume production as soon as possible', he added.

In the wave of strikes in October 2007, a number of foreign employers, in an effort to prevent strikes, requested the higher-level union to visit their companies and survey workers' demands on the grounds that workers have more confidence in the higher-level union than the workplace union and found it easier to talk to higher-level union officials. After demands had been listed, the employer negotiated with the higher-level union officials, who regularly informed workers about the process. It is claimed that many companies were successful in avoiding strikes by this initiative.

The Dong Nai federation of labour took this a bit further, focusing on group negotiation. In 2008, the provincial union initiated a dialogue with the Japanese and Korean business associations to request the latter to consider a wage increase for workers in the face of the high level of inflation. As a result, despite the wave of strikes in 2008, most Japanese and Korean companies in Dong Nai did not have strikes.

In an attempt to find a long-term solution to reduce strikes and create a workable mechanism for wage negotiation between employers and workers, the People's Committee of HCMC launched and funded a wage consultation experiment in 2008 designed by national industrial relations experts, DOLISA, and the HCMC union. According to the proposal, the city union would make recommendations to employers for wage increases, based on independent surveys of average salaries in the city. There would be two rounds of consultation and if they reached agreement, the employers would raise salaries and workers of participating companies would commit themselves not to strike for a wage increase. Companies would be encouraged to take part in the consultation on a voluntary basis. However, as of the end of 2009 nothing had happened to implement the plan.

Union activity is also co-ordinated with policing. In April 2007, in a further attempt to anticipate wildcat strikes, unions in the South established 'public opinion awareness' teams and 'self-managed' teams of migrant workers, following a similar model organised by the Party to get to know the mood of the public. Public opinion collaborators are generally heads of residential units, who are often retirees who know people in their units well, including tenants. The ostensible purpose of the public opinion and self-managed teams is to ensure security. The unions (accompanied by the local police) go to hubs of migrant workers and encourage them to join self-managed teams. An apparent benefit for migrants in joining these teams is security, since violence and crimes are pervasive in rented accommodation in poorer sections of the city. The collaborators will report to the unions on any changes among workers in their neighbourhoods, particularly about signals of wildcat strikes. In HCMC, for example, over 27 thousand migrant workers are organised into 390 self-managed teams. These teams receive legal advice from the district/IPZ unions and report to the latter on the situation of migrant workers in the region, for example: new migrant workers, where they come from, which company they are working for, violations of labour rights at workplaces and signals of wildcat strikes. With the information from public opinion awareness and self-managed teams, the unions hope to be able to predict strikes in the region. The HCMC union is planning to add more functions, particularly to organise workers, since VGCL is planning to revise the Union Law so as to allow workers to be members of higher-level unions directly.

In November 2007, VGCL submitted proposals for the revision of the 1990 Trade Union Law and in 2008 amended its own Constitution to give effect to a shift of responsibility from enterprise to higher-level unions, to allow higher-level unions to negotiate with employers on behalf of workers and even organise strikes if the primary unions fail to do so, although MOLISA opposed these proposals for fear that greater intervention of higher union bodies would discourage foreign investment. Moreover, given that higher union bodies claim to have insufficient funds and personnel even to fulfil their present limited functions, the proposal is unlikely to have much real impact, although there have been some initiatives at local level in the most strike-prone regions.

The 2008 strike wave further increased the pressure on VGCL from the government and the Party. 'Faced with the increasing trend of strikes spreading among a number of enterprises', on 5 June 2008 the Secretariat of the Party Central Committee issued Directive 22–CT/TW 'on enhancing leadership, providing direction for the development of harmonious, stable and progressive labour relations within enterprises', which had been drafted by MOLISA. In response VGCL drew up Plan 1233/KT-TLD, issued on 17 July 2008, which focused on recruitment of new members, establishment of workplace unions, assigning union officers to support workplace unions, and capacity building for union officers. The plan emphasised the collaboration of the union with local authorities in carrying out specific measures to improve the living standards of workers and requesting enterprises to raise wages or provide allowances and in the settlement of non-legitimate strikes, but also proposed that provincial federations should select suitable places to experiment in organising legal strikes.

In order to implement the Party Directive 22–CT/TW an inter-ministerial action plan on developing sound industrial relations was drawn up by MOLISA, VCCI, VCA and VGCL in August 2008 (English translation at http://www.amchamvietnam.com/2472). The Action Plan consolidated a wide range of initiatives, many of which already existed on paper, in the attempt to move away from fire-fighting strikes to the prevention of disputes. The VGCL's responsibilities under the Action Plan were primarily to extend trade union organisation, especially in the FDI sector, to 'identify clearly the trade union's role and responsibility of representing workers', identify means of increasing the effectiveness and strengthen the capacity of primary organisations, promote the practice of workplace collective bargaining and develop sectoral bargaining. The Action Plan also recommended that the Communist Party should pay special attention to strengthening its organisation in private and foreign-invested businesses, something that VGCL had long been pressing as a means of bolstering its authority in the workplace.

The global recession following the world financial crisis led to a halving of the number of strikes in 2009, which appeared to take the pressure off reform. Political differences over the direction of reform and over the rights and responsibilities of different agencies, particularly the Ministry of Labour and VGCL, also stalled the reform process. However, 2010 saw a renewed increase in the number, intensity and duration of strikes, with employers more ready to resist workers' demands and government more ready to back the employer. It remains to be seen what direction the reform will now take and what, if anything, its impact will be.

Support for primary trade union organisations

The unions in all three countries have come to recognise the need to strengthen their enterprise unions and to make them more responsive to the aspirations of their members, but at the same time their commitment to strengthening workplace unions is severely constrained by their limited leverage over their workplace union organisations and by their primary commitment to the maintenance of social peace. As we have already seen in the last section in the case of dispute resolution in Vietnam, and as we saw earlier in this chapter in the attempts to subsume workplace collective agreements under sectoral agreements, the tendency is rather for higher-level trade union organisations to displace their primary organisations, despite the fact that they lack the staff or the financial and political resources to have a significant impact.

In general, in all three countries, support for primary trade union organisations consists of the provision of legal advice, the circulation of information about union policy and relevant regulatory changes and the provision of training, mostly for the presidents of primary organisations. Higher-level trade union organisations can also be a very important resource for primary organisations in providing links with the relevant state authorities, whether it be state inspectorates, administrative departments or judicial and police apparatuses, to bring pressure to bear on employers. However, the use of such a resource presupposes, on the one hand, that the primary trade union organisation is willing to put pressure on the employer and, on the other hand, that the higher-level organisation is willing to make representations on its behalf. Since primary organisations are only rarely willing to risk antagonising the employer, even when they are not completely under the employer's thumb, it is more often the higher-level organisation that takes the initiative in the event of gross and blatant legal violations by the employer, though only to the extent that such an initiative does not risk incurring the disapproval of the local authorities.

In Russia, the leaders of the FNPR trade unions have long understood that the fate of the trade unions depends on their being able to reform and reinvigorate their primary organisations. However, the trade union apparatus is to a considerable extent insulated from dependence on its primary organisations because its income and resources derive much more from its substantial property and commercial activity than on the remission of membership dues from below. Even when higher-level trade union bodies seek to activate their primary organisations, the end of Party-enforced democratic centralism means that they have few levers of influence over their primary organisations, which derive their income and resources from their membership dues and the enterprise administration. So, for example, FNPR decrees targets for the spending of primary organisations on training, but very few achieve these targets and there are no sanctions if they do not. Moreover, while higher trade union bodies might encourage their primary organisations to be more active, they also set limits to this activism because of their commitment to the peaceful resolution of disputes on which their political position depends. For these reasons the support of higher-level trade union bodies to their primary organisations rarely involves direct intervention but primarily takes the form of the provision of training for trade union leaders, support in the negotiation of collective agreements and the provision of legal advice and support in the judicial resolution of individual and collective disputes. The higher-level trade union bodies also negotiate sectoral and regional agreements, which define minimum terms and conditions of employment for the industry and/or the region and provide a framework for the negotiation of enterprise-level collective agreements, lobby regional ministries and municipal administrations and participate in the management boards of various public bodies.

The ACFTU and VGCL both recognise that the weakness of their primary trade union organisations is a major barrier to their playing an effective role in moderating industrial conflict. However, higher trade union bodies have a very limited capacity and limited staff resources to reform primary trade union organisations from outside or even to protect primary union officers from victimisation by management. Similarly, higher levels of the Party have limited influence over the workplace since, even where there is a Party organisation in the enterprise, as is usually the case in SOEs and former SOEs, the Party Secretary is typically the Director or Deputy Director, and the trade union president is typically the Deputy Party Secretary (Zhang 2009: 206). Moreover, higher trade union and Party bodies are very reluctant to initiate changes which might provoke the conflict between management and the workplace trade union that could arise if the trade union genuinely represented the interests and aspirations of its members. Attempts to reform workplace trade unions have therefore been undertaken very cautiously.

According to VGCL, around 50 per cent of workplace trade unions have undertaken almost no activities since their establishment and about a third of primary trade union leaders have never received any trade union training. Initiatives at local level have tried to go some way to overcoming these barriers. District and IPZ unions in Binh Duong and Dong Nai visit inactive unions and urge them to start union work. They also send union officials to enterprises with newly established trade unions to support the new union board by training them in basic trade union skills and in making annual union plans. In Binh Duong IPZ, for instance, each year the higher-level union provides support to around 150 new primary unions. Binh Duong IPZ union organises review meetings with primary unions in each processing zone once a month. Regional union offices are often located a long way from the primary unions that they supervise. Recognising that this is a problem, Binh Duong, Dong Nai, and Hai Duong IPZ unions are setting up branch offices close to industrial zones to provide instant support to member unions.

The VGCL sees informing workers of their rights as one of the most effective means of protecting those rights (so shifting responsibility from the trade union to the workers themselves). The VGCL has developed new methods of informing private-sector workers of their rights, for instance: posters, leaflets, workers' meetings, internal bulletin boards, television and radio programs. The higher-level unions also integrate basic information about the labour and trade union laws into their recruitment programs and are particularly active in disseminating information about the labour law, and especially the legally prescribed methods of dispute resolution, in the wake of strikes, in the naïve belief that strikes take place because workers are ignorant of the proper procedures for resolving disputes.

The VGCL funds long-term training (four years for an undergraduate course at the Trade Union University, two to three years at union training institutions) for professional trade unionists, but these are overwhelmingly people working at provincial level. Most trade union training is traditional, based on lectures covering the history of VGCL, Party and VGCL policy decisions, and current labour and trade union legislation. There is no regular budget allocation from the VGCL for training of primary union leaders. However, unions in some of the most industrialised provinces, including HCMC, Dong Nai, Binh Duong, Da Nang, Hai Duong and Hai Phong, have used their own budgets to organise short training courses (two days to one week) for primary union leaders. In the best of cases these courses cover labour and union legislation, negotiation skills and collective bargaining, labour contracts, and dispute settlement procedures, but VGCL has an acute shortage of experienced trainers and appropriate training materials. In Binh Duong in 2006, the focus of these training sessions was how to organise union teams and sections at workshop level. In 2007, training sessions dealt with the new revision of the Labour Code and collective bargaining skills. A number of projects sponsored by international organisations (ILO, German Technical Cooperation (GTZ), Friedrich Ebert Stiftung (FES)) and foreign unions (Norway, Sweden, Denmark) are adding to these efforts by holding training-of-trainers courses through which core groups of union trainers will be developed.

Another means by which higher trade union bodies seek to improve the functioning of primary trade union organisations is for staff of the higher trade union body to play a more active supporting role, particularly in the preparation and negotiation of the collective agreement. Some initiatives in this direction have already been undertaken in China, though little significant in Vietnam. In Vietnam the ability of the higher trade union organisation to intervene is limited because it does not even have the right to visit an enterprise without an invitation from the primary organisation, so primary organisations are left to fend for themselves.

In 2006 VGCL experimented with the establishment of union funds to support workers who are illegally sacked and union officers who are victims of unfair labour practices, in the hope that this would reduce the dependence of workplace unions on the management. These funds are financed by union dues, contributions from employers, workers' voluntary contributions, and the state budget and were established in four provinces – Binh Duong, Dong Nai, Hai Phong and Hai Duong – and HCMC. The HCMC VGCL reported in its 2007 Annual Report that in the first year of its operation the Fund in HCMC had provided support to seven union leaders, all of whom had been dismissed illegally by the employers, but in a meeting organised by VGCL in June 2009 to review the experiment of union funds in four provinces, it was reported that there had been no beneficiaries, although VGCL decided to extend the model to other provinces.[1]

One of the barriers to the reform of primary union organisations in both China and Vietnam is considered by higher union bodies to be the fact that enterprise trade union presidents are paid by the employer, and not by the trade union, and are drawn largely from the ranks of managers. In Russia, trade union officers at the primary level are generally paid for their trade union work from the funds of the primary organisation, but this means that only large enterprises can afford to support full-time union staff, while trade union officers in smaller enterprises have to work on a voluntary basis, negotiating any facilities time with the employer, which clearly gives the employer considerable leverage over the trade union leader, both positive and negative. Although trade union officers enjoy legal protection, in practice the best that victimised union officers can hope for is modest compensation many months or years after the event.

There has been some discussion in both China and Vietnam of the possibility of placing professional trade unionists, paid by the higher trade union organisation, into the post of president of trade union primary organisations, at least in larger enterprises. However, it is claimed that higher trade union organisations do not have the money to cover such an expenditure, which in China is further constrained by regulations on the use of primary trade union funds, and little significant progress has been made in this direction. Article 23 of the 2004 regulations on collective contracts in China allows for 'professional personnel' (*zhuanye renyuan*) to negotiate on behalf of enterprise workers and management during the consultative process and this change could well either expand or challenge the role of higher union bodies. The provision is qualified by a limit on their participation to one-third of the negotiating team and they may not lead it (Brown 2006). The ACFTU has developed a

---

[1]   http://www.baomoi.com/Home/LaoDong/laodong.com.vn/Mo-rong-thi-diem-thanh-lap-quy-ho-tro-can-bo-cong-doan-co-so/2875680.epi

programme to train 'collective consultation consultants', who will facilitate collective consultation, but this is a recent innovation and it remains to be seen what, if any, effect it has (*China Labour Bulletin* 2007: 9).

In a pilot project in Guangdong province a district-level trade union has placed trade union officials – recruited 'from society', that is, outside the usual trade union cadre recruitment network – in three local enterprises in an attempt to improve the quality of trade union rights and representation work by reducing the financial dependence of primary trade union officials on the employer. Although the district trade union officials involved have acknowledged that the cost of placing such people will prohibit the widespread expansion of the scheme, they have nevertheless pressed ahead with the trial – a testament to their frustration at trade union dependency at the primary level. In interviews, they justified the experiment by pointing to their own lack of direct contact with workers, which in turn put the onus on primary trade union officials to report potential problems, a task that frequently results in the 'letting go' of such people by resentful employers exacting revenge. They argue that, if nothing else, the prompt reporting of violations will allow the district union time to gather accurate evidence for an arbitration hearing within the 60-day time limit.

Similarly, in Vietnam at its January 2008 meeting with 50 representatives from different enterprises in the region, the HCMC union announced a plan to place professional union organisers in enterprises. A full-time union official would be appointed to enterprises employing over 1000 workers to assist the local union executive board in communicating with workers, visiting sick workers, collecting relevant information for the union, and so on. The full-time union official would be eligible to be elected to become a member of the union executive board, vice chairman or chairman of the union. These union officials would either be nominated by the local union and management or selected and appointed by the city union. They would receive a salary of VND three million financed not by the union but by the People's Committee, in addition to any allowances from the management. However, the experience of such a scheme in Binh Duong Export Processing Zone was not entirely successful. If the professional leaders were too active, the management isolated them from the workers, while the workers were distrustful of somebody who had come from outside, so the professional leaders were soon voted out of office or neutralised. In June 2009, union officers in HCMC reported that their experiment had had the same negative result. The professional union officers were not able to get the confidence of the workers and after a few months, the district unions had to return these unionists back to work in the district union offices.

The strike waves of 2006–8 had a major impact on VGCL and provoked a substantial policy shift. After the third wave of strikes in October 2007, VGCL again tried to pass responsibility to the government, proposing that the Party Central Committee and the Government should address the union's legitimate recommendations on labour policy; adjust the minimum wage in the foreign-invested sector; introduce a policy on accommodation for workers; strengthen labour inspection and sanctions on violating employers; promote the *ad hoc* strike settlement model; provide training on labour law to workers and recruit more industrial workers to Party membership as a way to strengthen primary unions (VGCL Report to the Central Party Committee, 18 October 2007). However, the Report to the Tenth VGCL Congress in November 2008 marked a major shift, at least rhetorically, in the strategic priorities of VGCL in calling for the union to 'renew the methodology and contents of union activities at all levels; take the workplace as the fundamental site of actions; shift strongly toward the protection of the rights and interests of members and workers; develop sound, stable, and progressive industrial relations to contribute to the socio-economic development of the country'. The principal means of achieving this, however, was not so much to strengthen primary organisations as to increase the role of the intermediate trade union organisations.

To put this into effect VGCL proposed that by the end of 2013, over 70 per cent of enterprise unions should have concluded collective agreements that provide better working conditions for workers; that VGCL should promote higher-level collective agreements; that VGCL should recruit at least 1.5 million new members and by 2013, 70 per cent of eligible enterprises should have set up unions and 60 per cent of workers should have joined the union. The VGCL should participate effectively in the National Labour Relations Committee to protect the interests of workers and ensure regular reporting and information sharing at the workplace and among union levels; it should co-operate with relevant agencies to work out measures to develop sound industrial relations and prevent wildcat strikes; it should support enterprise unions to organise legal strikes; it should improve the quality of legal counselling services for workers; it should rearrange the personnel structure and define the functions and tasks of VGCL departments, regional federations and industrial unions; and it should increase the responsibility of the higher-level union in representing workplace unions and workers.

To these ends proposals were made for radical revisions to the union's 2003 Constitution and to the 1990 Trade Union Law to require all intermediary unions to 'support, assist, and guide enterprise unions in dispute settlement, negotiation with the employers, and the organisation of strikes as defined by the law'. The Constitution Revision adds one new function to the intermediary unions, which is 'to represent members and workers in negotiation and signing of collective agreements with business associations or representatives of employers in the industry'. Instead of putting the function of propaganda of Party and state policies as the top priority of workplace unions, the Revision defines the priority task of the union as being 'to represent workers in negotiating, signing, and monitoring the implementation of collective agreements'. Other new tasks include monitoring the compliance by the employers with the law on the rights of workers and unions; contributing to the work rules of enterprises; collecting the legitimate demands of workers; providing information and organising dialogue with employers; and organising and leading strikes in accordance with the legal procedures. The 2008 Amendment also substantially extends the mandate of district and industrial zone unions to 'settle labour disputes in the constituency, support primary unions to negotiate collective agreements, organise dialogue with employers, organise and lead strikes in accordance with the law' (2008 Union Statute, articles 26(4) and 27(3a)). VGCL issued an official guideline on the implementation of the Amendment on 6 May 2009 which, among other things, specifies that owners of enterprises, chairpersons of boards of directors and top executives in non-public enterprises are not allowed to join the union.

The most dramatic change in the pipeline in Vietnam is in the revision of the Labour Code, for which MOLISA has proposed that workers in non-union enterprises should be able to elect a group of representatives who would enjoy the right to represent workers in negotiation with employers over the collective agreement and the settlement of disputes, opening the door to freedom of association. The proposal has received support in the National Assembly, but has provoked vehement opposition from VGCL, which claims that to allow non-union representation would be 'to break the solidarity of the working class and the whole nation. Once the working class is divided, the social foundation of the Party will be destroyed and the leadership of the Party will be damaged' (*Lao Dong* 14 September 2009).

Trade union elections

The election of enterprise trade union leaders is one measure that has the potential to increase the responsiveness of the workplace trade union. In Russia and Vietnam the committee and officers of the primary trade union organisation are elected as a matter of course, but in China the issue has been very contentious and there has been a series of cautious experiments with the election of enterprise trade union leaders, usually but not always with some control of candidacy being maintained, and in some regions such as Guangdong, Shandong and Zhejiang union elections are commonplace (Howell 2008: 845; Pringle 2010). Temporary guidelines for union elections were formulated in 1992, prior to the lay-offs of the late nineties and dramatic increases in FDI leading up to WTO entry and beyond. Moreover the guidelines are vague on procedures and the legislative vacuum has left room for some guarded experimentation at the local level, but elections are generally not permitted where there is a risk that an elected leader might enter into a confrontation with management. For example, in Guangdong elections are not permitted where the trade union is newly established or where industrial relations are tense and there has previously been a mass action (Howell 2006: 18). Although elections can be effective in improving the quality of enterprise trade union leaders, it seems that the impact of elections on the character of workplace trade unions themselves has been quite limited.

A comparison of various models of trade union election procedures demonstrate – unsurprisingly – that participation and enthusiasm for the vote increases in direct proportion to the relaxation of restrictions on candidacy via vetting and checking procedures. In one enterprise, the naming of candidates from the floor of an election meeting – a practice known as *hai xuan* or 'throw in the sea' – led to an initial nomination of 47 candidates out of a total of 67 employees! In the context of this case study, involving largely private small and tightly knit enterprises notorious for their harsh labour practices, it is worth noting that the vetting of candidates is not always a bad thing as the process can exclude management placemen as well as the more recognised targets such as over-enthusiastic defenders of workers' interests. Moreover, we found subtle but important differences in vetting standards. In one enterprise the stress was very much on loyalty and implementation of Party, government and enterprise policies, but in another the emphasis was on the candidates' capacity to represent his or her constituency, dare to make criticisms, and have the capacity to accept them. New national guidelines on trade union elections were announced by the Xinhua News Agency following the ACFTU's fourteenth National Congress in 2003, but no time table was given and to date no progress in their drafting has been reported (http://www.hartford-hwp.com/archives/55/859.html; Howell 2006: 13).

The limitations of this approach to reform on its own are shown by the case of Vietnam. The provisional committee in a newly unionised enterprise is nominated by management and is generally headed by a senior manager, typically the HR director. As an official of one of the best IPZ unions explained, 'we have no idea about the people in the company, who can be union leaders; therefore, we have to ask the HR manager to do it. Any way, it is only the provisional union, not the official one.' The trade union leadership has to be elected within one year after the formation of a provisional trade union committee and there are subsequent elections every two years. Candidates are nominated by the union board, and workers can also make their own nominations, though the nominations are often vetted by management, who can also nominate their own candidates. 'We have to consult him [the employer] because sometimes the company would not like a person in a certain position to be union chairman due to management and production plan. If the employer disagrees with the list of candidates, we would negotiate. If he has good reasons for that, we would revise the list', the union chairman of a Korean company explained.

There is plenty of scope for management manipulation of the election process. In one Japanese company representatives at the union election meeting were appointed by the section managers. 'I have no idea who are members of the union board because only the team leaders were selected to attend the union congress. Workers were not allowed to go', a worker said. Management generally participates in the election meeting, which can be intimidating for workers. In a union election in a Vietnamese domestic company in Song Than Two Industrial Park, seven candidates were nominated for a five-member union board. Five candidates were nominated by the employer and two by the provisional union. In the presence of the director, workers initially kept silent at the suggestion by the IPZ union officials that they should make their own nominations, but after some persuasion, workers proposed two more candidates. Votes were counted in the room next to the meeting room by a member of the HR staff and a member of the provisional union. The director of the company kept on walking to their table, checking the ballot result, making sure that her candidates won. Though disagreeing with this type of election, the IPZ union official kept silent as he did not want to spoil his relationship with the company: 'Finally, that is their company, they are the host, we are guests, we have no way to force them to do it the way we want', he said. Since there is rarely any effective monitoring of the procedure, some companies do without it altogether. In a small strike-prone Taiwanese company the union was set up in 2006 with the warehouse manager as union chairman and HR manager as vice chair. But most workers we talked to had never attended any union meetings and had no idea how the union committee had been elected. One worker told us: 'I got to know from rumours among the girls in the factory that one day all managers, including line leaders, were invited to a lunch. After the lunch, a union committee was elected and their names were placed on the company bulletin board the next day.'

Even when elections are free and fair, given the character of workplace trade unions in Vietnam, workers tend to feel that it is appropriate that their trade union leader should be a manager, who knows how to interact with other managers, a view also held by elements within the higher trade union leadership. It proves very difficult to find any candidates for election who are not sponsored by management, because rank-and-file union members are afraid of victimisation, so the process of election makes very little difference to the character of trade union leaders. The overwhelming majority of trade union committee members in Vietnamese companies are managers or white-collar workers, with the few representatives of production divisions almost entirely being line managers, technicians or engineers, rather than ordinary workers. The only contact the union committee generally has with workers is in large companies, where there are separate union committees in each production unit, which are supposed to report to the main union committee, although 'consultation' is often a one-way process, with the main committee transmitting instructions to its subsidiary committees. This is why, when strikes occur in Vietnam the union committee is almost always taken by surprise, even though workers will often have known about the strike days in advance. Many employers, unable to rely on the union to communicate grievances from its members, use alternative methods, such as complaints boxes, surveys and even internet polling.

The limitations of democratic election on its own are also shown by the example of Russia. Following the 1989 miners' strikes new trade union elections were held throughout the coal-mining regions and many of the established trade union leaders were replaced by activists from the strike committees. However, these new 'radical' leaders were soon assimilated into the union apparatus, which continued largely to function in the traditional way. More recently, in post-soviet Russia, employers still have considerable power to manipulate union elections, from controlling the distribution of information and the selection of delegates to union conferences, refusing to negotiate with militant trade union activists and withdrawing facilities and resources from antagonistic trade union organisations. Thus we find repeated examples in Russia of militant trade union leaders being voted out of office and replaced by management nominees.

Extension of trade union organisation

The coverage of collective agreements is limited by the limited degree of trade union organisation in the new private and foreign-owned sectors, which have become the principal locus of strikes and worker protest since the turn of the century. In both China and Vietnam the trade unions have therefore come under pressure from the Party to extend their organisation and membership beyond the state and privatised sectors and beyond their traditional permanent urban worker membership. The ACFTU brought migrant workers, hitherto largely ineligible for trade union membership, into the trade union fold at its 2003 Congress and launched a campaign massively to expand its membership among migrant workers. At its own 2003 Congress VGCL similarly declared its main priority to be a campaign to recruit one million new members in the private sector, which it had hitherto largely neglected.

In both countries all enterprises are legally required to establish trade union organisations, at least if requested to do so by higher trade union bodies, and employers are legally prohibited from impeding the formation or activity of trade unions, though no penalties are prescribed for violation of the law. The typical way in which new trade union organisations are established is for the local higher trade union organisation to contact management to collaborate in establishing an enterprise trade union. Not surprisingly, the outcome is for the enterprise director to appoint the trade union president, typically a senior manager or the human resource director, so that the trade union is constituted as a tool of management. Even when striking workers demand the establishment of a trade union organisation, this will be organised in a similar top-down manner in collaboration with management. It is not surprising that the Chinese unions do not talk of 'organising workers' (*zuzhi gongren*) but of 'establishing trade unions' (*zujian gonghui*) the difference being that when trade union branches are established in private or foreign enterprises workers will only get to know of their new status as union members when a 2 per cent union fee is deducted from their pay packets.

China

A well-publicised exception to this practice has been the long struggle of ACFTU to establish a union organisation in Wal-Mart, where resistance from Wal-Mart management forced ACFTU to adopt an organising approach, recruiting individual employees to the union outside the workplace to provide the basis of a union branch. Nevertheless, even in this case ACFTU has been hesitant about moving beyond its traditional collaborationist model. Interviews with Wal-Mart trade union officials at the Jinjiang store, the first to organise a union branch, suggest the continued dominance of a traditional consensus-seeking approach alongside tantalising hints of a more adversarial stance induced chiefly by Wal-Mart's refusal to negotiate – or even meet with – union officials. While the Wal-Mart enterprise union in question received considerable financial, technical and political support from the higher-level union and city leaders, management confined communication to its human resources department. When the new union presented a draft collective contract, the management did not formally responded, indicating that the local management could not make decisions on such matters without the agreement of Wal-Mart headquarters. In the end a collective agreement was hammered out between Wal-Mart headquarters and ACFTU and the same agreement illegally imposed on all Wal-Mart stores, inducing one elected union chairperson at a store in Nanning to resign on the grounds that the national deal did not meet the aspirations of his members (Wei L.B. 2008).

The weakness of the 'organising' approach adopted with regard to Wal-Mart by the ACFTU was that it was driven by Wal-Mart's intransigence rather than by the ACFTU's initiative. Moreover, the enterprise union was unable to maintain its initial dynamism as it lost members, including committee members, to staff turnover as workers left for better-paid jobs. Wages at the Jinjiang Wal-Mart store remained static for two years, despite a shortfall of approximately 100 staff. The unionists' frustration was revealed in the creeping emergence of a 'them and us' attitude, despite a largely traditional approach to union work.

> At the moment, the biggest problem is that we need to get the enterprise's cooperation [to develop] our trade union activities and we have often sought consultation with them on this matter. But they always have an excuse to put it off. The usual reason is that they are too busy, or alternatively that they do not have the authority … This means that the progress we have made so far has been very superficial. (Wal-Mart trade union official, Wal-Mart Workers' Quarters, Jinjiang, 20 August 2007)

Two points stand out from this quote. First, the full-time union official interviewed refers to management as 'them'; and second, that management is continuing to frustrate the union's development, despite the political support the ACFTU has received from the Party. For example, the same interviewee noted that trade union committee members found it difficult to get permission to meet with visiting higher-level trade union leaders.

> It's also very difficult to get time off for union activities. Chairman He XX has to go through complicated procedures to get approval to take part in trade union [meetings] and on several occasions it has proved very difficult to get together with higher trade union leaders who come to inspect our work.

Although the Wal-Mart case has been widely proclaimed as a breakthrough in ACFTU's organising strategy, being followed up by a similar organising drive against Foxconn in Shenzhen, after the first union branches were established Wal-Mart signed a recognition agreement with ACFTU under which new branches would be established in the traditional way, in collaboration with management, although the preparatory committees include employee representatives and the agreement provided for the election of the trade union committee. Asked why Wal-Mart had agreed to allow unions a Wal-Mart spokesman reportedly said: 'The union in China is fundamentally different from unions in the West ... The union has made it clear that its goal is to work with employers, not promote confrontation' (*China Daily* 11 August 2006). It remains to be seen how effective Wal-Mart's and Foxconn's workplace trade unions will prove to be.

Vietnam

The VGCL has made extending union organisation to POEs and FIEs a priority in the belief that strikes are less likely to take place in enterprises with a trade union organisation, suggesting that the principal problem is not the character of the trade union but the absence of a trade union organisation in many POEs and FIEs. On the other hand, as trade union organisation extends in these sectors, an increasing number of strikes take place in POEs and FIEs that do have a trade union organisation, which VGCL considers to be a result of the inadequate knowledge and experience of trade union officers, which can be remedied through an expansion of training, and the inadequate legal protection of trade union officers. The VGCL Vice-President Mai Duc Chin noted 'There hasn't been any policy to protect union staff and most employers don't cooperate with unions ... Local union staff at non-state enterprises were not adequately qualified for carrying out their responsibilities. Most of them didn't devote much time to union activities and some lacked the courage and motivation to fight for labor rights' ('Illegal strikes increase following new labor law', *Vietnam News Agency* 19 June 2008, cited in HRW 2009: 12).

In Vietnam only about 12 per cent of employees in the private sector are trade union members. Over half of the VGCL membership (6.2 million) is concentrated in the public sector (including civil servants and state-owned enterprises). The ninth National Congress of VGCL in 2003 set itself the task of recruiting one million more members by 2008. By the end of 2007 VGCL had increased its membership by almost one and a half million, with membership in the non-public sectors more than doubled, from 1.1 million to 2.25 million. However, as the Steering Committee of the Campaign pointed out, the success of the recruitment campaign does not necessarily reflect a growth of the union's influence in the private and foreign-invested sectors because the union in the previous five years had recruited mostly from bigger companies and civil servants at community levels – areas where they generally faced few difficulties. The tenth National Congress of VGCL in 2008 set itself the task of recruiting a further 1.5 million union members by 2013.

According to Vietnam's Trade Union Law, any group of workers can form a union and then register with the higher-level union body, but according to the Labour Code and the VGCL Charter a new union organisation can only be established on the initiative of the higher-level VGCL organisation. In practice it is always the latter procedure that is applied and unions established on the initiative of workers are denied registration. Thus new organisations are established on the basis of a visit of a VGCL officer to the enterprise, so it is not surprising that new organisations are established through management and are subordinate to management. As a VGCL official explained at an ILO-sponsored tripartite roundtable in March 2006, 'when VGCL establishes a provisional trade union committee in a newly established company, we lack information about the people in the company. Therefore, we approach HR managers who must know workers better than anybody else.. Most VGCL officers see this as an advantage. As other officers said at the same seminar, 'trade union tasks take a lot of time. That is why administrative staff are appointed as trade union leaders'; 'It is better to have managerial staff as union leaders, because they can communicate directly with the employers'; 'We need a person who can bridge between managers and employees. That is why you appoint HR managers who know workers as well as employers'; 'most workers are not willing to run for the union election. Therefore, we continue to have HR managers as trade union leaders.' But the predominance of managers in union leadership positions is as much a symptom as a cause of the subordination of the union to management. In one case in Binh Duong Province an informal union leader emerging after a strike became the official union chairman. However, according to the IPZ union, he is now just like a typical VGCL union leader and he has been losing the workers' confidence ever since.

Most VGCL officers explain the low level of union organisation in the private and foreign-invested sectors in terms of the hostility of employers, who refuse to allow district trade union officers to meet with workers.

> Employers in the non-public sector have not supported and facilitated the union's activities. Some even caused difficulties and avoided union establishment as required by the law. (VGCL Political Report at the tenth National Union Congress, November 2008: 5)

However, a private employer in Da Nang put this claim in a different light, complaining that it is the municipal union that rarely comes to the grassroots level to talk to workers, not the employers who prevent them: 'if they [the union] came, we would welcome them because they can help us in talking to workers and stabilising labour relations. But they rarely come, except for strikes.'

In January 2008, Circular No. One of VGCL and MOLISA was issued. The regulation allows the higher-level unions to appoint a provisional union executive board in an enterprise that has operated for six months and employs at least five union members. The higher-level union no longer has to gain permission by the employer to set up unions; now, the employer will only be informed once the union establishment decision is made. However, it is unclear how VGCL could identify 'reliable' union leaders without the collaboration of the employer.

Russia

Despite the decline of union membership, the main emphasis of the FNPR unions in strengthening their trade union organisation at the base has not been on carrying out organising campaigns to build up trade union membership in the new private sector, where trade union density remains extremely low, but on expanding the coverage and quality of collective agreements and trade union representation in already organised workplaces, including the attraction of young workers to the union by organising social events, sports competitions and professional skill contests. The sixth FNPR Congress in November 2006 set the preservation and expansion of membership and the creation of trade union organisations in the new private sector as one of the union's priority tasks, following which the FNPR Executive Committee initiated a programme to expand trade union membership in small and medium enterprises over the period 2007–11, with a pilot project in the first two years, covering 12 regions and five branch unions organising in sectors where SMEs were particularly active. In the progress report on the first stage of the campaign, FNPR reported that there had been close collaboration with regional authorities and employers and their organisations within the framework of social partnership and that 494 primary organisations with a total of 43 228 members had been created, but that the success of the campaign had been limited by shortages of suitably qualified trade union staff, the resistance of employers and the passivity and fear of workers. The detailed progress report conveys the distinct impression that, although some regions trained trade union organisers and prepared recruiting materials, these new trade union organisations were set up in the traditional way, by collaboration with the employer (*Vesti FNPR*, 2, 2009: 74–90).

Conclusion

The trade unions in all three countries have taken considerable steps to adapt to their new role of representing their members in the conflicts that necessarily arise with the integration of formerly state controlled economies into the world capitalist order. However, this adaptation has primarily taken the form of attempts to extend the traditional model of trade unionism rather than transforming it. Although the principal barrier to effective trade union representation in all three countries is the weakness of primary organisations and their close dependence on management, higher trade union bodies have sought to adapt to this situation rather than seeking to strengthen and energise their primary organisations. This is partly a question of capacity, as higher trade union bodies have limited resources and limited leverage over their primary organisations, but it is also a question of timidity in the face of political constraints, since the higher bodies are afraid that more active primary organisations will exacerbate rather than confining conflict. Thus the primary strategy adopted by the trade unions in all three countries has been that of attempting to harness state powers in support of their members, rather than trying to build the capacity of their own organisation.

This conclusion might appear to be countered by the observation that in all three countries the trade unions have made the negotiation of collective agreements a primary focus of their activity and the primary indicator of the effectiveness of their regional and sectoral trade union organisations. The number of collective agreements signed has increased year by year and there has probably been a slow but steady improvement in their quality. However, as we have seen, collective agreements only very rarely represent an achievement of the trade union, being more fundamentally a formalisation of the personnel management policies of the employer, with the employer making few binding commitments. At best the process is what the Chinese call 'collective consultation' rather than collective bargaining. Rather than strengthening the role of primary organisations in collective bargaining, the trade unions in all three countries have sought to by-pass them either by negotiating sectoral and territorial agreements or by attempting to pass the negotiation of collective agreements to officers of the higher-level trade union organisation, in both cases relying on state agencies and minimum labour standards to pressure the employer to agree.

The limited capacity of the trade unions to achieve any improvement in wages and working conditions through collective agreements has led them to continue to rely most heavily on their traditional collaboration with government bodies and with administrative intervention, through which the state rather than the trade union takes responsibility for the protection of the rights of labour. This leads to a certain degree of ambiguity as to the relevant responsibilities of the trade union, on the one hand, and the Ministry of Labour, on the other. In all three countries the government has sought to move trade union lobbying outside the state apparatus, where trade union pressure can be counterbalanced by employer representation, so there have been attempts to develop mechanisms of tripartite consultation. In all three countries a major barrier to the development of effective systems of tripartite negotiation has been the weakness or absence of employer organisations. The most important policy areas in which the trade unions of all three countries have been active in relation to the representation of their members have been the determination of the legal minimum wage, on the one hand, and collaboration with the state labour and health and safety inspectorates, on the other.

In all three countries, the close integration of the trade union into the structure of management, and the traditional identification of trade union officers with the priorities of management, underlies a tendency for the enterprise trade union to seek to reconcile any differences of interest between employees and management within its own structures and so guarantee that its negotiations with management will be consensual. The traditional state-centred conception of the role of the trade union carries over into the approach of post-socialist trade unions to labour disputes, which is to pursue such disputes on behalf of members only when the dispute arises out of a clear violation of the law on the part of the employer and to seek to resolve the dispute through juridical channels. A central aspect of the trade union's responsibility to represent the rights and interests of its members is therefore seen as its provision of legal advice and representation in judicial proceedings, and in all three countries the trade unions have enormously increased the staff and financial resources allocated to such representation, though never by enough to handle the steadily increasing number of disputes.

Strengthening primary trade union organisations is a vital task, but it is easier said than done. In general, in all three countries, support for primary trade union organisations consists of the provision of legal advice, the circulation of information about union policy and relevant regulatory changes and the provision of training, mostly for the presidents of primary organisations, but none of this challenges the traditional role of the trade union. The election of trade union presidents, in place of their appointment by higher bodies, might make the trade union more responsive to the wishes of its members, but cannot overcome the dependence of the elected union leader on the employer. As trade unionists around the world know only too well, the extension of trade union organisation is a difficult, laborious and sometimes dangerous process, so it should not be surprising that the unions in all three countries follow the line of least resistance and organise new workplaces by agreement with the management.

Significant change in the trade unions will not come from above, but can only come from below, from workers taking their fate into their own hands and using the trade union as their representative in pressing their interests and aspirations on the employer. As we have seen, workers in all three countries, in particular regions and economic sectors, have taken these steps and have sought to forge their own organisations, to which the traditional trade unions have had to respond. In China and Vietnam the absence of freedom of association has meant that worker organisation has remained at the informal level, making it difficult to build on past experience and achievements, while in Russia informal worker organisation has been institutionalised in the alternative trade unions that have been a primary stimulus to the reform of the traditional unions. This is probably the principal reason why the Russian trade unions have progressed further in reforming themselves than have the unions in China and Vietnam. In the next chapter we will review these experiences to assess the limits and possibilities of trade unions in transition.

5
The Limits and Possibilities of Trade Unions in Transition

We have seen in previous chapters that the activities of the trade unions in all three countries are severely constrained by their political situation, on the one hand, and the dependence of workplace trade unions on management, on the other. The two barriers are closely linked, in that their commitment to the maintenance of social peace, born of their dependence on the state, makes the higher-level trade union organisations very reluctant to sanction or encourage activism on the part of workplace trade unions which might give rise to labour conflicts and even to strikes. The ACFTU and VGCL, which are subject to direct political control from the Party and local administration, are more rigidly constrained in this respect than is FNPR in Russia, whose legitimacy and political weight depends on its ability to show that it represents its members and which faces competition from alternative trade unions. These are the main reasons why the Russian trade unions have made considerably more progress in developing their proper trade union activities than have the trade unions in China and Vietnam. While there has been some local progress in developing more effective trade unionism in China and Vietnam, it is Russia that can give us a better idea of what is possible and so in this chapter we will concentrate on examples from Russia.

In all three countries the trade unions have sought to adapt to the transition from state-socialism to a capitalist market economy by adapting rather than transforming their traditional practices. On the one hand, workplace trade unions continue to function predominantly as a part of the personnel department of the enterprise, responsible for the administration of the enterprise management's social and welfare policy and keeping management informed of the mood of the labour force, but wages and working conditions are determined more by the concerns of management regarding labour turnover, the recruitment and retention of skilled workers, labour discipline and productivity than they are by any actions of the trade union in representing the interests of its members. On the other hand, higher-level trade union organisations are primarily concerned with lobbying state bodies over the state regulation of such issues as wages, contractual terms, working hours and health and safety and with collaborating with state bodies to secure the enforcement of regulations.

In each country there is more or less concern of higher trade union bodies with the development of more effective workplace trade unions. In China and Vietnam the preoccupation of the higher trade union bodies has been with bringing the millions of migrant workers in the new private and foreign-invested sectors into trade union membership, in the hope that trade union organisation will reduce the propensity of these workers to protest and to strike. However, the model of primary trade union organisation into which these workers are inserted is merely an extension of the traditional model of trade unionism inherited from SOEs, with the establishment and staffing of the trade union agreed with management, the collective agreement dictated by management, and, even in the best of cases, the trade union doing little more than organising social events, distributing limited welfare benefits, explaining management policy to their members and reporting workers' grievances to management. Higher trade union bodies provide very little support to their primary organisations, beyond the traditional training, provision of model collective agreements and circulation of policy documents. Instead of developing the capacity of their primary trade union organisations, ACFTU and VGCL have sought to increase the role of higher trade union bodies and to leave responsibility for the protection of workers' rights to state agencies. At the same time, in both countries the challenge of worker activism has meant that there has been some scope for more innovative activity at workplace and local levels, some of which was touched on in previous chapters.

In China the intensity of labour unrest has produced some innovation as the union has sought to restore peace to industrial relations, improve its labour rights work (*weiquan*) and increase the capacity of primary unions to represent their members, Such pilot projects have generally been confined to provinces where the foreign and private sectors are especially strong, such as Zhejiang and Guangdong.

As we saw in Chapter 4, ACFTU is charged with the task of channelling disputes into juridical channels of resolution. The risks that this strategy carries are exacerbated in a localised context. On the one hand, there is the risk that a successful intervention will encourage more unrest. On the other hand, a failed intervention will hardly serve to improve the ACFTU's credibility, especially among migrant workers who generally regard trade unions as an extension of management – if they regard them at all! Two further examples can illustrate the possibilities and limits of local innovation in China.

Exceptional circumstances can provoke an exceptional response. In Yiwu in Zhejiang province, the situation had been complicated by the emergence of 'place-of-origin' gangs such as the 'Anhui Gang', the 'Jiangxi Gang' or the 'Kaihua Gang' (for a more detailed account see Pringle 2010). According to Chen Youde, the chairman of the Yiwu Federation of Trade Unions (YFTU), this 'had a negative impact on the morale of the migrants and often led to inter-gang violence' (interview, Chen Youde, Yiwu, 21 March 2006). Home-town associations (*tongxianghui*) sometimes offer a questionable form of protection to migrant workers, usually in return for a compulsory fee. Luo and Zhou described a typical scenario in the town of Suxi, which falls under Yiwu administration.

The two hamlets of Hu and Jiang had over 8,000 migrant workers each, far outnumbering the local population. Most of these workers had arrived in large groups from the same villages outside the province and, as such, had recourse to powerful hometown 'forces' through which they protected their interests. Some ... paid a 'protection fee' of ten yuan per month to the hometown association which ... engaged in organised criminal activities including violent bullying [of other people] and even terrorizing employers. (Luo and Zhou 2007: 27)

Facing budgetary constraints and insufficient legally trained staff, the YFTU established a legal rights centre registered as a social organisation (*shehui tuanti*) under the Ministry of Civil Affairs, the first of its kind in China. The Yiwu Workers' Legal Rights Centre (YWLRC) was established in 2001, although its birth and early development were not without complications as employers and some 'relevant government departments' initially opposed it. Guided by Chen's strategy of socialising (*shehuihua*) trade union work, the YFTU drew on wider resources, including the media, the justice department and the courts, as it sought to overcome financial constraints and spread the risks of setting up the Centre, adopting a policy of accepting cases regardless of their complexity. Although not a solution to the problem of poor representation in the workplace, the YWLRC has opened up a new space in which migrant workers can settle complaints and claims against employers via union-sponsored mediation or through the formal dispute resolution system but with the help of legal support workers from the YWLRC. The Centre's emphasis on mediation and compromise has attracted opposition from more legally minded reformers in the ACFTU who wish to prioritise the task of upholding labour rights through arbitration and the civil courts.

While the Yiwu experiment was initiated by an enterprising ACFTU officer in the face of growing labour unrest, the second example is of official union intervention in immediate response to a potentially dangerous strike.

An effective 25-hour strike by 280 crane operators at the Yantian International Container Terminals (YICT) in Shenzhen illustrated how key institutions of the Party-state processed a labour dispute with the potential to disrupt not just local social stability but a key cog in the global economy – the sea routes for consumer goods from China to the West. The YICT was – and is – a joint-venture with working conditions and wages that lead the field in the port sector. However, management's arrogant attitude prevented workers from identifying with the company and its apparent commitment to corporate social responsibilities. In fact it was an incident of bullying that sparked the strike in the early hours of 7 April 2007, in which workers presented their case for improved pay and conditions and a trade union to keep management off their backs.

The Yantian crane operators' decision to strike was influenced by two previous strikes at nearby container terminals, one of which lasted three days. Both actions led to significant concessions from capital as workers sought to gain a share of the spectacular increase in turnover at the ports during China's export boom. At YICT, for example, tonnage reached 8.9 million tonnes in 2006, many times the figure for 1994 when the company was established, and making it the busiest port terminal in the world. When the strike broke out, work on fourteen ships stopped simultaneously and the impact on shipping timetables and routes was immediate.

The strikers' demand for a wage rise was based on prepared figures citing China's continued economic growth, the rise in tonnage at YICT, company profits and the cost of living in the Shenzhen area. It was flanked by further demands for improved rest time, working hours based on national guidelines for working at height and a commitment from the company not to take any measures against the strikers in the future. Crucially, the workers demanded a trade union be organised that was run by elected frontline workers with representatives paid for out of their own pockets.

The immediate intervention of Shenzhen Federation of Trade Unions (SFTU) was accompanied by senior representatives of the Shenzhen Party Committee and the Shenzhen City government. Considerable pressure was brought to bear on the company to negotiate, while the SFTU concentrated on repackaging the workers' demands – especially the demand calling for what amounted to independent trade union representation. The SFTU presented a rearranged and extended list of demands to YICT management that included calling on the latter to commit to future wage negotiations and refraining from arbitrary decisions over working conditions. Taking a line bolstered by the Party Committee, the SFTU acknowledged the workers' dismissal of the YICT staff association as a 'white collar club' but insisted that the new trade union must be set up according to the Trade Union Law.

During negotiations most of the demands on pay and conditions were met via a 3 per cent pay rise and concessions on rest time with the SFTU playing a mediating role at the negotiations between YICT and the workers' representatives. The strike was called off at two o'clock the following morning. The SFTU vice chair, Wang Tongyan, outlined three reasons for the swift settlement: the pressure brought to bear on management, local government and the SFTU itself by the workers' militant actions; management's speedy decision to recognise the validity of the workers' demands and negotiate them; intervention by the city authorities who applied considerable pressure to both sides to resolve the dispute through collective bargaining.

Although there was considerable disappointment among some crane operators over the subsequent election of union officials, the strike demonstrated how labour militancy can improve working conditions and kick-start the official trade union into life even in the face of powerful units of capital. The alacrity of the SFTU's response can be accounted for by the capacity of the crane operators to hold up international trade and the state's wish to preserve Shenzhen's leading position in a globalised export market. It is also clear that in the right conditions, class struggle is as important to improving trade union performance and credibility as legal reform and participation in formal channels of labour dispute resolution. It is too early to judge, but the sustainability of the collective contract that emerged soon after the initial agreement will depend on the newly established enterprise union's ability to remain independent of YICT management.

In Vietnam, VGCL had shown almost no inclination to make any significant effort to reform before an unprecedented wave of strikes broke out at the end of 2005. Even then, as we have seen, VGCL at the national level tried to shift responsibility for the strikes onto the government. However, at the provincial level, where the trade union is especially closely integrated into the local administration, the trade union came under more pressure to reform. Unlike at national level, at provincial level the union has a statutory responsibility to co-ordinate with other provincial departments to realise the decisions and plans of the provincial People's Committee, for which the union receives substantial funding from the provincial budget. The concerns of the provincial authority over wildcat strikes, therefore, are directly translated into tasks for the union. On the other hand, the implementation of the union's initiatives is secured by the power of the People's Committee. According to Nguyen Van Binh, a union official in the legal department of VGCL, 'the provincial federations of labour enjoy enormous autonomy to develop and implement their own solutions to the problems they are facing. They have to be active in this regard because they are under constant pressure from the local authority.' This power will be strengthened following a recent decision of the Party Central Committee that the provincial Party Committee (*tinh uy*) rather than the national VGCL will take responsibility for the appointment of key union officials at the provincial level.

In mid-February 2006 the VGCL Chairwoman toured the strike-affected provinces in the South and made important personnel changes, promoting more capable, reform-minded officers and moving them to the strike-prone regions. As a result we have found some new dynamism in some of the most advanced IPZs. Industrial Processing Zone union organisations constitute an intermediate level of organisation, between the workplace and the provincial union, supervising and supporting primary-level organisations in all the processing zones in the province. The IPZ unions have considerably more autonomy than is normal for VGCL intermediate structures, which gives them the freedom to experiment with new approaches.

Binh Duong is one of the three most industrialised provinces in the South of Vietnam, and also one of the most strike-prone, having recorded 116 wildcat strikes in 2006 and 216 in 2007. The IPZ union employs seven full-time officers, two of whom are responsible for finance and administration, the remaining five taking responsibility for union organisation in the 23 industrial-processing zones under their jurisdiction, with over 4500 companies and 440 thousand employees, 60 per cent of whom are migrants. The level of unionisation is low, with only 300 enterprise unions, only 14 per cent of which have registered collective agreements with the IPZ management board. Union officers spend a lot of time travelling around the province. As one of them explained, 'Normally, we spend all mornings visiting enterprise unions and companies for all kinds of purposes: setting up new unions, supporting enterprise unions in organising union congresses, investigating individual complaints, solving strikes, and so on. In the afternoon, we take calls from enterprises, counselling and providing information, and deal with paper work.' Apart from enterprise visits, most union work is done on the telephone. They get fifteen to twenty calls a day, mostly about workers' rights and legal questions. 'Binh Duong IPZ Union is friendly to the members, we are not bureaucratic like other unions. Others often require company unions to send official, written requests but in Binh Duong, we minimise paper work for them by counselling through the phone. This strengthens our relationship with the grassroots unions' (Vietnam Research Team 2007: 4). Union officers try to support new union organisations by providing some training for their presidents and encourage inactive organisations to engage in union activity, organising monthly meetings for the zone unions.

The union resolves problems primarily by using the administrative resources of the IPZ Management Board. When they receive complaints from workers, a union officer will visit the company to investigate and, if the employers refuse to co-operate, the union may refer the case to the Management Board, which may issue a warning or send inspectors to the company. In relation to strikes, the priority of the IPZ union is to restore order rather than to pursue workers' demands. In case of a strike, workers or union leaders may phone the IPZ union office to ask for help, in which case an officer will go to the company, persuade the employer to meet any demands that arise from the employer's violation of the law and persuade the workers that any demands beyond the provisions of the law are unreasonable. 'When we settle strikes, before negotiating with employers, we have to study carefully all workers' demands. We only select the legitimate demands that are related to employers' violation of workers' rights. For others, we have to explain to workers that their demands are inappropriate because the employers did not do anything wrong' (Vietnam Research Team 2007:7). In the strike waves the IPZ union was swamped and had to appeal to the provincial VGCL for help, although in general they are not happy with the bureaucratic style of the latter. 'VGCL never gives you an answer over the phone. They always ask for official correspondence which takes a long time and too much paper work for both sides' (Vietnam Research Team 2007:5).

The Binh Duong IPZ union is relatively proactive, but it still confines itself largely to bureaucratic procedures, formally establishing new union branches, monitoring the legal compliance of employers, and settling strikes. With each member of staff responsible for 900 companies, the overwhelming majority of which have no trade union, there is probably not much more that they can do, and the idea that they might have to take on even more of the responsibilities of primary union organisations without any additional staff horrifies them. Nevertheless, it appears that the increased activity of the Binh Duong IPZ union has had some effect. Whereas the number of strikes in other provinces in 2008 was half as many again as there had been in 2007, in Binh Duong the number of strikes fell dramatically, from 216 to 97.

We have to conclude that little progress has been made in either China or Vietnam in the development of more responsive and effective trade union organisation at the workplace level. Whether this situation is likely to change depends crucially on the extent to which experimental local innovations can be rolled out across the country as a whole. In general, these innovations have depended on two fundamental conditions. On the one hand, a high level of worker unrest, expressed in strikes, protests and labour turnover, which disturbs both the local authorities and the employers and makes them more inclined to tolerate relatively radical approaches that might succeed in reducing unrest. On the other hand, the success of such experiments depends on energetic, dedicated and charismatic individuals who have been ready to take the initiative and battle for their ideas. The danger is that when these innovations are translated into Party and trade union Directives and Resolutions their implementation will be purely formal and bureaucratic and their real impact negligible.

In Russia, despite the massive loss of trade union membership, FNPR has paid little attention to organising in the new branches of the economy, but has been concerned above all to retain membership in its traditional organisations. For this reason it has been much more concerned than have ACFTU and VGCL to ensure that its primary trade union organisations provide their members with value for money, so that they get something tangible in return for their trade union dues. The main emphasis in this respect has been on retaining the traditional social and welfare benefits provided by the enterprise and that the trade union distributes to its members, but there has also been a growing emphasis on the role of the trade union in protecting individual workers' rights, using laws and regulations as a means of securing additional benefits for members and in providing legal support to members to resolve not only work issues but also domestic problems. The FNPR has pressed its member organisations to encourage and support their primary organisations in negotiating more favourable collective agreements, each year setting targets for negotiation against which the quality of such agreements can be judged. On the other hand, the unions complain that the collective agreement is not a great recruiting agent since it applies to all employees, whether or not they are members of the trade union.

In the rest of this chapter we will look more closely at the progress that has been made in the development of trade unionism in Russia by looking at examples of the best practice of trade union organisations in the public and private sectors. In the public sector we use the example of the health workers' trade union, the most advanced of the public-sector unions, looking at its practice at national, regional and workplace levels. In the private sector we use examples from metallurgy and the construction industry, as well as the emerging role of alternative trade unions in the motor industry.

The Russian Health Service Workers' Trade Union

In the Soviet Union work in the health service, as part of the 'non-productive sphere', was always low in status and poorly paid. With the collapse of the Soviet Union and the enduring crisis of the Russian economy the financing of the health service was increasingly inadequate and pay declined relative to other sectors, working conditions deteriorated and the sector saw chronic delays in the payment of wages through the 1990s. The health service workers' trade union was an active and enthusiastic participant in the regular Days of Action organised by FNPR to protest against the non-payment of wages and the inadequate funding of public services and collaborated with the administration of the health service, from the level of the ministry down to that of local clinics and hospitals, to lobby for more adequate funding for the health service. In some regions, particularly Kemerovo oblast', the union supported strike action over the non-payment of wages, but while this may have been effective, it also cost the union members. As a militant trade union leader in Kemerovo noted, 'the most difficult task was to get people back in to the trade union after the strikes. It seemed that in the consciousness of people it was trade unions and strikes that led to the complete collapse of the economy'.

With the recovery of the Russian economy after 1998 the priorities of the trade union were unchanged, to restore the wages of health service employees relative to those of industrial workers and to secure adequate funding for the health service to enable health service establishments to pay a living wage, replace decrepit equipment and provide acceptable working conditions. However, the trade union also faced new challenges, in particular the proposal of the government to abolish the Unified Tariff Scale (UTS) that regulated the wages of all public employees, and to devolve responsibility for public-sector finances, and correspondingly for the level of provision of public services and wage-setting, to regional and local authorities, which would inevitably lead to large differentials in pay between more and less prosperous regions. The central demands of the trade union were that the Unified Tariff Scale should be preserved, to guarantee equal pay for equal work, and that the lowest point on the UTS should be set at the level of the subsistence minimum, to guarantee a living wage for all. In pursuit of these demands the union participated in protest actions organised by FNPR and the public-sector trade unions, sent appeals to the President, the government and legislative bodies and lobbied parliament. In February 2003 the public-sector unions claimed that two million people participated in their protest actions against the proposed abolition of the UTS. Further actions were organised around the country in September and October 2003 protesting at the refusal of the government to set the minimum wage at the level of the subsistence minimum.

These protests had no detectable impact on the government, so in 2004 the union turned to more radical measures, building up to a strike of health service workers. In June 2004 the union organised a series of meetings, demonstrations and pickets to present their case. In August 2004 they declared a collective labour dispute at the

Federal level and, faced with continued government refusal to consider their demands, in September the public-sector unions declared their intention to hold a five-day strike of health, education and culture workers from October 20. At this point the government resumed negotiations with the trade unions and proposed a programme to secure increased wages in the public sector. The government proposals did not satisfy the public-sector unions, who declared a one-day warning strike, in which they optimistically claimed over one million workers participated. At this point the government responded with the promise to present recommendations regarding public-sector pay to the Russian Tripartite Commission within one month. As a result, the lowest grade on the UTS was increased from 110 to 600 roubles and from 1 January 2005 public-sector wages were increased by 20 per cent. The 2006 federal budget somewhat improved provision for increasing public-sector wages, and included provision for increasing the wages of medical workers in the emergency services and rural medical-obstetric centres. Although the union leadership clearly believed that their actions had forced the government to respond, many rank-and-file union members were more sceptical. As one member in Perm' commented, 'there was not much sense in it, and we, by and large, did not achieve anything. Everything that we have achieved, once again I repeat, all this has been predetermined and programmed from above. We go by a schedule that has pretty much been preordained from above.'

The Program of Social and Economic Development of the Russian Federation for 2006–8 marked a major step forward in improving public-sector pay, incorporating proposals to increase public-sector real wages in stages by 50 per cent over the course of three years, but these were linked to proposals to increase the scope of incentive payments as a means of increasing the efficiency of public services; redundancies and closures of establishments to contain the overall pay budget; and an increased emphasis on collective agreements to further the devolution of wage-setting and provide increased pay flexibility. Of course the trade union claimed credit for the belated recognition by the government of the need to increase public-sector pay, but the issue as far as the government was concerned was not so much to secure social justice for public service workers as to introduce reforms, very much formulated within a neo-liberal ideological framework, which would save the public services from collapse. Unusually, the strong budgetary position meant that the government realised its promises to increase public-sector wages over this period, which included the parliamentary and presidential elections of 2007 and 2008.

In accordance with its new strategy, in 2007 the government offered a pay rise in the form of an increase in incentive payments of 15 per cent, which amounted to an average 7 per cent increase, instead of an increase in salaries. Following the lobbying of the trade union, the Ministry of Health and Social Development issued an order according to which the additional payment of 15 per cent of the rate or salary should be received by every worker. This situation was repeated in 2008, when inflation had again run ahead of wages. The trade union organised a campaign of petitioning the government and, more significantly, a media campaign against the proposal, threatening mass pickets and meetings across the country, and the Ministry again conceded that the increase would be paid to every worker.

In 2005 President Putin announced a series of priority National Projects, including major projects for health and education. The National Project for Health focused on the improvement of local provision of medical services and for the extension of general practice, with corresponding increases in pay for those employed in these areas of the medical services. The trade union claimed credit for the fact that the President had introduced such a project, but noted serious deficiencies in the proposals. On the one hand, the terms of the Project were very vague and no concrete mechanisms for its implementation were defined. On the other hand, increasing wages in the priority areas would lead to irrational and unjustified pay differentials which would lead to an outflow of medical personnel from unfavoured services such as hospitals, since a local general practitioner would be paid substantially more than a senior hospital specialist.

The Project was riddled with anomalies and contradictions which created an enormous amount of work for trade union organisations on the ground, which was co-ordinated through the central committee of the union. As a result of this co-ordination and the consequent lobbying of the government the union managed to secure amendments to the Project and directives from the ministry which ironed out some of the anomalies. It is noteworthy that many of these anomalies did not concern employees directly, but concerned the conditions for receipt of additional finance by medical establishments, which would enable them to pay additional wages. In this respect the union was lobbying as much on behalf of the employer as of its own members.

In the meantime, Federal law 122 of 22.08.04 provided the legislative foundation for the devolution of the provision and financing of public services to regional authorities, so taking the federal government out of the firing line. In practice this did not lead to an immediate change in wage-setting, since most regions initially implemented the federal tariff scale and in five regions rates were set above the federal level, but in the longer term the devolution of responsibility for wage-setting reduces the scope for trade union action at the federal level and puts increased responsibility on regional trade union organisations.

Regional trade union organisations

At the regional level the health service workers' trade union generally works in close collaboration with the regional Ministry of Health. The framework for wage-setting is built both by the policies and legislation of the federal government and by the social policy orientation of the regional administration. This has meant that a primary focus of regional trade union organisations has been lobbying the regional administration over public-sector pay and over the financing of the public sector from the regional budget. The health workers' union has tended to take the lead in organising collaboration with the other public-sector unions (education and culture) in such lobbying. During 2004–5 regional trade union organisations participated in the All-Russian protest actions of public-sector workers, but in general these actions attracted a poor turn-out and had a very limited impact. From 2006 the attention of the regional organisations of the union was turned towards resolving problems arising from the implementation of the National Project 'Health'. The most time-consuming work of the regional trade union organisations has been providing legal support for their member organisations in the negotiation of collective agreements and in pursuing individual disputes. The regional organisations are also active in carrying out inspections of establishments in collaboration with the state labour and health and safety inspectorates.

The scope for trade union action at the regional level is heavily dependent on the political orientation and policy priorities of the regional administration. To illustrate this, we look at the activity of the regional organisations of the health workers' union in three politically contrasting regions, Samara, Kemerovo and Perm'.

Samara

Samara oblast' throughout the 1990s was marked by its liberal democratic political orientation under the long-serving Governor, Konstantin Titov, and by the strength of the regional budget. The regional administration was committed to raising living standards by promoting economic growth and attracting investment on the basis of a liberal market regime, with employers and trade unions in the private sector encouraged to negotiate pay rises through collective agreements. Public sector pay is an important focus of negotiation between the regional administration and the regional trade union organisation in the framework of the regional Tripartite Commission, established in 1997, but successive regional agreements have been more a declaration of the good intentions of the regional administration than any negotiated settlement. In 1999 the regional administration began to supplement the wages of underpaid categories of public-sector workers from the regional budget and in 2005 increased wages across the sector by 37.5 per cent, against the increase awarded at the federal level of 26 per cent, so that by 2006 the lowest point on the pay scale was 60 per cent higher than the federal level and state employees in the countryside received an additional 25 per cent bonus. Nevertheless, in 2005 average pay in the health service was still 35 per cent below the regional average wage and 56 per cent of public-sector employees were still paid less than the subsistence minimum.

In 2007 Titov was replaced as Governor by Vladimir Artyakov, General Director of the auto-making giant Avtovaz. The priority of the new Governor was to restore the leading position of the oblast' by encouraging investment and making more efficient use of public money, which included a substantial increase in funding for health and education. The new Governor showed little interest in maintaining the close partnerly relations with the trade unions of his predecessor and the regional administration rejected trade union proposals to include an increase in the regional minimum wage above the federal level in the regional tripartite agreement for 2009–11.

The regional committee of the health service workers' union collaborates closely with the other public-sector unions and the regional trade union federation in campaigning over public-sector pay, lobbying the regional administration and the regional legislature, but the union sees no point in mobilising its members in protest actions, which would simply undermine its partnerly relations with the regional and local authorities, although they do participate, at least symbolically, in All-Russian trade union actions. It is difficult for the unions to claim credit for the pay policy of the regional administration, though they were successful in lobbying the regional legislature to amend the law when the supplement paid to rural employees came under threat because of budgetary problems in 2005 and also managed to secure the passage of a law providing budgetary financing for sanatorium treatment for all public-sector workers. The union also works very closely with the health service administration, the chair of the regional trade union committee being a member of the Board of the regional Ministry of Health, the Health Insurance Fund and all sorts of other bodies through which it is possible to press the case for increasing pay and improving working conditions as a means of improving the quality of the health service. However, the role of the trade union is more the traditional one of serving as a channel of information for the health service administration rather than being an effective source of pressure for the representation of workers' interests.

The introduction of the National Project 'Health' in 2005 created a host of problems for the trade union since the Project demanded major reorganisation of the health service while initially providing significant pay increases for fewer than 10 per cent of health service employees in the region. In the first year of the Project in Samara oblast' average nominal wages of health service employees increased by 29.4 per cent, but this concealed huge variations as those covered by the National Project received substantial increases, with a tripling of wages or more for the favoured categories, while others received small increases, and in 2007 the average wage in the health service was still only 72 per cent of the regional average wage. One effect of these changes was the move of hospital specialists into general practice and local health centres, exacerbating the already acute shortage of hospital specialists.

The fact that health service pay is basically determined at federal and regional levels means that there is little scope for primary trade union organisations to bargain over pay in negotiating collective agreements, so the emphasis at primary level is on monitoring the enforcement of labour law and regulations and resolving individual disputes. Much of the time of the regional committee is spent on helping their 168 primary organisations deal with these issues. The majority (70 per cent) of these cases concern miscalculation of wages, 15 per cent are related to health and safety, 8 per cent pension calculations and 7 per cent work records. The regional committee also collaborates with the state labour inspectorate in carrying out inspections of premises. In 2007 such checks identified 331 infringements of labour and health and safety legislation. The regional committee supported workers in pursuing 83 cases in court in 2007, in all of which the workers were successful.

Kemerovo

Kemerovo oblast' (Kuzbass) was the centre of the great strike waves of 1989 and 1991 and the birthplace of alternative trade unions, but from the mid-1990s the alternative trade unions in the region were effectively destroyed as the Regional Governor, Aman Tuleev, supported the traditional FNPR trade unions, on condition that they showed absolute loyalty to his administration, as the means of maintaining social peace in the region. Tuleev rules his region as an authoritarian populist, with a rigidly directive industrial strategy and a strong social orientation, maintaining strict control of all business structures. The social and welfare obligations of business are incorporated in social and economic co-operation agreements signed between the regional administration and all large companies, which were first introduced in 2000 and without which it is impossible to do business in Kuzbass. In such an environment the role of the regional trade union organisations is largely decorative. The regional tripartite agreement is dictated and monitored by the regional administration and it is the regional administration that presses enterprises to meet their social obligations, including the obligation imposed by the administration to pay a minimum wage not less than the regional subsistence minimum and for the basic wage to constitute not less than 50–70 per cent of earnings (a demand that FNPR has been pressing nationally for many years, to little effect). The trade unions routinely support the appeals of the Governor, encourage their primary organisations to incorporate such appeals into their collective agreements, and collaborate with the administration in monitoring their implementation, exactly as they did with regard to Party decisions in soviet times. The trade unions participate in FNPR's All-Russian Days of Action and occasionally in demonstrations focused at the regional level, but always and only with the approval and even on the initiative of the Governor.

The regional trade union organisations' capacity to engage in effective dialogue, let alone criticism, is very limited. Their participation in national trade union campaigns is generally limited to the formal endorsement of national appeals and forwarding them to the regional administration. A trade union organisation at any level can criticise the authorities at a higher or lower level (for a regional organisation, the federal government or a particular municipality), but would never dare to criticise their 'social partner' at their own level. Trade unions discuss the details of the implementation of the Governor's appeals to enterprises to increase pay and sign collective agreements, but have minimal impact on the process of pay determination.

The public-sector unions (health and education) in Kuzbass have had very poor relations with the regional trade union federation for some years. In 2005–6 they withdrew funding from the federation as an expression of dissatisfaction with the leadership. Following the election of a new Chairman, they continued to express their dissatisfaction with the passivity of the regional organisation, but in the political circumstances of the region the public-sector unions have not been able to be more active on their own account, confining themselves primarily to collaboration with administrative bodies and providing legal support for their primary organisations in negotiating collective agreements and in pursuing individual grievances. While they have been passive in relation to pay increases, which depend on federal and regional directives, they have been active in pressing their primary organisations to formalise all such directives in their collective agreements. Collaboration with the regional health authority is close, but frequent personnel changes in the latter have complicated the signing of a formal branch agreement which has been delayed for three years. In order to compensate for the absence of a regional agreement the union has encouraged its local organisations to sign agreements with their local authorities, although only two cities have agreements that are more than formal.

The regional organisation is very active in providing support in cases of individual labour disputes, usually finding that the employer has made a miscalculation or procedural violation so that the dispute can be settled informally, but occasionally the union has to take the case to court, particularly in cases of pension entitlements. When collective disputes arise the regional organisation is usually able to resolve them in collaboration with the regional health authority.

Perm'

Perm' krai had been noted for its highly developed institutions of social partnership, involving the close collaboration of regional and local administrations, employer organisations and the trade unions. The situation changed with the appointment of a new Governor in 2005 and changes in federal government policy, which included the abolition of the Ministry of Labour at federal and regional levels, which deprived the trade unions of their interlocutor and led to a substantial downgrading of social partnership and its reorientation from labour issues to social policy in Perm'.

The pay of health service workers in Perm' krai is below the national average and increasing pay has been a priority of the regional organisation of the health service workers' union. The union took part in the All-Russia protest actions of public-sector workers in 2004 and 2005. The first stage of the campaign involved pickets, meetings and demonstrations in June 2004. When these protests had no appreciable results, the union prepared for a one-day strike called by the public-sector unions nationally by holding meetings and conferences in their primary organisations in support of the demands and to decide about participation of the collective in the strike. However, most employers put strong pressure on workers, threatening them with suspension or dismissal if they participated in what had been deemed an illegal strike by the regional administration. In the only hospital in Perm' that managed to get the workers to strike, the hospital director supported the strike. The union provided explanatory leaflets and collected the signatures of a majority of employees in support of a strike. When the notice was submitted to the director he accepted the decision, 'since people have decided to participate in the strike', telling the union 'OK, I shall give you legal help so that nobody picks on you'. The overall result was that no more than 9000 health service workers participated in the strike, one-eighth of the number employed in the branch. Nevertheless, the regional legislature considered the issue of health service pay and resolved to pay an additional 10 per cent financed from the regional budget, though this remained only a paper promise until it was implemented by a decree of the Governor from 1 March 2006, predating an increase decreed by the federal government by two months. In preparation for the next stage of the action in October 2005 the regional committee proposed the establishment of a strike fund, but member organisations rejected the proposal that they should transfer money for such a fund. In the event, the October action was a dismal failure, with only 1000 people participating.

Alongside participation in All-Russian protest actions, the regional committee was very active in lobbying the regional legislature and administration, particularly around the adoption of a regional law on pay in the health service, which was passed in October 2005. The majority of amendments proposed by the trade union were accepted, but these were only minor changes. On the most significant issues the trade union proposals were ignored and the law, which only applies to regional establishments, led to little change in the level or mechanisms of payment.

According to the regional budget for 2007, adopted in 2006, public-sector workers should have received an increase in pay of 20 per cent, but pay was increased by only 10 per cent in May and a further 5 per cent in September. The trade union lobbied the legislative assembly and showered the deputies with telegrams, but it was only when they threatened to take people onto the streets that the administration agreed to pay the increase in full. This was not the end of the matter. When the federal government decreed an increase of 14 per cent in the wages of public-sector workers from 1 February 2008 the Perm' regional administration proposed to increase pay by only 4.35 per cent on the grounds of the previous increase (the only other region not to pay the increase in full was the Komi Republic). The union protested against this decision and the national union called an All-Russian protest action on 22 April 2008, although no other regions acted in support of Perm' and Komi, a major blow to illusions of trade union solidarity. In Perm', 500 public-sector workers picketed the regional parliament, and the Russian government amended its order to ensure that the increase was paid in full. However, Perm' krai was one of only two regions in which the increase was paid in the form of incentive payments rather than as an addition to basic pay. One side effect of the action was a notable cooling of the attitude of the regional administration to the trade union.

The failure of the union to mobilise significant numbers in protest actions and the lack of effect of such actions had already underpinned a substantial shift in the strategy of the regional trade union organisation away from protest towards participation in the implementation of the National Project 'Health', which provided opportunities to increase the pay of particular categories of work but was also riddled with anomalies and contradictions. The union intervened very actively in trying to resolve such anomalies and contradictions in the implementation of the Project by lobbying the regional administration, threatening to take cases to court and co-ordinating its work with the central committee of the trade union.

Primary organisations

The main problem facing health service institutions is grossly inadequate financing, which comes primarily from health insurance and the local budget, with some opportunities to raise additional funds by providing paid medical services. As a result, many institutions do not have enough money to cover even their most basic expenses, including wages, training and retraining, medical supplies and the maintenance and replacement of equipment and buildings, let alone being able to provide additional benefits for their employees. The shortage of money compounds the problem of what are still very low wages, leading to acute staff shortages, low staff morale and increased pressure on staff to cover for absent colleagues. In this situation there is very little scope for the workplace trade union to negotiate improved terms and conditions of employment and the best that the trade union can do is to ensure that their members at least receive the wages and benefits prescribed by federal and regional laws and regulations and work in a safe and healthy environment.

The long period in which pay in the health service was very low and there were chronic delays in the payment of wages created serious problems of recruitment, leaving the health service with an ageing labour force, serious labour shortages in key areas, poor morale and low motivation. In this context management has as strong an interest as the trade union in increasing pay, although its priorities might be different. Although pay scales are set at the federal and regional levels and there are strict regulations about the permissible expenditure of funds, many health service establishments in the past increased the pay of particular categories of employee through over-grading, but this practice was ruled illegal and the administration threatened with punitive sanctions for the misallocation of resources. An alternative approach was to pay discretionary bonuses from funds derived primarily from the provision of paid medical services, but the size of this source of income varied considerably between establishments and was generally unstable. The introduction of the National Project 'Health' provided a new means of increasing the pay of particular categories of employee, which could be extended to other employees by re-categorising their work or by redistributing some of the funds.

The National Project and the introduction of incentive payments have intensified social tension over increasing pay differentials that had already arisen with the payment of discretionary bonuses and income from paid services. This is a difficult issue for the trade union to address since it introduces divisions within the labour force and brings the union into confrontation with the administration, which wants to increase differentials to be able to recruit and retain key personnel.

Although there is often little scope for primary organisations to engage in pay bargaining, there is a large number of issues that can be the subject of local negotiation.

First, there is the question of the distribution of funds within the establishment, particularly of income that comes from the medical insurance system and from paid medical services and savings from unfilled vacant posts, which can be used to pay bonuses or increase staffing. If the institution has sufficient resources from paid medical services or savings from vacant posts the union can negotiate additional payments for particular categories of work, for example in hazardous conditions, holiday and unsocial working hours, overtime or working above the norm. The union can also press for the recertification of jobs, which can lead to upgrading of posts or additional payment and other benefits for working in hazardous conditions or with advanced technical equipment. The administration of health service establishments always has an interest in finding money to attract the best specialists, while the union is generally motivated by principles of social justice. The scope for making additional payments is limited by a plethora of regulations, but some collective agreements include illegal additional payments to particular categories of staff. In Kemerovo, the regional health authority carried out checks in 2006 and discovered that some medical institutions were making what were deemed to be illegal additions to wages. Where these payments were fixed in collective agreements they could not be abolished, but where they were not the establishment directors were punished for the unauthorised expenditure of money.

Second, there is the question of holiday entitlements. Health workers were granted 12 days annual holiday in 1974, in addition to the basic legal entitlement of 12–18 days. In 1991 the Law on Social Guarantees defined the national minimum holiday as 24 days, but the Ministry of Labour ruled in 1993 that additional holidays continued to be based on the previous norm of 12–18 days, so that those formerly benefiting had effectively lost their previous privilege. This interpretation was endorsed by the Ministry of Health and the State Labour Inspectorate. However, a court in Yamalo-Nenetsk ruled in 1994 that the health workers were entitled to the additional 12 days on top of the minimum 24 days holiday, a ruling confirmed by the Supreme Court in 1996. Although in a few regions the regional administration agreed to implement the ruling, elsewhere employers have consistently refused to recognise the health workers' right to additional holidays, pleading an inability to pay, and this plea was generally met 'with understanding' by trade union presidents, who continued to sign away their members' rights in collective agreements. More recently, increasing pressure from the members has forced a growing number of employers to include the additional holiday entitlement in the collective agreement, often following a successful application to court by individual employees, sometimes encouraged and represented by alternative unions.

Third, there is the provision of social and welfare benefits. It is important to incorporate all of these, even those over which management has no discretion, into the collective agreement because it is only possible to initiate a collective labour dispute over questions that are included in the collective agreement.

Finally, there are always disputes to resolve, around grading, the calculation of pay, pension entitlements and so on. As always in the health service, the leverage of the primary trade union organisation is limited. On the one hand, the core terms and conditions of employment are determined from outside the establishment so that disputes can only be resolved at the municipal, regional or federal level. On the other hand, health service workers are always reluctant to take strike action, because of its impact on their patients, and emergency service personnel are forbidden by law to strike, so the main bargaining tool for the trade union is the strict application of the Labour Code and other relevant laws and regulations. In Kemerovo the regional union committee tries to ensure that all medical institutions have an effective Labour Disputes Commission (KTS) but, according to a survey conducted by our colleagues, only half of medical staff know that they have a Labour Disputes Commission and appeals to them are very rare. As the lawyer of the regional committee commented, 'The problem of the Labour Disputes Commission is that workers, thinking that half the members of the KTS are representatives of the hospital administration, do not hope for the positive resolution of the question'.

Primary organisations face the problem of recruiting and retaining members, not only to secure an income but also to ensure that they retain the support of the majority of the labour force so as to secure their bargaining rights. The collective agreement, which is the principal achievement of an effective trade union, applies to everybody. Those on low pay cannot afford the trade union dues, while for those on high pay 1 per cent of salary is a significant amount. Traditionally the unions have not discriminated against non-members in providing advice and support and allocating benefits from trade union funds, but some primary trade union organisations have responded to the loss of members by restricting such benefits to trade union members.

Trade union presidents are generally part-time, most being managers or doctors in their main posts. The basic items of expenditure from the trade union budget are material assistance, gifts for holidays and the organisation of celebrations and awards. In Kemerovo oblast' a survey of primary trade union leaders found that about one-third of the trade union budget was spent on cultural activities, one-quarter on material assistance to members, and 15 per cent covered payment of trade union staff. The key features of an effective trade union primary organisation are an energetic trade union leader who has a thorough knowledge of all the applicable laws and regulations; a high level of participation of members in the activity of the trade union, through trade union groups, commissions and so on; a supportive higher-level trade union organisation; and recognition by management of the role of the trade union.

The most important role of the trade union is negotiating the collective agreement. Usually the draft collective agreement is prepared by a joint commission of management and the trade union on the basis of the previous agreement, and then circulated to the workforce for comment before being adopted at a union general meeting. The quality of the collective agreement depends very much on the effectiveness of the trade union president and the willingness of the administration to accept trade union proposals. In general the administration is reluctant to seal too many obligations in the collective agreement and will want to qualify items with the rider 'subject to the ability of the organisation to pay', while an active trade union will seek to include as much as possible in the collective agreement, consolidate existing gains and include additional benefits. However, in the last instance power lies with the administration and if the trade union proposals are rejected, particularly on the grounds of lack of funds, there is little the union can do.

Proposals for the collective agreement are collected from the members and then sorted and selected by the trade union committee. 'From ordinary workers proposals initially were the simplest things, such as "buy an overall" or "buy a pen". Therefore work was initially based on proposals from the management of divisions, and then once again a concrete draft was sent to the divisions to consider the proposals, proposals were discussed at meetings' (Kemerovo children's hospital). Gathering of proposals for the collective agreement is carried out traditionally: workers in branches are invited to make proposals: 'there they write everything, and we choose, and we work on the basis of these proposals, we make the collective agreement' (Perm' City Clinical Hospital).

Support from higher-level trade union organisations at municipal and regional levels is very important for the primary organisations. The regional committee of the union distributes information to primary organisations about changes in laws and regulations; issues model collective agreements and disseminates information about the achievements of the more successful primary organisations; organises training for trade union leaders and regular meetings of trade union presidents; co-ordinates inspection of establishments with the state inspectorates in response to requests from primary organisations; and provides legal advice to primary organisations, both with respect to negotiations with the administration and with respect to individual and collective labour disputes. Municipal (city and district) committees maintain the accounts for smaller primary organisations; provide expert advice and support; liaise with the regional committee; monitor the effectiveness of primary organisations and co-ordinate their activity.

Relations between the trade union and the administration

The role of the primary trade union organisation is largely determined by the attitude of the administration. In some cases the administration sees the trade union as a valued partner which will help with problems of human resource management. In such cases the trade union will be allocated various resources necessary for it to carry out its role. This does not necessarily mean that the trade union will be a passive instrument of the administration. Although most primary trade union organisations devote most of their time and money to carrying out their traditional role of providing material assistance and organising social and welfare functions, it is quite possible for the union to be assertive and bargaining to be intense on contentious issues. In many cases, financial limitations mean that the administration fails to provide even some of the benefits provided for by federal laws and regulations, such as free milk and additional holidays for those in hazardous occupations, the provision of work clothes, additional payment for overtime and weekend working and so on. In such cases the trade union may passively accept that it is impossible for the administration to afford such benefits, but a more active trade union will negotiate with the administration over these issues, while a militant trade union leader will complain to the local and regional health authorities and threaten legal proceedings to extract the benefits due. But in the final analysis the resources available to the establishment are limited and the permitted expenditure is restricted by federal laws and regulations, so the administration has the last word. Where there are possibilities of securing additional resources from the regional or local authorities, the trade union and administration will collaborate in substantiating claims for such resources, with the support of the municipal and regional committees of the trade union.

In other cases the administration is hostile to the idea of a trade union and can see no point in tolerating one. It is generally not possible to force out the trade union, which would be a violation of the principles of social partnership, but if the trade union organisation is deprived of resources and excluded from participation in decision-making it will most likely decay and disappear, or survive only nominally. Nevertheless, there are primary organisations which manage to survive and even struggle on behalf of their members in the face of a hostile administration. We can illustrate the possibilities and challenges facing the primary trade union organisation by looking at a number of examples of relations between the trade union and the administration.

Kemerovo city hospital: an effective traditional union. The trade union in a central hospital in a medium-sized coal-mining city in Kemerovo is very traditional, with close partnerly relations with the administration. As the hospital director noted, 'our trade union is the arbitrator and the guarantor in the observance of rights. Elena Nikolaevna [union president] is our partner in observance of the rights and interests of employees.' The hospital, whose facilities are dispersed across the city, faces acute financial difficulties and serious staff shortages. The primary role of the trade union, which takes up most of its time and money, is the distribution of social benefits provided by the administration, the organisation of social and cultural events and the distribution of material assistance, partially financed by the trade union. The trade union also provides legal assistance to members, for example in preparing documentation to secure a mortgage or make an insurance claim, as well as in ensuring that pay and conditions accord with the existing norms and regulations. Individual disputes, over such questions as grading, pay, pensions and holiday entitlements, are resolved between the trade union and management either on the spot or through the Disputes Commission. Nobody could remember there ever having been a collective labour dispute in the hospital.

The trade union president, who is simultaneously head of a department of the hospital, has been in post since 1989 and has overseen a gradual improvement in the work of the union, which she attributes to the increasing knowledge and experience of trade union cadres. Membership declined during the 1990s, but has since recovered gradually to reach a density of 85 per cent. Those who do not belong are either free-riders, particularly among the better-paid who do not wish to pay 1 per cent of their salary in dues, or those who want to see a more militant trade union. As one doctor, who is not a union member, commented, 'What is a trade union? I do not see any benefit. If they went onto the Square, demanded something … Some kind of action is necessary.'

The trade union takes the lead in the negotiation of the collective agreement, with support from the regional committee of the union, collecting proposals from the 56 trade union groups that make up the organisation and discussing them with the relevant departments of the administration before submitting the draft collective agreement to a general trade union meeting. In negotiating the most recent agreement the union was primarily concerned to retain the benefits from the previous agreement, despite the difficult financial situation, and was able to add some additional benefits, including sanatorium treatment for employees, bonuses for nurses engaged in emergency services (previously only paid to doctors) and additional holiday for some staff, but was not able to agree an increase in holidays and reduction in working hours for other staff because this was not provided for in the federal regulations. In general, financial constraints and regulations mean that it is very difficult for the trade union to secure any improvement in terms and conditions of employment beyond those provided by federal and regional norms and regulations. The trade union has no control over the allocation of income received by the hospital from the provision of private medical services, but would like to reach some agreement over this in the future.

Samara rural district hospital: traditional union under pressure from members. A rural district hospital in Samara oblast' has acute financial difficulties because it has insufficient financing from the local budget and the medical insurance system and little income from paid services. The trade union leader has worked at the hospital for 42 years, for 25 of which she has headed the trade union. The trade union has few benefits to distribute and little scope to extract concessions from management, but workers have confidence in their union. 'Nobody will listen to us singly, but the trade union is a public organisation, it has weight. The chair is very authoritative, knowing, and competent; they listen to her and respect her. I have no idea who could replace her' (senior nurse). The trade union trusts the administration and accepts that financial constraints make it impossible for management to fulfil all its obligations, and in turn, 'if there is even the slightest possibility, the administration always complies with the wishes of the trade union', said the deputy head doctor. In his view the interests of the administration and the trade union coincide completely: 'Both the trade union and the administration are interested in the hospital working and in wages being paid so that living conditions will be normal. Problems do not arise at our level, they come from above... we are so regulated that there is no place further to go. But we manage to find something from the money from paid services.' The trade union chair has full access to information and participates in all management planning meetings. Moreover, the trade union is involved in the allocation of additional money to pay various kinds of bonuses.

A serious problem arose in the hospital over the payment of compensation to employees for communal service charges, to which rural employees have been entitled since soviet times. In 2002 the hospital stopped paying this compensation because it did not have sufficient funds to do so, although from 2005 payment resumed with funding from the municipal budget. The trade union was understanding about the failure of the administration to repay the debt for 2002–4, but a group of disgruntled workers consulted a lawyer who advised them to take the case to court immediately, before the limitation period expired. This forced the trade union leader into action. On the advice of the regional committee of the union she told the director that court action was the only way forward, and he agreed, particularly because a court ruling would give him the right to divert funds from other sources to pay off the debt. The trade union prepared all the documentation and took the case to court, including a claim for compensation for inflation. In the event, the court ruled that the municipal administration was responsible for the payment, but the municipal administration did not have the money in that year's budget and the trade union and hospital management agreed with them that payment should be delayed till the following year. Impatient workers again by-passed the trade union and took the case back to the court, which warned the municipal administration that if the case went back to court their accounts would be frozen, the debt would have to be paid immediately and in full, and there would be additional penalties. Workers recognised that without the participation of the chairman of the trade union committee it would have been difficult independently to pass all the legal proceedings and to be successful in getting their debt back with compensation for inflation.

> Without the trade union, maybe, and it should be possible to do it on our own, in fact we started without the trade union. But the trade union protected our interests as a whole, across the hospital. I do not know if they would begin to listen to us one-by-one. (laboratory worker)

> Without the trade union it is not likely that we could have been successful, and it would be difficult for everyone to do it for themselves. The trade union became the organising force. Who would begin to run around, collect so many documents, go to the courts. It is easier to get rid of one, but you will not get rid of almost 300 people. (therapist)

She also managed to win for us a percentage for inflation. We demanded simply return of the sums. In summary, we have received more in view of inflation for all these years. (medical assistant)

The municipal administration asked the trade union for help with the problem and the union called a general meeting to discuss the issue, presenting a number of alternative solutions. The workers insisted that everyone should be treated equally and eventually agreed to withdraw their claims from court, with a guarantee that the debt would be repaid in quarterly instalments over the following year. The municipal authority carried out its promise to pay off the debt the following year, but financed it by cutting the budget of the hospital. Moreover, while paying off the debt it fell into arrears with the payment of compensation for the current year.

Samara central district hospital: from a hostile to a tough trade union leader. Of course, the attitude of the administration to the trade union depends in part on the character of the trade union and its leader. If the trade union leader rejects offers of collaboration on the part of the administration then he or she can only expect a hostile response. For example, the trade union in a large central district hospital in a prosperous city in Samara oblast' was headed by a combative trade union leader: 'our previous trade union organiser was like a tank. She did not want to make any compromises. Naturally, it was not possible for her to achieve anything.' The result was that the collective agreement only duplicated the standard set of social guarantees embodied in the Labour Code, while even some of the benefits provided by the employer were not included in the collective agreement, or their provision was qualified by the codicil 'if there is sufficient money'.

This trade union leader was replaced in 2004 by a more diplomatic leader, who was nominated by his colleagues, even though he had not previously even been a member of the trade union committee. The new leader took the job very seriously. In his opinion, the trade union should be in opposition to the employer, to be 'in a condition of permanent war with him', but he was willing to negotiate and compromise with the administration. According to the Vice-President of the regional trade union committee, 'despite his diplomacy, he is a pretty tough person; he quite often puts strong pressure on the employer, leaning only on the Labour Code and other normative documents'. The union president in turn is critical of the regional committee for being excessively loyal to the employers, failing to provide adequate selection and training of strong primary trade union leaders, failing to disseminate best practice in the protection of workers and failing to organise solidarity pressure on the employers.

The trade union carries out the traditional social and welfare functions, but also takes a firm position in negotiating with the director, relying on the provisions of the Labour Code backed up by threats of legal proceedings and even threats of strike action, although in the latter case the chairman of the trade union committee admitted, 'actually we were not going to stop work, it was pure pressure on the administration'.

As a result the new trade union president was able to resolve a series of problems that had remained unresolved for years.

With the expiry of the old collective agreement, the trade union leader prepared the draft of the new collective agreement himself, 'I have not advertised it yet, so that the administration does not cut it. There I have given a lot of thought to inserting reefs which, I hope, they will not notice at once. And then it will be possible to lean on it.' For this reason, the draft of the collective agreement was not circulated to the members for comment. 'For the worker who does not have a legal education, it is the result that is important, and it is all the same to him how it is achieved. And I know about the problems of the collective. I work here, I am a worker too, and all the problems affect me too... to acquaint workers with the collective agreement is not my problem, it is a lawful duty of the employer.'

The hospital has quite a substantial income from providing paid medical services, but in the past the money only went to those directly involved. The trade union president has persuaded the director that the distribution of this money should be included in the collective agreement and that the benefits should be spread to the whole labour collective, although in many medical institutions the trade union is not allowed to be involved in the distribution of money. The most contentious issue in negotiating the collective agreement was the payment of double pay for weekend working, to which the director agreed in principle, subject to financial constraints.

Despite the strong stand of the trade union leader, the director says

> On balance the trade union is useful to me. Well, now all social problems reach me with the method of their resolution already made out whereas, if people are on their own, many do not know their rights and the legislation, and the administration would have to deal with it. I think the chairman of the trade union committee solves most of the questions of our workers without me, he takes this work on himself, but if it were left to the administration, no problem could be solved without my participation.

Samara regional blood transfusion station: facing an authoritarian-paternalist director. The Samara regional blood transfusion station had a strong paternalist director and a traditional, but effective, trade union organisation that usually worked in close partnership with the director. However, a dispute arose when the administration asked the trade union president to sign a new regulation on the distribution of bonuses, financed from the income from the sale of blood products, which significantly increased differentials, particularly in favour of senior managers. The president refused to sign without consulting her committee and took the issue to an expanded meeting of the trade union committee.

> First people were in a fighting mood, they started to ask questions. Then the director spoke, he convinced everyone of his correctness. He managed to explain

to workers that the additional services are his achievement. People had come to demand what was theirs, but silently all accepted, and could not even plainly express what they wanted, I was simply surprised. They came to the trade union, asked us to help, the trade union was ready to insist, and they refused to support it. I found myself in this situation alone and without support. (chairman of the trade union committee)

In response to this challenge, the director cut off the trade union's access to financial information. As one union member noted, 'it is very difficult for her to protect our rights, she is under the head physician, and her salary depends on him'. Moreover, the workers look to their paternalist director rather than the trade union as the most effective guarantor of their interests. As the trade union president noted, 'he has complete command of an audience; as soon as something occurs and a dispute is going to arise, he goes to people and talks to them, explains everything, and people very much listen to him. He is very diplomatic, is able to convince and people believe what he says.' Nevertheless, workers have confidence in the trade union, as one of the workers explained, 'the trade union is certainly necessary, in such situations where else is there to go? Who will listen to us? And she is a competent person, knows the laws and knows where to appeal.' The only real leverage she has is to appeal to outside bodies. Thus, when there was a dispute about the redefinition of job descriptions for a group of workers, which implied a cut in pay, the workers involved appealed to the trade union committee and the chair took the issue immediately to the labour inspectorate. As one of the workers explained, 'the labour inspectorate sent a commission to the enterprise, with participation of the trade union. Certainly, the commission did not come to see us; they drank tea with the head physician in his office. But the instructions were then replaced with the old ones, and the money was paid to us.'

Samara children's' centre: extracting a collective agreement from a hostile management. The innovative children's consultative-diagnostic centre in Samara oblast' was spun off from the local polyclinic in the mid-1990s and built up by an energetic director, who was supportive of the traditional trade union, but was forced to resign in 2000 as a result of conflict with the city mayor. The new director was much less effective at raising funds by providing services for other medical establishments. As mounting financial difficulties led to increasing tension the director reacted by dismissing people who objected to his arbitrary management methods and his ignoring the trade union. With a high labour turnover and an anti-trade union policy on the part of the management, trade union membership declined, although it recovered as people rejoined when they came to see the trade union as their only defence. When the trade union president began to organise inspections of the establishment by the state labour and sanitary inspectorates the director forced her out. Under a new president the trade union asked the director to begin negotiations for a new collective agreement in September 2002. The director provided them with a supposed copy of the previous collective agreement, which was an obvious forgery, but refused to enter into discussion until the trade union submitted a formal request. He then presented the union with a completely inadequate draft collective agreement, demanding that they accept it without change. With the help of the regional committee, the trade union committee drew up an alternative draft, but the director refused to provide any information, even that required to be provided by legislation, constantly impeded the work of the committee and victimised its members. The director then tried to by-pass the trade union, since its membership had fallen below 50 per cent and it had failed to secure the endorsement of the majority of the labour force for its negotiating rights, by establishing a Labour Collective Council (STK) with which to conclude a collective agreement. At this point the trade union president resigned.

The director called a meeting to endorse his collective agreement, without informing the trade union, and intimidated employees into signing up to the agreement, eventually getting a majority. The trade union complained about a series of gross procedural irregularities to the state labour inspectorate, the city health administration and the regional trade union committee. The health administration administered a formal reprimand to the director, but directed the case to the labour inspectorate, which declared that it was outside its jurisdiction and referred it to the labour department. The labour department set up a commission, which included a representative of the regional committee of the union, which only met with the director and, not surprisingly, found that there had been no violations. The trade union president then appealed to the regional trade union federation, which referred the complaint back to the regional committee, which had originally failed to support its primary organisation on the grounds that the latter had allowed the situation to develop by permitting its membership to fall below 50 per cent. Eventually the case was considered by the Presidium of the regional committee, which passed a strong resolution of support, but still to no effect.

The situation was saved for the trade union by the fact that the centre was by now falling seriously into arrears in the payment of wages and in the course of subsequent investigations by the authorities many of the violations in the formulation of the original collective agreement were revealed. When the trade union threatened to take the issues to court, the head of the public health administration asked them not to do so, promising to resolve the issue by administrative methods, and the director was forced to resign under threat of dismissal, to be replaced as acting director by a branch manager, who was instructed to resolve the conflict. A general meeting of the labour collective was called, which decided to draw up a new collective agreement and mandated the trade union to do so on its behalf. After constructive discussions with the acting director a collective agreement was agreed, although the debts accumulated by the previous director meant that it was not possible to resolve all the problems immediately.

Everyone agreed that it was only the persistence of the trade union committee that achieved a result in this case, but the trade union president felt that all their appeals to higher state bodies had been in vain.

> All struggle through institutional channels, by and large, was not crowned with success, it was not possible to prove anything with the collective agreement. All of them closed their eyes to our complaints and listened only to his side. It is not possible to achieve anything by legal methods. We simply badgered everyone, so that the head physician was forced to leave.

She was not rewarded for her efforts. The following year the centre was merged with two other organisations and the management of the new organisation made strenuous efforts to ensure that she was not elected to the trade union committee.

Prokop'evsk city hospital: taming a new director. The experienced and active trade union president of a Prokop'evsk city hospital in Kemerovo oblast' is employed full-time as a doctor, which leaves her little time for trade union work. She has good relations with the functional departments of the administration, but faced problems with the appointment of a new director. The director complains of the emotionalism and unprofessionalism of the trade union president: 'She starts to carp and shout about trifles' and regards the union as an obstacle to his plans: 'I try not to pay any attention to them. If only they would not also impede me.' The new director was reluctant fully to implement the terms of the collective agreement concluded by his predecessor, but was forced to do so under pressure from the trade union. The director tried to put pressure on workers who appealed to the trade union for support. For some time the director sought to exclude the trade union from decisions about the allocation of money provided through the National Project, but was eventually forced to do so after the intervention of the city committee of the trade union, whose very active and authoritative head has held the post for more than twenty years. Gradually the new director was forced to recognise that he had to moderate his authoritarian style and play by the rules. 'But now it is getting better', said the trade union president, 'probably, it is necessary for him to learn how to conduct labour relations, how to negotiate', she said.

The trade union invariably supports workers in industrial injury cases and in disputes, which are resolved informally – the threat of a reference to the Disputes Commission is enough to persuade the director to back down.

Can a manager be an effective trade union leader? It is common for the leaders of primary trade union organisations to hold managerial positions in the health service. While it might be thought that this would immediately compromise the ability of the trade union leader to represent his or her members, this is not necessarily the case. We have found many examples of active, energetic and even militant trade union leaders who nevertheless occupy managerial positions. The trade union of the ambulance service in a mining city in Kuzbass is recognised as the strongest trade union branch in the city. The leader of the union, who was a manager in the ambulance service, participated in the organisation of militant strikes for the payment of wages in the mid-1990s. The trade union has a network of committees and commissions which ensure a high degree of participation of the membership in trade union work and is assiduous in monitoring health and safety and the proper payment of wages, in securing and maintaining social benefits, and in defending its members. Nevertheless, the trade union leader enjoys good relations with the administration. The director commented: 'I would say, that I learn from Alexander Dmitrievich (trade union president)… When I started work, there was much that I did not know, and we had disagreements. But for me the trade union is important, and I feel support', though he also noted that when he threatens to punish people, they say that they will go and complain to the trade union. Disputes, which are mostly over the proper calculation of wages, are always resolved amicably and informally. Far from being penalised for his activism, the trade union president was promoted to manage a substation in recognition of his organisational skills, and he finds it an advantage being a manager: 'Overlapping of administrative and trade-union work only helps in trade-union work. I as a manager always know about resources', although his enormous workload in his day job limits the amount of time he can devote to trade union work.

The very active trade union president of the Samara regional blood transfusion station, discussed above, is at the same time the manager responsible for health and safety. As she jokingly said about herself, 'in questions of labour safety I am employed both by the administration and by the trade union, it is like in that advertisement – "two for the price of one"'. The traditional, but active, president of the trade union in the Samara rural district hospital, also discussed above, is the head of a laboratory, while the very active president of the trade union in the Samara central district hospital is the head of a hospice and a member of the regional tripartite commission. The president of the union in the Kuzbass coal-mining city is simultaneously head of a centre.

A manager can also be vulnerable to victimisation. The Central City Hospital in another Kuzbass coal-mining city was reorganised in 2005 to embrace a number of formerly independent institutions. The reorganisation required the formation of a new trade union from the amalgamation of the previous trade union organisations, some of which had been moribund, some more active. The city committee of the health workers' trade union and the city health administration played a leading role in the creation of the new trade union organisation, seeking to preserve membership and disseminate the best practice of the more active of the previous organisations. When it came to identifying a president for the new trade union organisation the person elected was not an employee of the Central City Hospital, but a specialist in the public health laboratory, who was well known to the managers and specialists because of her work monitoring hygiene standards in the hospital. She regarded her independence of management as an important advantage, particularly as she had been made redundant from her post in the mid-1990s for her trade union activity, when her complaint to Moscow about the non-payment of wages revealed the failings of the accounts department.

The combative trade union leader of the Samara central district hospital recognised that the trade union has to represent not only the employees, but even the director, who is himself an employee: 'the employer, in my opinion, should not be in the trade union; he should have his own trade union. But in our case the chairman of the trade union committee has to protect both the workers and the employer, it is necessary always to observe a kind of balance.'

Trade unions in the private sector

There is considerable scope for collaboration between the trade union and the employer in the public sector, because both have an interest in securing adequate financing for the establishment. In the private sector, or in corporatised state enterprises, there is much less scope for such collaboration, since the priority of the employer is to maximise his profits. Nevertheless, the employer needs to recruit and retain a motivated labour force and so is subject to labour market pressures in the determination of wages and working conditions. A prosperous employer can tolerate a traditional trade union, which functions as a part of the personnel department, and in a tight labour market can negotiate collective agreements which provide improved wages and working conditions. A traditional trade union can also be of considerable benefit to a less prosperous employer, distributing social and welfare benefits as some compensation for inadequate wages, awarding honours to long-serving and exemplary workers, and explaining to the labour force the impossibility of providing adequate wages and working conditions in difficult financial conditions. Many workplace trade unions in the private sector in Russia continue to work in the traditional way, but there are also examples of trade union organisations which are more active in pressing their members' interests. To provide some examples of such trade union organisations we will look at cases from the construction and metallurgical industries and at the activity of alternative union organisations in the motor industry, before finally looking at trade union organisation in multinational companies.

Construction

The construction industry in Russia has been subjected to radical changes with the transition to a capitalist market economy. The privatisation of housing provision led to a massive decline in house construction during the 1990s, while the collapse of investment led to a similar decline in industrial and public construction. At the same time the privatisation of the industry led to the dismemberment of many of the large construction trusts which had formerly been responsible for construction and the proliferation of small private construction companies. In addition a substantial proportion of the labour force is now employed on short-term contracts and the industry employs a large number of undocumented migrant workers from former Soviet republics. This has all led to a massive decline in membership of the Russian Trade Union of Construction Workers and the Building Materials Industry, which today claims to have 700 000 members, against five and half million employed in the construction industry. Those primary organisations which have survived tend to be very traditional, so that the initiative generally lies with the central committee and regional organisations of the trade union.

One very positive initiative of the construction workers' union has been its response to the increasing employment of foreign migrant workers in the industry. By contrast to most of the rest of the Russian trade union movement, the construction workers' union has responded to the latter not by seeking to exclude migrant labour but by recruiting foreign workers into trade union membership, regardless of their legal status. A trade union card also serves as a useful identity document for such workers, providing some protection from police intimidation.

The main priorities of the construction workers' trade union are pay and health and safety. The union is committed in principle to the strategy of social partnership, but at the same time is prepared to back up its negotiating position by participation in FNPR Days of Action and by conducting strikes. As the chairman of the Central Committee of the union said in an interview, 'we have to be able to win through strikes, to threaten with strikes and to make sure that this threat somehow has an impact on the management... the more effectively we can stop production, the more successfully will we be able to influence the authorities. Such things make it possible to win.' However, the union has no strike fund to support striking workers and this makes it difficult to induce workers to take strike action. Nevertheless, in some cases the threat of strike action and the preparation for a strike is sufficient to induce the employer to back down.

The union puts a lot of emphasis on the negotiation of a branch tariff agreement with the employers' association, the Russian Union of Builders, with which it has good relations, though the agreement has limited coverage because few employers are members of their association. Nevertheless, the agreement can provide a point of reference for the negotiation of collective agreements at the level of the enterprise. By this means the union (rather optimistically) claims that the tariff agreement covers all of its primary organisations. The 2005–7 agreement included the provision that the minimum tariff rate for the industry should not be less than the subsistence minimum and that the differentiation of wages between the 10 per cent highest and 10 per cent lowest paid should not exceed four to six times. The 2008–10 agreement increased the minimum tariff rate to 1.2 times the subsistence minimum, specified that the average wage should reach five to six times the subsistence minimum and that pay should constitute 20–22 per cent of total costs (against an actual figure of less than 16 per cent in 2007). On health and safety the union has put the emphasis on lobbying the government to reintroduce a system of state regulation of health and safety in the construction industry.

In the conditions of the construction industry, with high levels of labour mobility, high levels of sub-contracting and often significant dependence on state orders, the regional committee of the building workers' trade union plays a very important role. What can be done is shown by the case of Samara oblast', which we contrast with the case of Perm'. In Kemerovo the regional organisation of the construction workers' union collapsed and the remaining primary organisations in the construction sector are now serviced by the regional committee of the Mining and Metallurgy Workers' Union.

Samara

Only one-sixth of construction industry employees in Samara oblast' are trade union members and only one-third are covered by collective agreements. About half the labour force is employed in small and medium private enterprises, many of whom are employed informally, not paying tax or social insurance contributions.

The leader of the regional construction workers' union is an outstanding personality who has been a trade union activist for his whole life. Although he is heavily engaged in the institutions of social partnership and is a member of the oblast' tripartite commission, he is a pure anarcho-syndicalist who believes that social partnership can only be built from the bottom up, on the basis of strong primary organisations.[1]

Discussion around a regional agreement only began following the creation of a regional branch of the employers' organisation in 2004, but was then stalled when the regional construction agency was abolished and its functions incorporated into a new regional ministry. In the absence of a regional agreement, the union encouraged its primary organisations to persuade the employer to apply the federal tariff agreement in their enterprise by incorporating its terms into their collective agreement. A regional tariff agreement for 2006–7 was finally signed in March 2006, which basically reproduced the terms of the federal agreement.

The conditions in the industry also mean that it is unrealistic to expect to be able substantially to increase union membership, although the regional committee makes serious efforts to create new primary organisations and to revive those which have collapsed by intervening whenever it hears of disputes arising. For example, one of the largest groups of companies building high-cost housing, which was closely linked to the former governor, lost its connections and contracts when the governor was replaced, leading to the non-payment of wages and large-scale lay-offs. The regional committee intervened and managed to establish primary organisations in four of the

---

[1]   When he was deputy president of the union he described social partnership as 'a fig leaf on the body of wild capitalism. It's not a compromise, but a complete sell-out' (Ashwin and Clarke 2002: 176).

companies of the group, which decided to picket the headquarters of the group in August 2008, followed by a picket of the regional administration on the first anniversary of the appointment of the new governor. As a result the regional administration agreed to buy equipment from the group to the value of the unpaid wages, which was immediately transferred to the workers of the four companies through the regional committee of the union.

In this context the focus of the regional committee of the union is on preserving, activating and mobilising its existing primary organisations. The construction workers' union is one of the most active in the oblast' in this respect. As the chairman of the regional committee declared, 'we must give up any indulgence in moods of dependency, as if it was not tempting to see us as benefactors – the trade union is a fighting organisation, not a charitable one. The main tasks are not solved by humiliatingly eliciting crumbs. Only competently organised pressure upon employers brings a positive result.' However, the union is not averse to establishing new organisations in collaboration with the employer, on the grounds that any organisation is better than nothing.

The regional committee is exceptional in supporting the activism of primary organisations, right up to strike action. On average the union has conducted about five collective disputes a year, winning the vast majority of their demands. The most famous victory was in 2001, when the union managed to stop the bankruptcy of a large building materials combine, owned by a major Russian conglomerate, where pickets, meetings, threats of litigation and road blocks persuaded the conglomerate to sell the combine to a new owner as a going concern. A similar struggle was won when the threat of a strike persuaded the employer to withdraw the threat of making 400 workers redundant. In 2006 the Mayor of Samara City threatened to liquidate an enterprise which occupied a big prestigious site. Again, the threat of mass picketing was sufficient to persuade the Mayor to withdraw his proposal, claiming that he had been 'misinformed'. Despite their successes, the regional committees are still not satisfied with their work: 'We are static – something happens, we react, but it is necessary to act in anticipation.' The regional federation has tried to combat the subordination of trade union leaders to management by extending trade union training from trade union presidents to the members of trade union committees.

It is estimated that about 40 per cent of employees in the industry are on non-standard employment terms, moving from employer to employer on short-term contracts. In order to deal with this situation the regional committee has established a form of direct union membership without attachment to a particular primary organisation, which is used to keep redundant workers in membership. A new means of dealing with the wild construction labour market was initiated when a construction brigade asked the regional committee to recommend a 'normal' employer, that is, one 'which pays a normal salary and which does not cheat'. Now there are several such brigades which are placed with a new employer by the regional committee when each contract ends.

Perm'

The construction workers' union in Perm' now embraces fewer than 10 per cent of those employed in the industry. The regional organisation has gradually had to scale back its ambition to reflect the realities it faces, so it has abandoned its previously ambitious plans, which contained 'unreal parameters which do not inspire the chairmen of trade union committees', to concentrate on securing the implementation of the branch tariff agreement at the level of enterprises. During the 1990s the regional committee concentrated on training trade union presidents to analyse the finances of their employer as a basis for negotiating more favourable collective agreements, but this had little success. Since 2001 the union has shifted the emphasis to the centralised regulation of wages. The chairman of the regional committee sits on the commission which sets the tariff rates to be applied to construction contracts financed from the regional budget and through this the union has secured more favourable pay rates for such contracts than are provided for by the federal branch tariff agreement. The chairman has also managed to ensure that the level of pay and conformity with the branch tariff agreement will be taken into account in considering tenders for public construction contracts.

The regional committee has taken few effective steps to increase trade union membership. In sharp contrast to the Samara organisation, its approach is to recommend to primary organisations that they should take on functions which would show their usefulness to the employer (organisation of industrial competitions and competitions of professional skill, struggle for labour discipline and so forth).

The most successful primary organisations are in large privatised construction trusts, which retain the traditional soviet management styles and traditional collaboration between management and the trade union. One large construction company is now owned by its managers, with the director, who began his career as an ordinary construction worker in the company, as the majority shareholder. The company is prosperous and expanding and the management style is paternalistic. The trade union, of which almost all employees are members, is almost merged into the management structure and the trade union president is committed to collaboration and compromise, 'I think the trade union, certainly, should co-exist. Not only to take the side of workers, but also the side of the management. Because only in such tandem can the enterprise also develop. And our enterprise is an example of this.' Nevertheless, the collective agreement incorporates the terms of the branch tariff agreement, so that pay is above average for the sector, and in addition provides many more benefits than are the norm for construction enterprises. Workers are encouraged to put forward proposals for the collective agreement, either through the trade union or through their line manager.

One of the largest construction trusts in the region survived the crisis of the 1990s because of its traditional close links with the regional administration, through which it secured public construction contracts. Although the labour force is stable, trade union membership has declined to about 30 per cent of the labour force as established workers are reluctant to pay dues, while young workers have no interest in joining. The trade union is very traditional and has not persuaded the management to incorporate the terms of the regional or the branch tariff agreements into the collective agreement, and pay increases are entirely at the discretion of the employer ('Increase of tariff rates and official salaries of workers of the enterprise is made within the limits of available resources of the payment fund on the decision of the Employer', reads Item 5.7 of the agreement), although pay is above average for the sector. As the trade union president comments, 'I can do nothing here, because the employer here is the owner. And it is his duty, it is really his right. He can decide whether or not to allocate money … we take the proposals from the divisions to him … he says either drop it or cut it … the Commission does not work here.' The trade union does not even pursue disagreements to the extent of including a report of such disagreements as an annex to the collective agreement. The adoption of the agreement at a general meeting is a formality.

Following the lead of the regional committee, the trade union tries to secure its place by persuading the employer that it is useful to him, but with little success. The president complains,

> I cannot really convince him that we do not work for someone else, we work for his workers. All these competitions, doing things for pensioners, the money we give out, holidays we organise, tickets, we constantly give out vouchers, constantly for children, adults. … Well, it would be nice if the employer … saw that we are trying to work … Not that we incite people, but on the contrary … Well, we had wage delays … the trade union comes to a site, they [workers] are all immediately like dogs, they pour everything possible out onto us. And we also had to justify the employer: 'Well, wait, well, be patient, they are getting a loan … from the bank … money for wages'. There were such cases, where we calmed people down.

The only lever the trade union president has is to apply gentle pressure by referring to the law and the threat of sanctions imposed by the state inspectorates. Another tactic that she used successfully was to organise line managers to submit a co-ordinated request to the general director to increase the pay of their workers, though this avenue has now been blocked by the director.

Metallurgy

The metallurgical and metal-working industries were the traditional core of the Russian economy, dominated by giant industrial enterprises traditionally paying relatively high wages to their skilled labour forces. Most of these enterprises were privatised in the 1990s and fell into the hands of Russian conglomerates, some having subsequently been sold to foreign owners. The collapse of industrial training in the

1990s meant that these enterprises have faced shortages of skilled labour, which has enhanced the bargaining position of their workers despite the weak labour market situation overall.

Enterprises in the metallurgical sector were traditionally affiliated to the Mining and Metallurgy Workers' Union (GMPR), while those in metal-working were affiliated to the union of their branch of production. Thus auto enterprises were affiliated to the Auto and Agricultural Machine Building Trade Union (ASM) and those in aviation to the aviation industry trade union. The transition to a market economy potentially benefitted workers in the metallurgical industry as their employers profited from cheap Russian energy and raw materials and access to global markets, while shortages of skilled labour enabled workers to achieve relatively high wages. Thus GMPR had a tense relationship with FNPR through the 1990s, leaving FNPR at the national level in 1992 over the FNPR leadership's opposition to market reform, and only rejoining in 2000, since when it has been the most active and independent branch trade union, regularly negotiating the most favourable branch tariff agreements and encouraging and supporting its primary organisations.

The GMPR branch agreement with the employers' association is the strongest in Russia, the agreement includes norms for wages and a mechanism for increasing salaries, as well as a significant volume of social benefits. The agreement is only binding on employers who are signatories to it, but it provides a point of reference for the negotiation of collective agreements throughout the industry. Negotiations over the renewal of the collective agreement in 2009 were very tense, as employers sought to cut costs in the face of the global crisis. Giving up any hope of negotiating an improved agreement, the union proposed an extension of the existing agreement, but the employers proposed to suspend 35 points. In the end it was agreed to freeze 12 points, mostly concerning pay, for the duration of the crisis.

In the wake of the crisis many employers put workers on short-time and laid workers off, paying them only two-thirds of basic pay, rather than two-thirds of average pay (which can be two or three times as much), in violation of the law. GMR secured a legal ruling from the Public Chamber that employers were liable to pay two-thirds of average pay and circulated the ruling to its regional and primary organisations, which were able to use it to force employers to meet their obligations. In many other industries laid-off workers were paid only a meagre retainer or were not paid at all, without their unions taking any effective action at all.

In the vast majority of privatised enterprises, even in the metallurgical industry, the trade union has continued to play its traditional role as a branch of enterprise management and has continued to concentrate on its traditional functions. However, there are cases where the traditional union takes an independent position in pressing for improved terms and conditions of employment.

Siberian Ore

Siberian Ore was formed in late 2002 as the mining division of a large Russian metallurgical holding company. Siberian Ore brought together seven mines and two concentrating factories across three regions of Western Siberia. The constituent enterprises of Siberian Ore have retained their own primary trade union organisations and there is no general whole-company trade union committee – all trade union branches have equal rights – but the primary organisations in Novokuznetsk, where the management of the company is based, play the leading role in co-ordinating the activity of the unions across the company and there is a common collective agreement for the whole company. Seventy-three per cent of the 11 000 employees are union members.

The effective leader of the trade union in the company is a woman who is an economist by training. In 1998 she was elected vice-president of the trade union committee of a large Siberian metallurgical combine, where the union conducted a serious struggle against the management and at the same time actively resisted its takeover by new owners. In 2001, under pressure from the regional authorities and the owners, the conflictual trade union committee was not re-elected and she moved on to work at a concentrating enterprise as deputy head of the labour department. When Siberian Ore was created, the Mining and Metallurgy Workers' Union, GMPR, suggested that she should head the trade union committee and she has headed this organisation ever since. Although formally she is only leader of one of the trade union organisations in the company, in practice she is recognised by all as the leader of the trade union in the company as a whole. The trade union is widely recognised as one of the strongest in GMPR and, indeed, in Russia as a whole and is often held up as a model of what can be achieved even in Russian conditions. As the Deputy Chairman of GMPR said, 'due to them, I can give examples not from remote history, not from foreign experience, but at the same enterprises which live in the same conditions'.

Because the company is spread across three regions, with different economic and political conditions, it is difficult to co-ordinate the work of the trade union committees in the different enterprises. Nevertheless, there is a constant flow of information, regular co-ordinating and report-back meetings and a dense network of active trade union committees and commissions throughout the enterprises of the company. Part of the reason for the success of the union is the personality of its leader and its high level of organisation, but it has also been helped by the fact that the regional administration in Kemerovo pursues a 'socially-oriented' policy which insists that companies in the region should recognise and negotiate with FNPR trade unions (provided that these unions are loyal to the regional administration).

Negotiation with the company is difficult because, although the company is willing to co-operate with the trade union, there are frequent changes of management personnel and the company management is not empowered to make any major decisions, which have to be referred to the holding company in Moscow.

The trade union signed a three-year collective agreement in October 2004 in which it agreed that pay would only be increased in line with inflation while the company implemented a major investment programme to modernise the plant and equipment. The unions had also signed an agreement in April 2006 that they would not demand any pay increases while the company was loss-making. The owners of Siberian Ore had subscribed to the 2006 branch tariff agreement a week after the agreement was signed, but then refused to implement the pay increase included in the agreement, claiming that there was no money for such an increase. In September 2006 the company moved into profit and the union proposed negotiations for a 2007 salary increase, in accordance with the branch agreement, arguing that the wage-freeze agreed in the 2004 collective agreement was void because the company had not fully implemented the promised investment programme. The company refused to enter negotiations, which became the legal basis for the declaration of a collective labour dispute in the company in November 2006. This was a very high-profile dispute, which involved lawyers and officials of GMPR as well as the government and the employers' association at regional and federal levels.

The dispute began with a one-day picket on 14 December 2006 in all the cities in which the company had affiliates, which involved a large number of workers. The pickets did not produce any results, so mass protest meetings of workers of the company were held on 25 December in which several thousand workers participated, although production was not interrupted and only those who were off-duty took part. Solidarity messages were organised from other enterprises and in response to an appeal from the mass meetings, the Governor of Kemerovo oblast' pressed the company to settle the dispute. Agreement was reached in February 2007, providing a 20 per cent pay increase for all workers and the implementation of the social standards provided in the branch tariff agreement. In the longer term it was decided that pay at the enterprises of the company should increase by not less than 30 per cent of the subsistence minimum in the given region. Finally, as a result of negotiations, a decision on payment of a lump sum bonus in February for non-loss-making work was adopted. However, this agreement was only a prelude to difficult negotiations over the collective agreement in the autumn of 2007.

The trade union won a 38.2 per cent pay increase for 2008 in the 2007–9 collective agreement, but in December 2008 and again in June 2009 agreed to suspend some of the provisions of the collective agreement, including deferring the payment of wage increases to compensate for inflation, because of the financial difficulties faced by the company in the wake of the 2008 financial crisis. In exchange the company made a number of concessions, including a guarantee not to extend out-sourcing for the duration of the agreement.

Perm' Metallurgist

Perm' Metallurgist is a prosperous metallurgical enterprise with an autonomous trade union. The enterprise union left the regional organisation of FNPR in 1992 and later, in 1999, it left the branch trade union organisation, GMPR, since when it has not been affiliated to any higher or alternative trade union organisation, though it does participate in the trade union co-ordinating council of the city. The dispute with the higher trade union organisations arose primarily over the functions of the latter. The higher trade union organisations viewed their role as being solidaristic, to use the fees received from richer enterprises to support weaker primary organisations, which meant that Perm' Metallurgist was paying substantial trade union dues and was getting very little in return. Part of the money saved in this way has been used to employ a lawyer as part of the trade union apparatus.

The trade union organises 84 per cent of the labour force, but managers are not members of the union. The exclusion of managers from membership of the union was on the initiative of the enterprise director, but the trade union president feels that it is appropriate. The trade union derives its strength from its record of having actively protected the rights and interests of its members through the 1990s under its former president, who had been in post since 1987, and the extensive involvement of the membership in its activities through active shop trade union committees. Under the collective agreement, chairmen of shop trade union committees and members of the company trade union committee are released for trade union work for one day a week, but full-time trade union officers are paid entirely from trade union funds.

As economic conditions improved in the late 1990s the union became more active in demanding and securing regular pay increases. Although not a member of GMPR, the union managed to include a commitment to adhere to the branch tariff agreement in the collective agreement of the enterprise. In 1999 the enterprise acquired a new owner, who refused to implement the pay increase provided for by the branch tariff agreement and the trade union initiated a collective labour dispute, including the threat of declaring a strike and, simultaneously, appealed to the governor, the mayor and the public prosecutor of the city and the mass-media. The management conceded in June and conceded a further increase in response to a second collective labour dispute in August. The following year, the new owners tried to convert Metallurgist into a subsidiary of an enterprise in a neighbouring city, which the trade union successfully resisted through appeals to the governor, the mayor and the deputy of the state Duma, with the threat to demand an investigation into the privatisation of the enterprise.

The procedure for the negotiation of the collective agreement is typical for large industrial enterprises. The draft collective agreement is sent to shop meetings for comments and proposals. Foremen and chiefs of shops look at the proposals and filter out those that can be resolved at their own level, 'but those things which are really necessary, which we resolve in the collective agreement, about work clothes and such things, that is, which are concrete, which require an investment of money, which do not depend on our level, on the level of the chief of shop, those things, you see, are sent further, for the consideration of the administration of the combine' (foreman). In the negotiation for the last collective agreement a dispute arose over holiday entitlements for those working in harmful conditions, which the union won after the declaration of a collective labour dispute and three months of negotiations. The union has also managed to secure agreement that nobody should earn less than the subsistence minimum, the earnings of those who would otherwise get less being made up to the minimum with a special bonus.

Auto industry

The auto and agricultural machine-building trade union, ASM, is one of the more conservative and traditional of the Russian branch trade unions, only signing a branch tariff agreement covering the agricultural machinery sector and supporting very traditional primary trade union organisations. This meant that the union was ill-equipped to divert the conflicts that arose in the auto industry into the institutional channels of conflict resolution, leaving a space for the emergence of alternative trade unions. However, only one such trade union, the trade union of Ford workers in Vsevolozhsk, outside St Petersburg, has been able to overcome the opposition of management and the traditional trade union to act as the recognised representative of the labour force.

Avtovaz

The longest established independent union in the motor industry is Yedinstvo (Unity) in the giant Avtovaz plant in Togliatti. Yedinstvo was created in November 1990, in the wake of a September 1989 strike involving 20 000 workers, which was followed by the repression of the strikers, with the traditional ASM union supporting the management. The union initially affiliated to Sotsprof, but soon declared its independence of the latter before affiliating to the All-Russia Confederation of Labour (VKT). The leader of Yedinstvo, Anatolii Ivanov, was elected to the State Duma as an independent candidate from Togliatti in 1999 and was replaced as union leader by Petr Zolotaryev, who was narrowly defeated in the election for Mayor of the city in 2004.[1] Under the aegis of VKT Yedinstvo participated in the formation of the Inter-regional Trade Union of Motor Industry Workers (MPRA) in July 2006, of which Zolotaryev was co-President alongside Alexei Etmanov, leader of the Ford trade union in Vsevolozhsk.[2]

---

[1] In the 2007 election, fought entirely on party lists, Ivanov was returned to the Duma on the ruling United Russia list.

[2] At the 2009 MPRA Conference Etmanov was elected President and Zolotaryev Vice-President.

Yedinstvo has always been the minority union in Avtovaz. At first the management ignored it, but after it had stopped the main track in major strikes in 1994 and 1996 the management took it more seriously and since then it has been constantly under pressure both from the administration and from the ASM union. Its membership peaked at 3425 in October 2000, on a new wave of strike activity, though many people retained their membership of ASM as well to cover themselves against victimisation. Since then membership has fallen below 1000 of the 105 000 employed in the plant as management has cleaned shops of Yedinstvo members by depriving them of overtime, bonuses and promotion opportunities and ASM has banned dual membership.[1] There are now Yedinstvo trade union committees in only a handful of shops. On the main track Yedinstvo now has only 83 members, whereas in the past it had 1500. This loss of membership has deprived Yedinstvo of resources to pay its five full-time staff and to finance effective campaigning and it has never had the resources or desire to match the enormous spending of ASM on social, welfare and cultural activities and benefits. In April 2010 its membership was reported to have fallen to 300.

Throughout the period of its existence the management has refused to negotiate with Yedinstvo, either ignoring or rejecting its appeals, and Yedinstvo has never had the strength to force management to the negotiating table. In 1995 it managed to begin negotiations on the draft collective agreement, however the conference of the labour collective then voted in favour of the ASM draft. In 2006 Zolotaryev found out about the meeting of the collective agreement commission, but when he tried to attend he was thrown out with the threat to call security. In 2007 it was reported in the factory newspaper that the new general director had had a friendly discussion with Zolotaryev and agreed to include Yedinstvo in the negotiation of the next collective agreement, but nothing came of this. Yedinstvo has therefore had to use the same methods as the traditional unions in seeking to resolve individual disputes on the basis of the law, by reference to the Labour Disputes Commission and ultimately to the courts and state inspectorates. Yedinstvo's main priority, however, is pay and, being excluded from the negotiating process, it can only press its claims through mass protests and strikes. The 2003 Labour Code has made it impossible for Yedinstvo to organise a legal strike, which requires the support of the majority of the entire labour force, so now they can only overtly organise pickets and protest meetings.

Avtovaz was privatised in the early 1990s and through a complex system of cross-shareholding effectively owned itself. The company faced a rapid decline in market share from 2003, as foreign imports grew, at the rate of 10 per cent a year. Moreover, the company had enormous tax debts and maintained a gigantic social infrastructure. At the end of 2005 the state took control of the company and installed new management in the hope of making it more attractive to outside, and preferably

---

[1] The ASM union has 160 000 members, but almost half of these are pensioners and employees of hived-off establishments.

foreign, investors. The new management developed a programme of investment in new models, the devolution of non-core activities, in particular the social welfare infrastructure, and the 'optimisation' of the number of the labour force, in other words mass redundancies. However, the new management trod cautiously for fear of stoking up social tension, and discussed its plans in detail with ASM, but the crisis was mounting. By the middle of 2007 Vaz's share of the Russian market had fallen to 28 per cent, from 63 per cent only four years before, and the excess stock of unsold cars had reached 130 000.

The ASM trade union is a traditional union, fully integrated into the management structure as its social and welfare department, with personnel managers at Avtovaz traditionally being recruited from the trade union apparatus. The ASM supported management plans to make 25 000 employees redundant, though preferred to achieve this by natural wastage rather than compulsory redundancy, and sought guarantees that pay and employment in the hived-off social and welfare facilities would be preserved, to which the then-director, now Governor of Samara oblast', Vladimir Artyakov, agreed. The ASM recognises that it can only avoid mass redundancies by moderating its pay demands. 'We have two problems. We can achieve a significant pay increase, but alongside that the number employed will be reduced. If we demand preservation of jobs, the question of increase of pay will not be solved. We try to observe a balance. Gradually to raise the salary, and to make reductions through natural wastage. We try to agree that there should be no mass redundancies' (president of the ASM trade union committee). The ASM regards Yedinstvo with disdain, but nevertheless the existence of a competitor keeps it on its toes, as the ASM president said, 'the fact that two trade unions work, do not relax, is kind of positive and stimulates development. We do not rest on our laurels any more. So we publish booklets for those who are not trade union members, all the time we should think of something to involve people. I relate to all this so: if they have success somewhere, it means we have worked badly.'

As inflation was eroding real wages, the collapse of the market in 2007 meant a sharp fall in earnings of assembly workers as they lost overtime pay and production bonuses, which had comprised up to half their earnings. The ASM president demanded that management should restore the purchasing power of wages and threatened, for the first time in the union's history, to initiate a collective labour dispute if management did not comply. Meetings were held in the shops to support the demand, in which ASM claimed 74 000 people participated. Yedinstvo supported these demands and proposed to ASM that the two unions should jointly prepare for a strike, circulating leaflets to this effect through the shops. However, management immediately conceded a modest increase in pay and full indexation of salary and the collective agreement was amended accordingly.

When workers received their pay slips for June they were outraged to see how small the increase was and workers on the main track began talking about a strike. Zolotaryev warned them that a wildcat strike would be illegal and proposed that they call on ASM to organise a legal strike. The workers did this, but got no reply. The ASM held explanatory meetings in the shops to try to head off the strike. Meanwhile, leaflets with the workers' demands were distributed through the factory and two Yedinstvo activists were detained by the factory police for distributing 'extremist literature'. A mass meeting of one of the assembly shops in which there was a Yedinstvo organisation decided to carry out a short warning strike on 1 August and asked Yedinstvo to lead the strike. In the event between 150 and 500 people, according to different sources, walked out of three of the assembly shops to meet outside on the street, and some stopped work but remained at their posts, though this did not stop the track and Zolotaryev called off the strike after a little more than an hour. Two people were dismissed as a result of the strike, with the support of ASM, and 300 were reprimanded and deprived of their bonuses. The ASM and the management of Avtovaz denounced the strike and Yedinstvo as being politically motivated in the run-up to the elections, while Zolotaryev insisted that the strike was spontaneous and he had acted only as an adviser, since Yedinstvo had too few members to influence the situation, pointing out that the strike leader in one of the shops was actually the ASM group organiser. Although the strike had no obvious immediate impact, it was probably no coincidence that the following month ASM had 'agreed to the employer's proposal' to increase tariff rates from 1 October.

The impact of the 2008 global financial crisis only deepened the problems at Avtovaz. Production was suspended from the middle of December 2008 to the end of January 2009 and short-time working was introduced when production resumed, with consequent reductions in pay. Prime Minister Putin visited the plant in March 2009 and promised massive government subsidies to enable Avtovaz to survive, while the management complained that they were not able to make the compulsory redundancies necessary to make the plant viable because of their social impact on the city, although they did transfer their catering staff to a new company. In order to protect jobs, ASM agreed in January 2009 to suspend the point in the collective agreement providing for the indexation of wages. In August 2009 the ASM trade union conference approved a new collective agreement which reduced the benefits provided for Avtovaz workers. The conference was picketed by only three representatives of the alternative union. In September the first 5000 compulsory redundancies, of engineers, managers and office workers, were announced, with a further 22 000 redundancies planned for 2010. Yedinstvo was not consulted about any of these actions and was not able to take any action because the Avtovaz workers, fearing redundancy, were not willing to resist the cuts in their pay and conditions. As the crisis deepened, Yedinstvo organised protest meetings and warned of the devastating impact on the local economy of redundancies and even more of the proposed takeover of Avtovaz by Renault, which would reduce the factory to an assembly plant and devastate the local component suppliers, but the alternative union was powerless to do anything.

GM-Avtovaz

GM-Avtovaz was established as a joint-venture of the two companies, supported by the European Bank for Reconstruction and Development, in 2001 and its plant in Togliatti, which assembles the Chevrolet Niva and Viva models, came on-stream in September 2002. Although the plant produces outdated models with second-hand equipment, the company presented itself as entirely modern, in contrast to Avtovaz. The new enterprise was marked by a rigidly hierarchical, authoritarian management system which had no place for trade unions, where dissent was met not with negotiation but with dismissal. The pay system was opaque, with considerable scope for the award of discretionary bonuses. Overall, pay was initially a little higher than at Avtovaz, but the work regime was much more intensive, discipline strict and subsequent increases in pay did not match inflation.

The management responded with horror to the attempt of the regional committee of ASM to establish a trade union organisation through Avtovaz – 'better that troops come in, but never a trade union' the then-director was quoted as saying – and ASM gave up the attempt. Petr Zolotaryev, leader of Yedinstvo, also sought to encourage the formation of an independent union, with support from the CIS Representative of the International Metalworkers' Federation, but at first was unable to find anybody willing to take on the job. Eventually he was contacted by a dissatisfied manager in the Sales Department, Andrei Lyapin, who had been threatened with dismissal for challenging the work practices of his department, but had decided to stay and fight. Lyapin could get no support from other managers, who were afraid for their jobs, so decided to contact production workers. Yedinstvo helped Lyapin to produce and distribute leaflets in April and May 2006, citing the positive example of the Ford workers. In July 2006 the union was founded on the basis of the ten people who had responded to the leaflet. Five representatives of different production departments constituted the union committee and Lyapin was elected president. The priority was to expand the organisation, to get a majority of the labour force into membership so as to achieve bargaining rights. The union restricts membership to ordinary workers, excluding any managers who have the right to impose disciplinary sanctions or significantly to change working conditions, unlike ASM which admits all employees to membership. 'The position of the regional committee is that all hired employees can be members of the trade union, from workers up to the director, the director in fact is also a hired employee' (chairman of the regional committee of ASM). Within a year the new union had about one hundred members out of five hundred production workers and had trade union committees in two of the three shops.

At the beginning of August 2006 the new union officially notified the management of its creation, but received no reply. Instead management launched a wave of repression of trade union activists, disconnecting the telephone and work email of the president, transferring two committee members to other jobs and impeding the entrance of committee members to the factory at the checkpoint. The union held a press conference to publicise its existence and, on the intervention of the State Duma Deputy and former leader of Yedinstvo at Avtovaz, Anatolii Ivanov, the Public Prosecutor ordered the factory to stop the illegal inspection of committee members at the checkpoint. Only after this did the union receive a response from management, refusing recognition on the grounds that the union was not legally registered. At the same time, in September 2006, a branch of the traditional ASM union was suddenly established at the factory, headed by the Health and Safety Coordinator of the company, and was immediately recognised by management, although the ASM union was not legally registered and attracted few members, basically engineers and line managers, although line managers tried to persuade their workers to join. One of the women workers from the paint section said: 'our chief of shop went to persuade everybody. All the chiefs, brigadiers, foremen have joined ASM. They did not especially press workers, they simply deceived them. There are a lot of us who need housing, many newcomers. There were rumours that they would only consider giving places in the VAZ hostels to members of ASM. But at VAZ there are not even places in the hostel for their own people. And people joined, they wanted to write an application for the hostel, but then they said to them that applications were closed.' The ASM membership peaked at 30, but the union was almost completely inactive and by May 2008 membership had fallen to 22. The ASM leaders insist that 'there is no obvious oppression of workers at our enterprise, and a very good dialogue is established with the administration'.

While the ASM union enjoyed obvious management support, the leaders of the alternative union were subjected to repeated intimidation. As a precursor to dismissal, repeated reprimands were issued against Lyapin and in November the deputy president of the trade union committee, Il'ciyar Sharafutdinova, was dismissed for absenteeism, on the grounds that a sick-note was supposedly improperly formulated (in March 2007 she was reinstated by order of the court).

The new union at GM-Avtovaz approached VKT for support and joined the newly created Inter-Regional Trade Union of Motor Industry Workers (MPRA), which they hoped would help them to secure state registration. At the beginning of September 2006, VKT organised a picket of the GM-Avtovaz offices in Moscow in solidarity with the victimised unionists. Especially after the dismissal of Sharafutdinova the campaign intensified, with picketing of GM offices and dealers in Moscow, St Petersburg and Samara. Appeals were posted on internet sites and over 3000 letters of solidarity were sent to the management from all over the world. GM-Avtovaz bosses were bombarded with SMS after their cell phone numbers were publicised and VKT threatened GM that it would organise a boycott of all GM products. This campaign did not secure recognition for the union. In April 2007 MPRA decided to affiliate to the International Metalworkers' Federation (IMF), which it achieved in November. Through the IMF, the GM-Avtovaz union was able to get access to the management of GM Europe and to participate in meetings of the GM European Works Council. In response to the union's complaints, GM Europe transferred the General Director of

GM-Avtovaz to another enterprise and informed VKT and Lyapin that they were conducting an internal investigation of alleged anti-trade union activity at the enterprise.

Despite the refusal of recognition and harsh intimidation, the union immediately pressed its demands for an increase and indexation of pay, collecting 331 signatures in support of its demands in a petition in September 2006. Management did not respond officially, but did announce a small increase in pay. Following a well-publicised picket in November 2006, which included demands for pay increases, management announced a further small pay rise from January 2007, although the General Director had previously declared that no increases were proposed for 2007. The union also campaigned over health and safety issues, particularly in the paint shop. Again appeals to management met with no response, but an inspection following a complaint to the State Labour Inspectorate led to the Inspectorate demanding remedial measures. At the end of May 2007 a group of women paint shop workers, led by Il'ciyar Sharafutdinova, stopped work because, in the absence of effective air conditioning, the temperature had risen above the legal limit. After three hours of negotiations and threats the women agreed to resume work on condition that air conditioning was installed within two weeks. Although the strikers were promised that they would not be victimised, all received formal reprimands and their access to social benefits was withdrawn, although the air conditioning was installed within the agreed time.

This turned out to be the high point in the activity of the alternative union. Andrei Lyapin moved to Moscow in the summer of 2007 to work for IUF and his sudden departure demoralised the members and decapitated the organisation at GM-Avtovaz, with nobody willing to take over the post of president of the union.[1] Zolotaryev, as president of Yedinstvo and MPRA, was supportive but had very little time to devote to GM-Avtovaz. Management refused the union's request to collect dues by check-off, and the activists were unwilling to collect dues in cash, 'we now do not have any activity. Why collect payments? What can we say to people? To collect for a strike fund? But we are not going to strike. I will not risk it', said the vice-president of the union. As a result of high labour turnover at the enterprise the union lost many of its members as they quit their jobs, and as a result of continued management pressure was unable to recruit new members, so that by March 2008 only about 20 members remained, in the assembly and paint shops, while in the welding shop, where the union had had a strong presence, not one member remained. Nevertheless, individual workers still approached Il'ciyar Sharafutdinova with their problems, even if they were not members of the union, and management left her alone.

[1] Lyapin moved to the MPRA the following year as the person responsible for international activity and returned to Togliatti.

They do not press me, they do not touch me, most likely they do not want to communicate, because I know my rights, and I am afraid of nobody. ... People do not want to protect their rights. The employer knows this and his oppression squeezes everything that he can out of people. But they are careful in their relations with me. They do not give me false papers, do not deceive me. At worst they ignore me, or agree. They cannot propose anything illegal either to me, or to the collective where I work. And that we [the independent trade union] exist at this factory gives workers some hope ... . They know to whom to run. And for the employer it is a kind of brake, they know that we know our rights and they operate cautiously.

Eventually a volunteer came forward to chair the union branch, assembly shop foreman Sergei Yartsev. In August 2008 one brigade in the assembly shop stopped work because the temperature was above the legal norm, stopping the track for half an hour, though management refused to install air conditioning on the grounds that it was too expensive and in November dismissed one of the organisers of the stoppage, Sergei Pavlyuchkov, a deputy president of the MPRA union, although his dismissal was ruled unlawful by the local court in March 2009.

When the workers returned from their New Year break in January 2009 they found the plant swarming with security guards and were brusquely informed that half the labour force would be laid off in March, with the agreement of the ASM union. Needless to say, MPRA members, including Yartsev and Sharafutdinova, were first in line for redundancy though, according to the law, union officers can only be dismissed with the approval of their union. The President of IG Metall, Berthold Huber, sent a letter of protest to the Personnel Director of GM-Avtovaz and MPRA organised a picket of the main entrance to the plant, but to no avail. When 25 of their activists were dismissed in March, MPRA took the case to court, but the GM-Avtovaz management denied the very existence of the union and in September the court turned down the appeal of all the MPRA activists, except for Sharafutdinova, who was dismissed once again as soon as she tried to return to work.

In August 2009 the shutdown at Avtovaz meant that GM-Avtovaz also stopped production, suspending the workers on two-thirds pay, returning to a five-day week single shift working in September.

Ford

The most successful workplace trade union in the first decade of the twenty-first century was that of the Ford assembly plant at Vsevolozhsk, outside St Petersburg. The plant was opened in 2002 to assemble the Ford Focus for the Russian market, initially employing 400 people, reaching 1700 by the middle of 2005. Pay is far below that of Ford's other East European plants, but a bit above the average for the local labour market, though work is intensive and good money can only be made with long hours of overtime. Originally there were none of the plan fulfilment bonuses that Russian workers are used to.

A trade union was established on the initiative of a disgruntled sales manager soon after the plant opened and affiliated to the FNPR engineering union, Rosprofmash,[1] but the union turned out to be entirely traditional, organising vacations and gifts for children, and by the middle of 2005 had only 112 members and so had no bargaining rights. On hearing of the formation of the Russian trade union, the trade union of Ford Brazil invited the Vsevolozhsk organisation to send two delegates to a conference of trade unions of Ford of the Americas. The visit was organised and funded by Transnational Information Exchange (TIE). Since the union president was not able to go, two ordinary workers grabbed the chance of a free trip to Brazil, where they were amazed and inspired by what they heard from other Ford unionists – for the first time they realised what a real trade union could be. On their return they reported to a trade union meeting and in October 2005 one of them, Alexei Etmanov, a welder, was elected President of the union with a new committee of activists, all ordinary workers. Their first priority was to get the majority of the labour force into the union, to secure recognition, and within a month they had recruited 800 members by going around the shops and talking to workers about the need for an active trade union that would stand up to management.

Almost immediately the trade union drew up a set of demands, including for a 30 per cent pay rise on account of inflation and the productivity increase associated with the intensification of work. The company immediately tried to buy off the union. Etmanov was appointed a section chief and there were suggestions that the company would give the union a new automobile. Some committee members wavered and were replaced, but the union stood firm. Agreement was not reached in the conciliation commission and at the beginning of November 2005 the union held a token one-hour strike, followed by a five-day work-to-rule. In December the management conceded some of the union's demands, but offered only a 12 per cent pay rise, so the issue of pay remained unresolved. It was only after another work-to-rule in March 2006, during which the company brought in 200 agency workers, that the dispute was settled with a 16 per cent pay rise and improved bonuses, although the company dismissed four union activists and the union lost about 40 members.

The new trade union committee had a tense relationship with the regional Rosprofmash organisation, which had not supported their actions and which they regarded as a bureaucratic, conciliatory structure which provided no useful services in exchange for the 35 per cent of union dues which they demanded from the primary organisation. As a result the Ford union left Rosprofmash in January 2006 and, finding it impossible to register as an independent union, affiliated to Sotsprof, later transferring their affiliation to VKT and participating in the formation of the Inter-

---

[1] Rosprofmash and ASM decided to merge in April 2008 and the decision was confirmed at their Congresses that were held in parallel on 17 February 17 2010.

regional Trade Union of Motor Industry Workers (MPRA), of which Etmanov is president.

The trade union committee is committed to building the union from the base, so that initiatives will come from below, and the trade union committee will only have to organise workers to carry them out:

> We have set things up so that the people decide. I spend all day in the shop, I approach people, I show them the work schedule, and I say what possible ways are there: we strike, or they sell this schedule + 30 per cent. Will that be enough for you? No. Will it be enough if they sell the schedule + 45 per cent? Yes, that's enough, I shall not strike. Dialogue with people. And if they say, for example, + 70 per cent, but people are not satisfied, then yes, we shall lead, we shall go on strike. But the protest should be born from within. And in negotiations, they give us something – sign that, and we say: no, we cannot, we sound out the opinion of our people and should agree everything with them … . We have taken as a rule for ourselves the principle of the Polish trade union 'Solidarity' where there is a rule not to meet management in private, because they play such interesting games, can compromise at any moment. Here it is important: if you are caught in a corridor and have discussed some question on the run with the heads, it is not so terrible, but if you go to a meeting, you only go with someone else. (Alexei Etmanov)

At the end of 2006 the union put forward an ambitious set of demands, including for a 30 per cent pay increase and strict control of the conditions of outsourced agency labour, supplied by Adecco. In February 2007 a mass meeting voted overwhelmingly in favour of a one-day strike in pursuit of the demands, almost all of which management immediately accepted, though only meeting just over half of the pay demand. In the agreement, the number of workers from out-sourcing agencies who can work at the enterprise was agreed, it was agreed that they would be paid the same basic salary as regular workers, and their rights and the opportunity for them to transfer to the ranks of basic workers was stipulated. (Even such a vigorous traditional trade union as GMPR, faced with the proposal of the management of the Russian giant Evrazholding to transfer about 30 thousand employees to out-sourcing organisations in 2007, could offer almost nothing.) A further one-day strike on 7 November 2007 in pursuit of the 30 per cent pay rise, amongst other things, was ruled illegal by the court, but was followed by an indefinite strike from 20 November following all the legal procedures. The management kept production going, at much reduced capacity, by organising scab labour. The strike was called off on 14 December and negotiations resumed, management finally agreeing a substantial pay rise in February 2008. The workers on strike did not just sit at home, but had daily meetings at which they discussed the strike tactics and planned and organised pickets and demonstrations. The strike, which was the longest strike in modern Russian history, was also more aggressively policed than the previous Ford strikes had been.

In December 2008 Ford workers were surprised to discover that a new trade union, a branch of the 'Inter-regional Trade Union of Autotransport and the Automobile Industry' (MPAAP), affiliated to Sotsprof, had been established in the factory, claiming to have 30 members, although none of these members, other than the President, could be identified. The establishment of the Sotsprof union was seen as a clear government-inspired provocation. It was probably no coincidence that Etmanov was physically attacked twice in November 2008 and once in April 2009.

Ford claimed to have been hit as hard as other auto producers by the slump in the market following the 2008 global financial crisis and refused to offer any pay increase or provide employment guarantees in the negotiations for the 2009 collective agreement. The union demanded a pay increase to compensate for inflation but had little choice but to accept management's collective agreement in March, appending an extensive memorandum of disagreement. In June Ford went on to a four-day week, threatening those who would not agree with dismissal. The MPRA union objected to this short-time working, which it did not consider the management had justified, but recognised that a strike threat in such circumstances was inappropriate, instead pursuing the issue through the courts, the case dragging on for months. Through 2009 production was repeatedly suspended for two weeks at a time, with production workers being laid off on two-thirds pay, and in the autumn Ford moved to working only two shifts, with those on the night shift, the best paid and most individualistic workers, being redeployed or forced to leave. Faced with such a loss of earnings many Ford workers quit. As short-time working and inflation continued to erode Ford workers' wages the union vainly sought to negotiate improvements in pay and working conditions, discussion over the 2010 collective agreement again breaking down in March, but following a short work-to-rule, management agreed in April a 12 per cent pay rise and guaranteed that there would be no redundancies while dispatched workers were employed at the plant.

The trade union at Ford owed its success to a number of factors. First, it has an energetic, committed and charismatic leader in Etmanov. The loss of such a leader effectively destroyed the union at GM-Avtovaz. Second, the union actively engages the members at all times, so that it is a participatory rather than a bureaucratic organisation. This contrasts with the neighbouring Caterpillar plant, which established its union organisation at the same time as Ford, but the union at Caterpillar depended on a handful of activists who were easily neutralised by the management. Third, the union organises the majority of the labour force, which gives it bargaining rights and some legal protection, whereas the leaders of other militant Saint Petersburg unions, at Heineken, Coca Cola and the Postal Service, could all be dismissed. Fourth, the union has enjoyed sympathetic coverage in the mass-media and, while it has not enjoyed the active support of the local administration, it has not faced significant opposition from the local authorities, in both cases primarily because it is facing a foreign employer.

The success of the Ford union has inspired workers in many other factories, particularly in the immediate neighbourhood of the Ford plant, to try to emulate the Ford workers, although none has so far managed to achieve the breakthrough of organising a majority of the labour force that is required to achieve recognition. Indeed, even at Ford only a bare majority of the 2400 employees were MPRA members in April 2010. Moreover, employers have also learnt the lesson of Ford, that if they want to avoid confronting a militant trade union they have to nip it in the bud. The MPRA branch established at the Taganrog Automobile Plant in October 2007 was met with severe repression, including repeated beatings; MPRA activists at Tsentrosvarmash and the Wagon Building Factory in Tver faced dismissal, FSB investigation and court action for extremist activity; an MPRA branch was established at GM-St Petersburg with 70 members of the 900 employed in December 2008. The branch president, Evgeny Ivanov, immediately received telephone threats and was assaulted soon after. Following a work-to-rule in November 2009, Ivanov was dismissed and the management created a 'yellow' union, although in March 2010 the local court ruled the dismissal illegal. Activists seeking to consolidate MPRA branches at Tenneco Automotive Volga in Togliatti, Tikkurila Paints in St Petersburg,[1] Nissan in St Petersburg, Nokian Tyres at Vsevolozhsk and Avtoframos (Renault) in Moscow have all faced concerted management opposition and each only managed to enlist a handful of members. One major problem has been that MPRA has recruited predominantly young inexperienced workers who seek to confront management before they have built up their organisation. The most promising new development has been at Volkswagen in Kaluga.

Volkswagen

The VW assembly plant in Kaluga was opened in November 2007. The VW had originally planned to pay relatively high wages, but the oblast' administration pleaded with them not to pay significantly above the local average for fear of the consequences for other employers. Following a meeting in Moscow between the General Director and Personnel Director of Volkswagen Rus, management and trade union representatives from the VW Works Council in Germany and the leaders of ASM and MPRA; in May 2008, an MPRA union was established in VW Kaluga in June and had soon recruited 150 members, but VW management kept stalling over the provision of facilities for the union. An ASM union organisation was established in March–April 2009 with about 60 members, but management would not negotiate a collective agreement with either union since it claimed that neither represented more than 20 per cent of the labour force (as at Ford, a substantial number of VW employees are agency workers, hired through Adecco). On 13 June 2009 Alexei Etmanov and Petr Zolotaryev spoke at a meeting of VW workers in Kaluga organised

---

[1]   At its 2009 conference MPRA amended its constitution to allow it to organise outside the motor industry.

by MPRA and attended by about 80 people, at which the workers present decided to demand a doubling of their pay. The MPRA installed thermometers in the shops and a week later, on the initiative of the MPRA union, 50 assembly workers stopped work on the pretext of the excessive temperature on the track. Following negotiations, management agreed to workers taking a five-minute break every hour whenever the temperature rose above 28 degrees. In essence the stoppage was a legal means of protesting at the earlier loss of their May bonus suffered by all the workers at the factory as a result of the failure to reach production targets, which the workers blamed on management. After the strike the management began to put pressure on MPRA and threatened that if the plant did not meet its target there would be lay-offs, but MPRA membership increased to about 250. Three weeks later the President of the German metalworkers' union, IG Metall, and the head of the VW Works Council visited VW Kaluga and met both unions separately, inviting them to take part in a seminar in Germany from 21 to 25 of September, attended by seven delegates from each union, at which VW management signed an agreement to collaborate with both trade unions.

Dealing with multinationals

We have already seen some of the problems and possibilities faced by alternative trade unions dealing with branch plants of multinational companies in the motor industry. Attempts to organise the plants of notoriously anti-union foreign companies such as Macdonalds and Coca Cola have faced the familiar difficulties of repressive management. In other cases foreign management has proved accommodating to traditional Russian trade unions. But the organisation of trade unions in large national and multinational companies faces particular problems in Russia because the trade unions are organised on a regional and sectoral basis, while legislation provides for the negotiation of collective agreements at enterprise level and for higher-level sectoral and regional agreements, but not for company-level agreements. The traditional unions see the problem not so much as one of establishing a militant trade union in the face of the corporate employer as of establishing a framework within which to continue to carry out their traditional role.

The emergence of foreign and Russian corporations owning several plants in different industries and different regions presents a challenge to the primary trade union organisations of the various plants, which may be affiliated to different sectoral and regional trade union organisations, but which face a common management policy dictated by the head office of the company. One solution to this problem has been the creation of a Co-ordinating Council of trade union organisations of the corporation, which meets regularly for the exchange of information and co-ordination of collective bargaining strategies of the various primary trade union organisations, which remain the bargaining units according to Russian law. Such Co-ordination Councils have been created in a lot of Russian and foreign-owned companies, such as Alcoa, JTI,

Gallagher, RUSAL and Eurocement. Some companies have gone further and created corporate trade unions – inter-regional or even international trade union organisations uniting and consolidating the actions of primary trade union organisations of the enterprises included in the corporation. The International Association of Trade union Organisations (MOPO) of LUKOIL includes 364 primary and about thirty unified trade union organisations of affiliates of the company in 25 regions of the Russian Federation, and also in Azerbaijan, Ukraine, Bulgaria, Romania and Moldova (almost 170 thousand people). Among Russian companies which have set up such corporate trade unions are Gazprom and Sibur.

Where the various plants are in one industry, the primary organisations might delegate their bargaining powers to the central committee of the sectoral trade union, as was the case with Rusal, where the primary unions delegated their bargaining powers to the Central Committee of the Mining and Metallurgy Workers' Union. Where there is a uniform inter-regional trade union organisation it is possible to conclude a uniform general collective agreement as, for example, in Gazprom or Russian railways, which is applied to all enterprises of the holding company, in which the primary trade union organisations delegate the right to sign such a General Agreement to the unified elected body of the trade union organisation of the company. In practice this is frequently impossible because, although the company represents a more or less integrated organism, the position of its subsidiaries may be very different (regional features and profit, on whose size the financing of the collective agreement depends). In such conditions it is possible to prepare a framework document with average parameters and on the basis of such a document to conclude a General Agreement between the employer and trade union association (LUKOIL), according to which the terms of collective agreements should not be inferior to those established in the General Agreement (http://mopo.lukoil.com/main/default.asp).

In a situation when the primary trade union organisations of the enterprises which are included in the company belong to different branch trade unions and there is no unified representative trade union body it is impossible to conclude a General Agreement, but there are other methods of unification of collective agreements. In TNK-BP, for example, on the initiative of the corporate centre, a standard (model) collective agreement has been developed, which has a recommendatory status, but in practice the collective agreements signed at the enterprises of the company are no more than a registration of the social programs authorised by the corporate centre, with very little discretion for local negotiation. This leads to an improvement in conditions in the less successful enterprises of the holding company, but a deterioration for enterprises with traditions of wide social support of workers. If it is possible to defend established positions so that they are included in the draft of the business-plan, as a rule, this is perceived as a joint victory of the plant administration and the trade union. The content of collective agreements is strictly supervised by the company and no local 'spontaneous action' is allowed: 'Social policy, key parameters of the collective agreement are developed at the head office in Moscow. At the enterprise we can put forward proposals, but nothing in it can really change if it is not decided in Moscow and is not included in the business-plan. We constantly entered indexation of salary in the corresponding section of the draft of the Collective agreement, but the Company also constantly deleted this item.'[1]

In such corporations social policy is determined in the head office, so that the enterprise trade unions have lost their traditional participation in decision-making in this sphere,[2] though they continue to play a major role in their implementation. 'The social development department, personnel service and the trade union – we are like a single whole.' Since workers basically value the trade union for its role in the distribution of social benefits and services, for trade unions visible participation in such activity is one of the basic conditions for preserving trade union membership. The employers, meanwhile, value the trade union as a feedback channel: 'people can say things to the trade union they will not say to the employers ... Thanks to the trade union we find out about problems, imminent conflicts, long before the situation becomes critical. And the earlier you find out about a problem, the easier it is to solve it.' The trade unions are also very active in facilitating organisational reforms and the introduction of new labour practices. 'If the impression is created somewhere that the trade union wants to take too much on itself, it is incorrect. The trade union takes exactly as much and exactly what the administration is ready and wants to give it.' Trade union leaders acknowledge and even celebrate their renewed role as a transmission belt, no longer as the 'school of communism', but as the 'school of capitalism'. 'Trade unions are a cementing part between workers and employers. And personally my task consists in supporting the image of the Company among workers, to explain to them the policy of the Company. In fact it is much easier for the trade unions to make contact with the worker than for someone else, because we have informal relations with workers. Therefore the role of trade unions cannot be underestimated.'

The trade union more often acts as a buffer between workers and the administration than really protecting labour rights. The trade union is ready to support workers in their demands for wage increases in the face of inflation, but only as the transmitter of the workers' moods, in the form of a statement of the problem to the management of the company. For example, when the service enterprises of Nizhnevartovsk raised the question of a wage increase with the head office of TNK-BP, the trade union

---

[1]   Under the law the content of a collective agreement is determined by the parties, that is, administration and trade unions of the enterprise, and any outside intervention, including from higher structures, is not allowed.

[2]   An exception is the Russian management of TNK-BP, which has established Corporate Co-ordinating Councils at national and regional levels in which representatives of management and trade unions can discuss the business strategy and social policy of the company so that 'the opportunity to take local problems directly up to the management of the company has appeared, without risking losing half the information through the hierarchy'.

supported the demand. At that moment in fact a pre-strike situation had developed, but the trade union leaders categorically refused to qualify it as such: '26 chairmen of trade union committees have signed a letter declaring their readiness to start picketing. They were not prepared to declare a strike as it was economically not favourable either to the company, or for workers. They only mentioned the possibility of picketing, and that is not at all the same as a strike.'

The protective role of trade unions in multinational companies is almost exclusively in the resolution of individual problems, most of which are not work-related: 'workers come here with all problems: someone has been treated badly, someone has not paid everything due'. Among the requests are appeals to draw up letters, court papers, preparation of documents for the privatisation of a summer house, sale of an apartment. For this purpose the trade union organisations have established legal departments – 'In the organising committee we have opened free-of-charge legal consultation, we have specially taken lawyers onto the staff. In total over the year there have been more than 100 requests not connected with production.' Thus, the trade union acts as a service organisation reacting to potential inquiries of its clients.

Participation in a transnational company opens up opportunities for international co-operation, often co-ordinated by the regional offices of the Global Union Federations. International contacts provide opportunities to learn about the possibilities of effective trade unionism. Alexei Etmanov, president of the Ford trade union, was inspired by a visit to a conference of Ford workers in Brazil:

> There I have seen such a situation. The chief of a section approaches a worker and says: 'Come on!' – 'I am not obliged to do it. We shall meet in the trade union committee'. The chief at once says: 'Well. You should not do it'. This is an indicator! Security, material and moral. I saw real trade-union work. … It became insulting for Russia. We are people, not some kind of monkeys! … I saw. It was insulting. It lit me up.

The leader of the traditional union at one of Alcoa's Russian plants similarly, though less radically, said 'I have found out for myself that we lag behind in the level of our organisation, those requirements which the organisation demands from us. I have understood that we should work a lot with people.' The success of the union at the Ford factory in Vsevolozhsk owes a lot to the support of trade union colleagues from other Ford factories, throwing letters at the head office and refusing to increase production to make up for losses from the Russian plant during their strikes. French trade unions acted in support of the dismissed chairman of the trade union committee of the Moscow hypermarket Ashan, sending a declaration to the management of the head company.

However, the traditional trade unions are much more cautious about engaging in international solidarity action. The head of the Alcoa trade union quoted above rejected a proposal from the Canadian trade union of the company to unite their efforts to press the employer to increase wages because the Russian union was very conscious of the fact that Alcoa had bought their plant because of their lower wages. The same trade union organisation also refused to co-ordinate their wage bargaining with that of Alcoa's other Russian plant, on the grounds that the latter paid substantially lower wages because the local cost of living was less and the labour market was less competitive there. Such a rejection of solidaristic bargaining is not a universal feature of traditional trade unions. The trade union organisations of a major Russian metallurgical holding company have sought to equalise pay and conditions across the various plants of the company, while it is not uncommon for traditional trade unions to attempt to preserve pay and conditions when some functions, typically the social apparatus of the enterprise and services such as cleaning and power supply, are hived off or out-sourced.

Conclusion

Russia's traditional trade unions continue to be bureaucratic organisations, committed to the principles of social partnership, in almost every case subservient to the state and to management. Yet, despite such constraints, there is no doubt that they have made some progress in representing their members through lobbying government and pressing, if rarely confronting, management. When the traditional trade union is unwilling to confront management, particularly in demanding pay rises, Russian workers turn to the alternative trade unions, but more militant action faces a strong reaction from employers, who have shown themselves ready to go to court to declare strikes illegal, to victimise and dismiss activists and even to hire thugs to threaten and assault leaders of alternative trade unions. Nevertheless, the Russian example shows that it is possible for trade unions to make progress, even in such unfavourable circumstances, with a strong leader and active involvement of the membership.

6

Labour Activism and the Reform of Trade Unions

What has been the role of labour activism in driving forward the reform of the trade unions in Russia, China and Vietnam? In the most general terms one can say that the reform of trade unions has been driven by worker activism, because the primary objective of reform of the traditional trade unions has been to confine worker activism within peaceful constitutional channels of trade union representation. In China and Vietnam this objective has been imposed on the trade unions by the Communist Party, whereas in Russia it has been an objective imposed on the trade unions by threats and opportunities presented by the state. The Chinese Party, perhaps haunted by the memories of Tiananmen and challenged especially by SOE worker protest (Pringle 2001), has been much more anxious about the political dangers posed by industrial unrest than has the Vietnamese Party, which has until recently taken a more relaxed view of strikes and worker protests, and ACFTU has accordingly come under much more concerted pressure to reform than has VGCL. The political weight of VGCL may also have put it in a stronger position to resist pressure to reform.

In China and Vietnam the subordination of the trade unions to the Communist Party has meant that the unions have enjoyed the political support of the Party in their attempts at reform, whereas the Russian trade unions have had to reform themselves on their own initiative and using their own resources, albeit under pressure from the state. At the same time, the trade unions in China and Vietnam have been severely constrained by the Party in the steps they can take to reform their own structures and practices, for fear that such reform might encourage rather than restrain worker activism.

In all three countries the principal barrier to the development of the representative role of trade unions has been the subordination of the workplace trade union to management, which makes it very difficult for the trade union to reform in response to pressure from below. Attempts to initiate reform from above have been impeded by the limited leverage which higher trade union bodies have over their primary organisations, even in China and Vietnam where the trade unions are still governed according to the principles of 'democratic centralism'. This limited leverage makes the higher-level trade unions in China and Vietnam even more reluctant to risk activating their primary organisations for fear that they will lose control of such organisations, so they continue to endorse management control as the lesser of two evils. Thus, they create new trade union organisations in close collaboration with management, even, or especially, when workers themselves demand the creation of a primary organisation, and resist worker demands to democratise their trade union organisations. Even in Russia, where the trade unions are nominally independent, higher trade union bodies are often reluctant to encourage grass roots activism for fear of compromising their political alliances with employers and arousing the hostility of the local or federal government.

The most dramatic difference that subordination to the Party makes to trade union activity is in the political sphere, where the trade unions in China and Vietnam are excluded from playing an independent political role, at least in public, while the Russian trade unions have sought to constitute themselves as an effective political force in lobbying regional and federal legislatures, participating in tripartite structures of consultation and by mobilising their members in symbolic 'days of action', which require the unions to develop their representative capacity. Of course, this does not mean that the trade unions in China and Vietnam do not play a political role, but this role depends on their privileged position within the Party structure rather than on any claims to be representative of their members.

In Russia, the failure of the traditional unions to represent the interests of their members in the workplace created the space within which alternative workers' organisations arose and in which alternative trade unions were able to organise to harness worker activism. 'Freedom of association' was not granted to soviet workers by the state, it was a right appropriated by workers as the soviet repressive apparatus crumbled in the face of unrest. The first independent trade unions registered as 'social organisations', akin to sports clubs, and were subsequently able to constitute themselves as trade unions because the 1990 Trade Union Law defined trade unions as independent self-governing bodies which were not required to register with the state, unintentionally creating the space for trade union pluralism. Alternative trade unions have never been a major force in Russia, and have never constituted a serious threat to the traditional unions, but they have been important as the means by which worker activism has presented a challenge to the traditional trade unions, particularly in the negotiation of collective agreements and the defence of trade union members, and the alternative unions have pioneered new forms of trade union action, most particularly through picketing and hunger strikes and in the use of judicial procedures to represent workers in individual and collective labour disputes, all of which have been taken up by the traditional unions.

We can see embryonic forms of freedom of association in China in the legal advice centres set up by NGOs to pursue individual and collective labour disputes, which have induced ACFTU to set up their own such centres, and in the informal networks which underlie strikes in China and Vietnam, but the impact of such activities on the practice of the traditional trade unions is restricted by the narrow limits within which independent activism is confined by state repression.

The limitation of the right to strike has been by no means as significant a factor as the absence of freedom of association in inhibiting worker activism and the reform of the trade unions in China and Vietnam. The important issue is not so much whether or not a strike is legal, but whether or not it is effective. In China and Vietnam strikes have proved to be an extremely effective method for workers to achieve their immediate demands, as the authorities refrain from repressing strikers for fear of exacerbating the situation and press employers immediately to meet the workers' demands to prevent the strike from spreading. However, the victimisation of worker activists and suppression of independent worker organisation means that strikes are not effective as a means of building the workers' organisational solidarity, which might otherwise present a serious challenge to the traditional trade unions. The Vietnamese authorities probably have a more realistic understanding of the political significance of wildcat strikes than do their Chinese counterparts, in taking a relatively relaxed attitude to strikes, while clamping down on independent worker organisation. On the other hand, such wildcat strikes will continue to escalate unless or until workers achieve the freedom of association that will enable them to articulate, represent and negotiate their grievances within the workplace. In Russia, the state has been much more successful in limiting the right to strike precisely because freedom of association means that most strikes have identifiable organisers who can be taken to court and punished for conducting strikes that are not in accordance with the legislation.

The main barriers to trade union reform in all three countries are the inertia of the trade union apparatus and the dependence of primary union organisations on management. There is progress in all three countries, the most substantial being in Russia where workers have enjoyed freedom of association, the trade unions have a longer experience of independence and have faced less direct political constraint, but even in Russia progress is very slow, while in Vietnam the very limited extent of trade union reform means that the leading role in the regulation of industrial relations has been played by MOLISA.

Finally, it should be noted that international trade union co-operation has played an important role in fostering the reform of trade union language, structures and practices in Russia through international dialogue and training programmes. The FNPR and the two principal alternative federations, VKT and KTR, affiliated to ICFTU in 2000. Today about 30 of the 42 Russian branch (industrial) unions are affiliated to Global Union Federations, five of which have permanent representatives in Moscow. Although the Vietnamese trade union confederation, VGCL, continues to be affiliated to the Communist-era WFTU, it has developed an extensive programme of collaboration with ITUC-affiliated national trade union centres and with Global Union Federations.[1] The ITUC only began to explore the possibility of collaboration with the Chinese ACFTU in December 2007 and connections remain at the exploratory level to date. The ILO has been active in supporting institutional development in all three countries. The most effective international trade union

---

[1]   Vietnam's Postal and Telecommunication Workers' Union affiliated to UNI in August 2008, the first Vietnamese union to affiliate to a Global Union Federation.

collaboration has been in support of the training of trade union officers, particularly in health and safety and in methods of collective bargaining. Because the driving force for change has been located at the local and workplace levels international trade union collaboration is most effective when it is targeted at the exchange of experience at these levels, rather than the exchange of high level delegations.

The recession following the 2008 global financial crisis has had a significant impact on the dynamics of trade union reform. On the one hand, cutbacks in production and employment in the leading sectors of the economy have weakened the labour market position of workers, so that fear of unemployment inhibits them from taking industrial action. On the other hand, increased pressure from employers seeking to restore profitability increases the potential for conflict. In the background, the state is increasingly wary of the political risk of industrial and social unrest. In all three countries the economic crisis produced an increase in tension and conflict, but a fall in the number of strikes, and an increasing reliance of the state on policing and extra-legal forms of repression to contain unrest. However, in China since late 2009, economic recovery has somewhat ameliorated the tension between union reform and political stability, at least for the time being. Renewed labour shortages have boosted workers' confidence to take effective action and increased pressure on the ACFTU to reform ineffective traditional practices. Should the recovery falter, then it is very likely that the reduced possibilities of strikes and constitutional protest in China, as well as in Russia and Vietnam, will lead to a politicisation of conflict, a greater polarisation of forces and more rigid constraints on trade union reform.

References

ACFTU 2005. *Chinese Trade Union's Safeguarding the Legitimate Rights and Interests of Workers and Staff Members 2004*. Beijing: Statistics Publishing House.

ACFTU 2007. *Work Statistics of the Chinese Trade Unions in 2006*. Beijing: ACFTU.

Ashwin, S. 2004. 'Social Partnership or a "Complete Sellout"? Russian Trade Unions' Responses to Conflict'. *British Journal of Industrial Relations* 42: 23–46.

Ashwin, S. and Clarke, S. 2002. *Russian Trade Unions and Industrial Relations in Transition*. Basingstoke and New York: Palgrave.

Baek, S. 2000. 'The Changing Trade Unions in China'. *Journal of Contemporary Asia* 30: 46–65.

Beijing Federation of Trade Unions 2003 *Zhonghua zong gonghui guanyu jianli kunnan zhigong bangfu zhongxin de yijian* (ACFTU Opinion on the establishment of Workers' Support Centres).

Belser, P. 2000. *Vietnam - On the Road to Labor-Intensive Growth?* Washington DC: The World Bank.

Biddulph, S. and Cooney, S. 1993. 'Regulation of Trade Unions in the People's Republic of China'. *Melbourne University Law Review* 19: 253–92.

Brown, R.C. 2006. 'China Collective Contract Provisions: Can Collective Negotiations Embody Collective Bargaining?' *Duke Journal of Comparative and International Law* 16: 35–79.

Butler, W.E. 1988. *Soviet Law*. London: Butterworths.

Chan, A. 1993. 'Revolution or Corporatism? Workers and Trade Unions in Post-Mao China'. *The Australian Journal of Chinese Affairs* 29: 31–61.

Chan, A. 1998. 'Labour Relations in Foreign-Funded Ventures, Chinese Trade Unions, and the Prospects for Collective Bargaining' in Leary, G.O. (ed.) *Adjusting to Capitalism: Chinese Workers and the State*, 122–49. Armonk, NY: M.E. Sharpe.

Chan, A. 2000a. 'Chinese Trade Unions and Workplace Relations in State-owned and Joint-venture enterprises' in Warner, M. (ed.) *Changing Workplace Relations in the Chinese Economy*, 34–56. Basingstoke: Macmillan.

Chan, A. 2000b. 'The Nature of the Chinese Trade Union and the International Labour Movement' *Conference on the Chinese Labour Movement and its Relations to the Hong Kong Labour Movement*. Hong Kong: Asia Monitor Resource Centre.

Chan, A. 2001. *China's Workers Under Assault*. Armonk, NY: M.E. Sharpe.

Chan, A. and Nörlund, I. 1998. 'Vietnamese and Chinese Labour Regimes: On the Road to Divergence'. *China Journal* 40: 173–97.

Chan, C.K.C. 2008. *The Challenge of Labour in China: Strikes and the Changing Labour Regime in Global Factories*. PhD Thesis. Coventry: University of Warwick (http://www.warwick.ac.uk/fac/soc/complabstuds/russia/ngpa/Chanthesis.pdf).

Chan, C.K.C. 2009. 'Strike and Workplace Relations in a Chinese Global Factory'. *Industrial Relations Journal* 40: 60–77.

Chan, C.K.C. and Pringle, T. 2008. 'Centres of Contention: Labour Rights Work in China'. AMRC Seminar, January.

Chang, K. and Zhao, J. (eds) 1995. *Laodong guanxi, laodongzhe he laoquan dangdai zhongguo de laodong wenti* (Labour Relations, Labourers, Labour Rights: Problems of Labour in Contemporary China). Beijing: China Labour Publisher.

Chen, F. 2003. 'Between the State and Labour: The Conflict of Chinese Trade Unions' Double Identity in Market Reform'. *The China Quarterly* 176: 1006–028.

Chen, J. 2002. 'Paying the Price: Worker Unrest in Northeast China'. *Human Rights Watch* 14, 6C (http://www.hrw.org/reports/2002/chinalbr02/).

Chen, J. 2006. 'Is there a labour movement in China'. *Asian Labour Update*, 59 (http://amrc.org.hk/alu_article/focus_on_china/is_there_a_labour_movement_in_china).

Cheng, Y.Y., 2004. 'The Development of Labour Disputes and the Regulation of Industrial Relations in China'. *The International Journal of Comparative Labour Law and Industrial Relations* 20(2): 277-95.

Chetvernina, T., Smirnov, P. and Dunaeva, N. 1995. 'Mesto profsoyuza na predpriyatii'. *Voprosi Ekonomiki* 6: 83–9.

China Institute of Labour Movement. 1993. *Xin shiqi gonghui gongzuo zhongyao wenjian xuanbian* (Selection of Important Documents about the Trade Unions' Jobs in New Period). Dept. of Trade Union Science.

China Statistics Publishing House 2007. *China Labour Statistical Yearbook*. Beijing: China Statistics Publishing House.

Chiu, S.W.K. and Frenkel, S.J. 2000. *Globalization and Industrial Relations and Human Resources Change in China*. Bangkok: ILO Regional Office for Asia and the Pacific.

Christensen, P.T. 1999. *Russia's Workers in Transition*. DeKalb, IL: Northern Illinois University Press.

Clarke, S. 1990. 'Crisis of Socialism or Crisis of the State?' *Capital and Class* 42: 19–29.

Clarke, S. 2001. 'Russian Trade Unions in the 1999 Duma Election'. *Journal of Communist Studies and Transition Politics* 17: 43–69.

Clarke, S. 2006. 'The Changing Character of Strikes in Vietnam'. *Post-Communist Economies* 18: 345–61.

Clarke, S., Fairbrother, P., Burawoy, M. and Krotov, P. 1993. *What about the Workers? Workers and the Transition to Capitalism in Russia*. London: Verso.

Clarke, S., Fairbrother, P. and Borisov, V. 1995. *The Workers' Movement in Russia*. Cheltenham: Edward Elgar.

Clarke, S. and Kabalina, V. 1995. 'Privatisation and the Struggle for Control of the Enterprise in Russia' in Lane, D. (ed.) *Russia in Transition*, 142–58. London: Longman.

Clarke, S. and Lee, C.-H. 2002. 'Towards a System of Tripartite Consultation in China?' *Asia-Pacific Business Review* 9: 61–80.

Clarke, S., Lee, C.-H. and Do, Q.C. 2007. 'From Rights to Interests: The Challenge of Industrial Relations in Vietnam'. *Journal of Industrial Relations* 49: 545–68.

Clarke, S., Lee, C.-H. and Li, Q. 2004. 'Collective Consultation and Industrial Relations in China'. *British Journal of Industrial Relations* 42: 235–54.

Clarke, S. and Pulaeva, O. 2000. 'Vyborg Cellulose Paper Combine' (www.warwick.ac.uk/fac/soc/complabstuds/russia/documents/VBK.doc).

Connor, W. 1996. *Tattered Banners: Labor, Conflict and Corporatism in Postcommunist Russia*. Boulder, CO: Westview.

Cooke, F.L. 2002. 'Ownership Change and Reshaping of Employment Relations in China: A Study of Two Manufacturing Companies'. *Journal of Industrial Relations* 44: 19–39.

Cooney, S. 2007. 'China's Labour Law, Compliance and Flaws in Implementing Institutions'. *Journal of Industrial Relations* 49: 673–86.

Ding, D.Z., Goodall, K. and Warner, M. 2002. 'The Impact of Economic Reform on the Role of Trade Unions in Chinese Enterprises'. *International Journal of Human Resource Management* 13: 431–49.

Do, Q.C. 2007a. 'Evolution of a New Pattern of Strike in Vietnam' *NGPA Project Research Report* (go.warwick.ac.uk/russia/NGPA/strike_mapping.doc).

Do, Q.C. 2007b. 'Independent Worker Activism in Vietnam and Its Influence on the Strategy of the Government and Traditional Union' *NGPA Project Research Report* (go.warwick.ac.uk/russia/NGPA/Vietactivism.doc).

Do, Q.C. 2008. 'The Challenge from Below: Wildcat Strikes and the Pressure for Union Reform in Vietnam' *Vietnam Update 2008 Conference, Labour in Vietnam*. The Australian National University, Canberra (go.warwick.ac.uk/russia/ngpa/ChallengefromBelow.doc).

Do, Q.C. 2010. *The Challenge from Below and the Transformation of Vietnamese Industrial Relations*. PhD Thesis. University of Sydney.

Fair Labor Association 2004. *Annual Public Report: Freedom of Association in Vietnam* (www.fairlabor.org/2004report/freedom/vietnam.html).

FNPR 1996. Ot vtorogo k tretemu sezdu profsoyuzov Rossii (FNPR). Moscow: FNPR.

FNPR 2001. Informatsiya o tarifno-dogovornoi kampanii 1999–2000 godov. Moscow: FNPR.

Gallagher, M.E. 2005. *Contagious Capitalism: Globalization and Politics of Labor in China*. Princeton, NJ: Princeton University Press.

Godson, J. 1981. 'The Role of the Trade Unions' in Schapiro, L. and Godson, J. (eds) *The Soviet Worker: Illusions and Realities*, 106–29. Basingstoke: Macmillan.

Goodall, K. and Warner, M. 1997. 'Human Resources in Sino-Foreign Joint Ventures: Selected Case Studies in Shanghai, Compared with Beijing'. *International Journal of Human Resource Management* 8: 569–94.

Greenfield, G. 1999. 'Vietnam's black gold'. *International Viewpoint* 314: 18–20.

Gritsenko, N.N., Kadeikina, V.A. and Makukhina, E.V. 1999. *Istoriya profsoyuzov Rossii.* Moscow: Akademiya truda i sotsialnykh otnoshenii.

Guillermaz, J. 1972. *A History of the Chinese Communist Party.* New York: Random House.

Haynes, V. and Semyonova, O. 1979. *Workers Against the Gulag.* London: Pluto.

Hendley, K. 1996. *Trying to Make Law Matter: Legal Reform and Labor Law in the Soviet Union.* Ann Arbor, MI: University of Michigan Press.

Henley, J.S. and Nyaw, M.K. 1986. 'Introducing Market Forces into Managerial Decision-Making in Chinese Enterprises'. *Journal of Management Studies* 23: 635–56.

Hobsbawm, E. 1964. *Labouring Men, Studies in the History of Labour.* London: Weidenfeld and Nicolson.

Howell, J. 1998. 'Trade Unions in China: The Challenge of Foreign Capital' in Leary, G.O. (ed.) *Adjusting to Capitalism*, 150–72. Armonk, NY: M.E.Sharpe.

Howell, J. 2003. 'Trade Unionism in China: Sinking or Swimming'. *Journal of Communist Studies and Transition Politics* 19: 102–22.

Howell, J. 2006. *New Democratic Trends in China? Reforming the All-China Federation of Trade Unions.* Brighton: Institute of Development Studies, University of Sussex.

Howell, J. 2008. 'All-China Federation of Trades Unions beyond Reform? The Slow March of Direct Elections'. *China Quarterly* 196: 845–63.

Human Rights Watch 2009. *Not Yet a Worker's Paradise: Vietnam's Suppression of the Independent Workers' Movement.* NY: Human Rights Watch (http://www.hrw.org/sites/default/files/reports/vietnam0509web.pdf).

Hurst, W. 2004. 'Understanding Contentious Collective Action by Chinese Laid-off Workers: The Importance of Regional Political Economy'. *Studies in Comparative International Development* 39: 94–120.

IHLO 2001. *The Revised Trade Union Law in Mainland China: Progress or Regression for Worker and Trade Union Rights?* Hong Kong: IHLO.

Klump, R. and Bonschab, T. 2004. 'Operationalising Pro-Poor Growth: A Country Case Study on Vietnam': AFD, BMZ (GTZ, KfW Development Bank), DFID, and the World Bank (http://www.dfid.gov.uk/pubs/files/oppgvietnam.pdf).

Lau, R.W.K. 2001. 'Socio-Political Control in Urban China: Changes and Crisis'. *British Journal of Sociology* 52: 605–20.

Lee, C.K. 2007. *Against the Law: Labour Protests in China's Rustbelt and Sunbelt.* London: University of California Press.

Lee, L.T. 1986. *Trade Unions in China.* Singapore: Singapore University Press.

Li, J.P. 2005. Zhonghua quanguo zong gonghui guanyu ji yibu jiaqiang jiceng gonghui gongzuo de jueding' xiangguan wenti jianda'. (Answers to Questions Relating to the 'ACFTU Decision on Strengthening the Work of Primary Level Trade Unions'). Beijing: China Workers Press.

Li, Q. 2000. *A Study of Labour Relations in State-owned Enterprises in China: The Continued Dominance of the State and the Failure of the Collective Contract System*. PhD Thesis. Hong Kong: City University of Hong Kong.

Liu, M.W. 2007. 'Union Organizing in China, Swimming, Floating or Sinking?', Warwick-ILR Brettschneider PhD Seminar, University of Warwick, 4 May.

Luo X. and Zhou S. 2007. 'Zai zhengfu he nongmingong zhijian: shichang jingji xiagonghui shuang zhong shen xi de pingwei' (Between the Government and Migrant Workers: Evaluating the Twin Role of Trade Union in a Market Economy). *Labour Union Bimonthly* 6: 25–30

Mandel, D. 1991. 'Revolutionary Reform in Soviet Factories' in Mandel, D. *Perestroika and the Soviet People*. Montreal and New York: Black Rose.

Mandel, D. 1995. 'The Russian Working Class and Labour Movement in the Fourth Year of Shock Therapy'. Mimeo. Montreal.

MOLISA 2007. *Employment Policy Department Report*, October.

Moses, J.C. 1987. 'Worker Self-Management and the Reformist Alternative in Soviet Labour Policy, 1979–85'. *Soviet Studies* 39: 205–28.

Ng, S.H. and Warner, M. 1998. *China's Trade Unions and Management*. Basingstoke: Macmillan Press.

Ng, S.H. and Warner, M. 2000. 'Industrial Relations versus Human Resources Management in the PRC: Collective Bargaining with "Chinese Characteristics"' in Warner, M. (ed.) *Changing Workplace Relations in the Chinese Economy*, 100–16. Basingstoke: Macmillan.

Ogden, S. 2000. 'China's Developing Civil Society: Interest Groups, Trade Unions and Associational Pluralism' in Warner, M. (ed.) *Changing Workplace Relations in the Chinese Economy*, 263–97. Basingstoke: Macmillan.

Pan, Y. 2005. 'Quanguo zong gonghui 2006 yuandan chunjie song wennuan huodong qidong' (ACFTU's Charitable Activities on the Eve of the 2006 Lunar New Year). *People's Daily*, 12 December.

Perry, E. 1993. *Shanghai on Strike: The Politics of Chinese Labor*. Stanford: Stanford University Press.

Pringle, T. 2001. 'Industrial Unrest in China – A Labour Movement in the Making?' *Asian Labour Update* 40, July – September 2001 (http://www.amrc.org.hk/alu_article/industrial_action/industrial_unrest_in_china_a_labour_movement_in_the_making).

Pringle, T. 2010. *Chinese Trade Unions: The Challenge of Labour Unrest*. London: Routledge.

Pringle, T. and Frost, S. 2003. 'The Absence of Rigor and the Failure of Implementation'. *International Journal of Occupational and Environmental Safety and Health* 9: 209–316.

Qiao, Y. 2005. 'Zujin zai jiuye' (Encourage Re-employment). *Workers' Daily*, 19 January.

Rose, R. 1998. *Getting Things Done with Social Capital.* Glasgow: Centre for the Study of Public Policy, University of Strathclyde.

Ruble, B. 1981. *Soviet Trade Unions: Their Development in the 1970s.* Cambridge: Cambridge University Press.

Shen, J. 2006. 'Analysis of Changing Industrial Relations in China'. *The International Journal of Comparative Labour Law and Industrial Relations* 22: 347–68.

Socialist Republic of Vietnam 1990. *Law on Trade Unions* (www.osh.netnam.vn/luatphap/ENG_cd.htm).

Socialist Republic of Vietnam 1994. *Labour Code of Socialist Republic of Vietnam* (www.ilo.org/dyn/natlex/docs/WEBTEXT/38229/64933/E94VNM01.htm).

Socialist Republic of Vietnam 2002. *Labour Code of Socialist Republic of Vietnam* (http://www.global-standards.com/Resources/VNLaborCode1994-2002.pdf).

State Council 2004. *Laodong baozhang jiancha tiaoli.* (Regulations on the Inspection of Labour Safeguards 2004), http://www.jincao.com/fa/12/law12.52.htm

Taylor, W., Chang, K. and Li, Q. 2003. *Industrial Relations in China.* Cheltenham: Edward Elgar.

Vesti FNPR, bi-monthly, Moscow: FNPR (various issues).

Vietnam Research Team 2007. Case study: Binh Duong industrial-processing zone union. Hanoi. February, http://www.warwick.ac.uk/fac/soc/complabstuds/russia/ngpa/BinhDuongEPZ.doc

Warner, M. 1995. *The Management of Human Resources in Chinese Industry.* Basingstoke: Macmillan.

Warner, M. and Ng, S.H. 1999. 'Collective Contracts in Chinese Enterprises: A New Brand of Collective Bargaining under Market Socialism'. *British Journal of Industrial Relations* 37: 295–314.

Wehrle, E. 2008. 'Awakening the Conscience of the Masses: The Vietnamese Confederation of Labour and International Labour, 1947–1975'. *Vietnam Update 2008 Conference, Labour in Vietnam.* The Australian National University, Canberra.

Wei, J. 2000. *Renzhen xuexi guanche dang de shiwu ju wu zhong quan hui jingshen. Jin yi bu jia kuai xin jian qiye gonghui zu jian bufa.* (Conscientiously Implement the Spirit of the Fifth Plenary Session of the Fifteenth Central Committee and Speed up the Organising and Establishing of Trade Unions in New Enterprises), Beijing: Beijing Federation of Trade Unions (http://www.bjzgh.gov.cn/jianghua/5_jianghua_13.php).

Wei, L.B. 2008. 'yige jiceng gonghui ruhe yu Wo'erma douzheng?' (How Does a Grassroots Union Take on Wal-Mart?). *Southern Weekend*, 17 September 2008.

White, G. 1996. 'Chinese Trade Unions in the Transition from Socialism'. *British Journal of Industrial Relations* 34: 433–57.

Wilson, J.L. 1990. 'The Polish Lesson: China and Poland 1989–1990'. *Studies in Comparative Communism* XIII: 259–79.

Xia X.Y. 2005. 'Wenling gonghui: weiquan cong fensan xiang jihe kuayue'(Wenling Trade Union Makes the Leap from Upholding Individual to Collective Rights), *Zhejiang Workers' Daily*, 12 July.

Yi, B. and Yue, S. 2010. 'Jiti tanpan: zhongguo laozi maodun huajie lu', (Collective bargaining: the road to industrial harmony in China). *Caijing*, 17 March 2010 (http://dycj.ynet.com/article.jsp?oid=64142217).

Yi, M. 2007. *Zhonghua quan guo cong gonghui lai wo xian tiaoyan hangye xing jiti hetong gongzuo* (The ACFTU Investigation into Collective Sector-Level Contracts in Fuping County) (old.fuping.gov.cn/fpzw/Article_Show.asp?ArticleID=3125).

Yu, L. 2004. 'Zhejiang Wenlingshi: laozi shuangying jinxing shi', (Wenling city, Zhejiang: A Win-Win for Labour and Capital). *Southern Weekend*, 23 September.

Zhang, Y. 1997. 'An Intermediary: the Chinese Perception of Trade Unions since the 1980s'. *Journal of Contemporary China* 6: 139–52.

Zhang, X. 2009. 'Trade Unions under the Modernization of Paternalist Rule in China'. *Working USA* 12, 2: 193–218.

Zhou, Q. 2009. 'Quan shi geji fayuan shouli zhenyi anyuan tongbi shangshen 159.18%' (City Courts Process an Increase in Cases of 159.18%). *Caijing,* 14 January 2009 (http://www.caijing.com.cn/2009-01-14/110048077.html).

Zhou Y. 2002. 'Guanyu gonghui dangqian xuyao renzhen yanjiu de ji ge wenti' (Several Problems Presently Requiring Diligent Research by Labour Unions). *Workers' Daily*, 3 September.

Zhu, J. 1996. 'Zai laodong guanxi xietiao gongzuo zuotanhui shang de jianghua' (Speech Given at the Working Forum of Co-ordinating Labour Relations) in Wang, J. et al. (eds) *Zhongguo laodong nianjian: 1995–1996*, 99. Beijing: Zhongguo laodong chubanshe.

Zhu, Y. 1995. 'Major Changes under Way in China's Industrial Relations'. *International Labour Review* 134: 37–50.

Zhu, Y. and Campbell, I. 1996. 'Economic Reform and the Challenge of Transforming Labour Regulation in China'. *Labour & Industry* 7: 29–49.

Index

All China Federation of Trade Unions (ACFTU), 3, 14, 16, 20-1, 29, 40, 42, 57-8, 62, 65, 77, 78, 86-90, 92, 94-5, 103-4, 106, 108, 112, 114-15, 121-2, 132, 134, 138, 140-2, 147-9, 153, 202, 203, 204, 205

agreements
  collective, 5, 19, 16, 21, 24, 27-8, 30, 32, 33, 37, 54, 77-101, 113, 125, 131-2, 134, 136, 140, 144-5, 148, 151, 153, 155, 157, 158, 159, 157-60, 163, 165, 175-7, 179, 181, 197-8, 203
  enforcement 106, 113, 115
  sectoral, 77, 79, 82, 84-5, 101-2, 131, 180-1

All-Russia Confederation of Labour (VKT), 53-4, 185, 190, 193, 204

anarcho-syndicalism, 47, 57, 177

arbitration, 21, 25, 27, 30, 44, 47, 57, 66, 76, 87, 105, 115, 120-3, 125, 127, 135, 149

Artyakov, Vladimir 157, 187

Auto and Agricultural Machine Building Trade Union (ASM), 181, 185-90, 192-3, 196

authorities
  local, 6, 8-9, 30, 33, 51, 55, 60-1, 63-5, 74, 79, 86-90, 92-3, 96, 105-7, 109, 112, 119, 122, 125-6, 128, 130-2, 143, 147-8, 150-1, 153-4, 158, 160, 164-6, 168-9, 172, 174, 195
  provincial, 41, 72, 74, 86, 89, 93-4, 96, 104-5, 121-2, 124, 126, 129-30, 133, 151-2
  regional, 29-30, 33, 43, 85, 106, 119, 156-63, 178-9, 182, 196

Avtovaz, 157, 185-92, 195

benefits, 1, 5, 7-10, 18, 24, 35, 39, 44, 58-9, 61, 77, 82-4, 91, 94, 97-8, 100, 106, 108, 114, 118, 124, 148, 153, 162-7, 169-70, 174-5, 179, 181, 186, 188, 191, 199

Binh Duong, 68, 69, 71, 73, 102, 128, 132-5, 143, 151-2

bonuses, 30, 98, 157, 183, 185, 197

Beijing Workers Autonomous Federation (BWAF), 58

China Enterprise Confederation (CEC), 104

Chinese Enterprise Directors' Association (CEDA), 94

China Enterprise Management Association (CEMA), 88

Chen Youde, 148

Chengdu, 94

China Labor Watch, 120

China Labour Bulletin, 92, 120, 135

collective bargaining, 64, 72, 76, 87, 89-90, 97-102, 108, 130, 133, 145, 150, 197, 205

collective consultation, 19, 42, 87-1, 93, 95-6, 135, 145

command economy, 1, 3-4, 10-12, 17-18, 80

Communist Party, 1, 8-11, 16, 18, 20, 22, 29, 31, 34, 36, 40-2, 46-7, 52, 56-7, 59, 65, 67, 79, 87, 130, 20
  leadership, 2, 9, 11, 14, 18, 20, 31, 66

conciliation, 21, 25, 27, 30, 47, 68, 123, 125-6, 193

Confederation of Labour of Russia (KTR), 53-54, 204

consultation, 20-1, 26, 38, 44, 47, 83, 86, 90-2, 94-5, 97, 104-5, 116, 127, 129, 135, 139, 141, 200, 203

corruption, 11, 36, 53, 58, 61, 109, 124

courts, 25, 44, 109, 114, 118-21, 123, 125, 159-60, 162-3, 168-9, 172, 190, 192, 194, 196, 200-1, 204

Corporate Social Responsibility, 97

Cu Thi Hau, 126

Cultural Revolution, 58

Da Nang, 128, 133, 143

Daqing, 61, 62

democracy movement, 15, 45, 58

democratic centralism, 15, 28, 51, 57, 132, 202

democratisation, 1, 3, 13, 15, 47

demonstrations, 27, 30, 44, 46, 54, 61, 95, 103, 122, 154, 159-60, 194

Deng Xiaoping, 11, 12, 16, 20, 58, 59

discipline, 7, 9, 35, 37, 39, 44, 51, 55, 57, 74, 80, 98, 102, 115, 147, 179, 189
dismissal, 8, 20, 23, 26-7, 41, 116-17, 119, 150, 160, 172, 189-90, 192, 195-6
doi moi, 17
Donbas, 46, 47
Dong Nai, 68-9, 71-2, 102, 128-9, 132-4
Dongguan, 121
Duma, 24, 26, 31, 53, 103, 184-5, 190
employers, 1- 4, 10, 12, 17-19, 21, 23, 25-6, 28-9, 31-4, 39-41, 43, 45, 49-50, 52, 56-7, 64-6, 70-1, 77, 79, 81-6, 88, 90, 92, 94-5, 97, 100, 102-5, 107-9, 113, 121-2, 124-31, 134-7, 139-40, 142-4, 149, 152-3, 157, 160, 163, 169, 176-8, 181, 183, 196, 199, 201, 203-5
employment
    creation, 59, 62, 77, 78, 114
    relation, 1- 4, 6, 10, 19, 27, 77
    terms and conditions, 4- 6, 10, 19, 21, 23, 25, 27-8, 70, 75-6, 79-80, 83, 85, 87, 91, 98, 102-3, 105-9, 132, 145, 162, 164, 167, 181
enterprise, 6-8, 10-14, 16-18, 20-2, 26-8, 30, 32-4, 36-45, 48-9, 51-2, 55-7, 59-62, 64-5, 67, 69, 72, 77, 79-80, 82-5, 88, 89-91, 93-96, 98-101, 103, 110, 112-13, 117-18, 120, 122-5, 128, 130-2, 134, 136-8, 140-1, 143, 145, 147, 151, 153, 160, 166, 168-82, 184, 186-7, 189-91, 194, 197, 199, 201
    director, 7-8, 12, 35-6, 38-41, 71, 73-4, 81, 90, 99-100, 138, 140, 179-80, 184, 189
Etmanov, Alexei, 185, 193-6, 200
Foreign Direct Investment (FDI), 11, 12, 54, 66-7, 74, 108, 126, 130, 137
Friedrich Ebert Stiftung (FES), 133
Federation of Independent Trade Unions of Russia (FNPR), 22, 24, 26, 29-33, 37, 48, 52-4, 56, 77, 81-2, 84-5, 103, 106, 110-11, 117-18, 120, 131, 144, 147, 153-4, 159, 176, 181-2, 184, 193, 204
foreign-invested enterprises (FIEs), 4, 14, 17, 42, 63, 68, 70, 75, 92, 100, 104, 107, 112, 131, 135, 142-3, 147
freedom of association, 2, 5, 23, 34, 45, 100, 137, 146, 203, 204
Freetrend, 72, 107

Fuping County, 96
Fushun, 61-2
Guomindang (GMD), 56
Gongli, 96
Gorbachev, Mikhail, 11, 15, 24, 46-8
government, 5, 14, 16, 18, 23-6, 28-33, 43, 46, 48-52, 54, 56, 58-62, 63, 70, 76, 79, 86-7, 94-6, 99, 102-8, 112, 115, 122, 125, 127, 130-1, 135, 138, 145, 149-51, 154-6, 159-61, 177, 183, 188, 195, 201, 203
Great Leap Forward, 58
group of four, 12, 40, 67
Guangdong, 65, 96, 121-2, 135, 137, 148
Hai Duong, 124, 128, 133-4
Hai Phong, 128, 133-4
Hangzhou, 93
Hanoi, 66, 68, 73, 98, 102, 112, 125, 128
health and safety, 5-6, 8-9, 18-19, 23-4, 29-30, 33, 44, 51, 63, 77, 82, 103, 105, 109-12, 115, 145, 147, 157-8, 174, 176, 191, 205
Ho Chi Minh, 66
Ho Chi Minh City (HCMC), 42, 68-74, 97, 100, 102, 105, 112, 123, 125, 128-9, 133-5
holidays, 6, 37-8, 108, 163, 166-7, 185
home-place networks, 63, 148-9
housing, 6-10, 19, 31, 80, 85, 125, 175, 177, 190
Human Rights Watch (HRW), 142
Hu Jintao, 29, 65, 87
Hundred Flowers Movement, 58
IG Metall, 192, 197
Independent Workers' Union of Vietnam (IWUV), 75
industries
    autos, 157, 181, 185, 195
    aviation, 50, 52-3, 120, 181
    coal-mining, 15, 35, 45-8, 52-3, 84, 101-2, 118, 139, 166, 173-4, 182
    construction, 84-5, 113, 153, 175-9
    docks, 50, 52-3, 64, 120, 149-50
    education, 50, 56
    engineering, 49, 71, 193
    footwear, 71, 72, 74, 107
    garments, 71, 101, 102
    health, 154-5, 163
    metallurgy, 177, 194, 198
    postal service, 195

railways, 9, 50, 52-3, 198
ship-building, 101
transport, 49, 52-3, 98, 119
inflation, 14, 18, 48, 58, 70-1, 77-8, 84,
98, 105, 107-8, 128-9, 155, 168-9, 183,
187, 189, 193, 195, 199
informal organisation, 5, 34, 37, 45, 63,
69, 72-3, 98, 203
intimidation, 4, 50, 63, 72, 176, 190-1
Industrial Processing Zone (IPZ), 71, 125,
128-9, 132, 138, 143, 151-2
Institute for Comparative Labour
Relations Research(ISITO), 38, 82
Inter-regional Trade Union of Motor
Industry Workers (MPRA), 185, 190-2,
194-6
International Confederation of Free Trade
Unions (ICFTU), 3, 33, 53-4, 204
International Federation of Chemical,
Energy, Mine and General Workers'
Unions (ICEM), 33
International Labour Organization (ILO),
54, 97, 126, 133, 143, 204
International Trade Union Confederation
(ITUC), 3, 33, 204
International Union of Food workers
(IUF), 191
Ivanov, Anatolii, 185
Ivanov, Evgeny, 190, 196
Jinjiang, 141
Kaluga, 196
Karaganda, 47
Kemerovo, 47, 53, 82, 118, 154, 157, 159,
163-6, 173-4, 177, 182-3
Khramov, Sergei, 53-4
Klebanov, Vladimir, 46
Klochkov, Igor', 52
Komi, 53, 161
Labour Department, 21, 41, 69, 70-4,
98-9, 113, 123-4, 128-9
labour disputes, 21, 22, 24, 55, 57, 70, 76,
79, 98, 115-18, 121, 126, 137, 146, 165,
203
collective, 5, 24, 27, 116, 121-2, 125,
132, 160, 178
individual, 5, 25, 27, 116, 157-8, 160,
186
resolution, 4, 5, 19, 27, 92, 96, 104,
115, 120, 122-3, 126, 131, 133,
149-50, 185

labour law, 9-10, 13, 19-28, 32-4, 36-7,
40, 53-4, 66-8, 70-3, 79-83, 84-6, 88-9,
93-7, 101, 103, 106, 109-13, 115-7,
119, 121-6, 128, 133, 136-7, 140,
142-3, 145, 152, 156, 158, 161, 163-4,
169, 180-1, 186, 192, 197, 199
enforcement, 5, 21, 28, 32, 44, 63, 109,
110, 112-14, 125-6, 147, 158
labour shortage, 2, 7, 63, 71, 75, 77, 128,
162, 205
labour unrest, 1-2, 4-5, 18, 28, 32, 51,
57-8, 62, 76-7, 91, 118, 122, 148-9,
153, 202-3, 205
Laomiao, 96
lay-offs, 51, 60-1, 66-8, 77-8, 114, 137,
177, 197
leaflets, 63, 69, 71-2, 133, 160, 187-9
legal advice, 37, 77, 79, 116-7, 121-2,
124, 129, 131-2, 146, 165, 203
legal regulation, 23, 27, 76, 79, 86
legal violations, 70-1, 109, 113, 122, 125,
128, 131
legislation, 5, 10, 19, 21, 24-7, 31, 44-5,
55, 82, 93, 103, 105, 109-15, 117-18,
124, 126, 133, 156, 159, 170, 172, 197,
204
Lenin, Vladimir, 18, 79
Liaoyang, 61, 62
liberalisation, 17, 51
Li Lisan, 57
lobbying, 1, 9, 103-6, 132, 154, 161
Lyapin, Andrei 189-91
Mai Duc Chin, 126, 142
management, 3-4, 8-9, 11-13, 16-19, 22-4,
26-8, 30, 33-9, 41-6, 49, 51-2, 54, 57,
60, 63-5, 67-9, 71, 73-4, 80-3, 86-7, 89-
94, 97-103, 107, 109, 111, 115-20,
125-7, 132, 134-5, 137-51, 162-8, 171,
173-4, 176, 178-82, 184-202, 204
democratic, 1, 12-13, 15-16, 17, 30, 51,
57-8, 71, 80, 95, 172
line managers, 35, 72-3, 116, 139,
179-80, 190
personnel management, 39-41, 73, 97,
100, 124, 138-9, 143
Mao Zedong, 20, 58
market economy, 1- 12, 15, 17-19, 27, 31,
34, 39, 43, 48, 50, 86-7, 92, 102, 115,
126, 147, 175, 181
material assistance, 10, 37, 164-6

mediation, 21, 27, 30, 44, 66, 73, 76, 115-16, 120, 125, 127, 149

migrant workers, 4, 7, 45, 59, 62-5, 67, 75, 77, 93-5, 125, 128-9, 140, 147-9, 176

minimum wage, 5, 32, 65, 70-1, 76, 78, 84-5, 92-4, 99, 102, 105-8, 125, 128, 135, 154, 158-9

Ministry of Labour, 10, 16, 24, 29, 33, 49, 68, 70, 78, 81, 86, 88, 94-5, 97-8, 101, 103-4, 108-9, 112, 127, 130-1, 137, 143, 145, 160, 163, 204

neo-liberalism, 26, 105, 155

Nguyen Van Binh, 151

Ni Zhifu, 16

Ningbo, 121

non-governmental organisations (NGOs), 11, 15, 122, 203

North-East China, 59

Novocherkassk, 46

Novokuznetsk, 182

overtime, 6, 21, 23, 71, 73, 76, 109, 163, 166, 186-7, 193

Party-state, 1-4, 9, 11, 13-16, 18-19, 34, 44-5, 51, 57, 77-8, 87, 89, 92, 102-3, 126-7, 149

Pavlyuchkov, Sergei, 192

pensions, 6, 9, 32, 37, 102, 158, 160, 164

perestroika, 11, 15-6, 46-7

petitions, 44, 61

Pham Minh Huan, 108

picketing, 178, 183, 190-2

police, 27, 41, 55, 61, 64, 69, 72, 74, 129, 131, 176, 188, 205

press, 34, 41, 55, 74, 70, 90, 95, 107, 113, 127, 186

private sector, 12, 17, 26, 40, 57, 59, 61, 77, 79, 82, 85, 92-5, 97, 108, 112, 123, 126, 140, 142, 144, 148, 153, 157, 175, 177

privatisation, 4, 16-18, 50-1, 59, 68, 175, 184, 200

protests, 4, 13-17, 27, 32-3, 44-6, 52, 56, 59-66, 76-7, 96, 107, 109-10, 122-3, 148, 153-4, 157-61, 176, 183, 186, 188, 192, 194, 202, 205

public order, 69, 74, 77

public sector, 6, 22, 33, 38, 42, 78, 85, 142, 143, 153, 155-7, 175

Putin, Vladimir, 31-3, 52, 106, 156, 188

redundancy, 59-60, 62, 67, 187-8, 192

re-employment centres, 59, 114

regions, 15, 37, 45, 47-9, 59, 63, 71, 76, 83, 85, 103-4, 125, 128, 130, 137, 139, 144, 146, 151, 154, 156-7, 161, 163, 182, 197

repression, 15, 45, 50, 61, 63, 185, 189, 196, 203, 205

right to strike, 2, 25-6, 34, 53, 100, 120, 203

riot, 64, 72

Russian Confederation of Free Trade Unions (RKSP), 53

road blocks, 61

Rosprofmash, 193

Russian-American Fund, 49

Samara, 53, 82, 103, 157-8, 167, 169-71, 174-9, 187, 190

sectional interests, 9, 49, 52

Sergeev, Alexander, 53

Shandong, 137

Shanghai, 89, 121

Sharafutdinova, Il'ciyar, 190-2

Shenzhen, 65, 89, 107, 121, 142, 149, 150

Shmakov, Mikhail, 29, 31-3, 52, 120

social insurance, 17-8, 21-2, 24, 28, 51, 59, 96, 98-9, 102, 109, 113, 124, 126, 177

social partnership, 5, 18, 25-6, 28-34, 44, 52, 77, 81, 144, 160, 166, 176-7, 201

social peace, 2, 5, 28, 30, 32, 34-5, 44, 46, 51, 69, 77, 118, 131, 147, 159

social welfare, 7-10, 21, 28, 31, 35, 39, 44, 51, 59, 77, 80, 82-4, 91, 147, 153, 159, 163, 165, 169, 175, 187

socialist competition, 30, 80, 82

socialist market economy, 6, 11-15, 17, 21

solidarity, 25, 37, 49, 58, 61, 72, 137, 161, 169, 190, 200, 204

Sotsprof, 49, 53-4, 185, 193, 195

Soviet Union, 7, 9, 11, 13, 15, 17, 22-3, 30, 42, 45-8, 50-1, 79, 154

social stability, 16, 20, 29, 87, 90, 109, 124, 149, 205

Stalin, Josef, 46, 79

state apparatus, 1, 48, 102, 104, 118, 145

state inspectorates, 5, 24, 32, 79, 103, 105, 109-12, 131, 145, 157-8, 163, 165, 171-2, 180, 186 state-owned enterprises (SOEs), 4, 11-12, 14-19, 40, 42, 44-5, 51, 58-63, 67-8, 74, 77, 82, 85, 88-9, 93, 97, 101, 106, 112, 114, 142, 175, 202

state-socialism, 1-11, 18, 27, 36, 44, 59, 77, 109, 115, 147

State Trade and Economic Commission (STEC), 88, 94

strikes, 4, 14, 15, 19, 20, 24-6, 30, 32, 37, 41-2, 44-50, 52, 54-9, 63-78, 95-6, 98-100, 107-10, 113, 115, 118-20, 123-31, 133, 135-6, 139-40, 142-3, 147-54, 159, 160, 164, 169, 174, 176, 178, 184-7, 191, 193-5, 197, 200-5

   wildcat, 14, 27, 46, 69, 71-2, 74, 98, 100, 108, 119, 127, 129, 136, 151, 187, 204

Sun Yatsen, 56

Taganrog, 196

Tet, 71, 98, 108, 128

Tiananmen, 14, 16, 42, 58-9, 61, 202

Titov, Konstantin, 157

Togliatti, 185, 189, 191, 196

Tomsk, 82

trade union

   committee, 13, 20, 36, 43, 117-18, 138-9, 141-3, 158, 165, 168-73, 175, 178-9, 182, 184, 186-7, 189-90, 193-4, 200

   collaboration with employer, 3, 35, 40, 42, 76, 83, 140, 142, 144, 169, 175, 178-9, 202

   collaboration with state, 24, 30-2, 76, 78, 102-3, 105, 110, 113, 118, 130, 144-5, 156, 160

   dependence on employers, 5, 11, 14, 33-4, 36, 38-9, 41, 43, 63, 74, 91, 116, 127, 134-5, 144-7, 204

   dependence on state, 8, 14, 18, 25, 33, 147

   dues, 29, 49, 132, 134, 153, 164, 167, 180, 184, 191, 193

   elections, 40, 96, 137-6, 150, 159, 185

   higher trade union bodies, 5, 43-5, 84, 118, 132, 148

   organising, 2, 5, 15, 28, 50, 56, 58, 64, 66, 77, 79, 92, 119, 130,140-2, 144, 146, 153, 168, 194, 196-7, 200, 203

president, 35-8, 40, 42, 73, 83, 92-3, 98, 119, 132, 134, 140, 146, 163-7, 169-74, 178-80, 184, 193

reform, 1-5, 15, 33, 44-6, 65, 78-9, 101, 131-2, 134, 138, 146, 151, 202-5

training, 30, 42, 54, 59, 70, 80, 82, 111, 113-17, 131-3, 136, 142, 146, 148, 152, 162, 165, 169, 178-80, 182, 204

workplace, 69, 78, 100, 119, 128-31, 134, 136

Trade Union Law, 13-14, 16, 19, 22, 29, 43, 86, 90, 102, 104, 120, 130, 136, 143, 150, 203

trade union organization

   primary, 25-6, 37, 44-5, 49, 55-7, 78-9, 81, 83-4, 87, 94-5, 100, 110, 113, 117, 124, 127, 130-7, 144, 146, 148, 151-3, 158-60, 163-6, 169, 172-3, 176-9, 181, 182, 184-5, 193, 197-8, 202, 204

   regional, 9, 30, 37-8, 53, 81, 85, 111, 117, 124, 156-9, 161, 169, 172, 197-8

   territorial, 9, 43, 81-2, 85, 145

trade unions

   alternative, 1, 3, 5, 15, 23-6, 32, 34-5, 38, 41, 45, 48-50, 52-4, 69, 77-8, 80, 117, 119-20, 139, 146-7, 153, 159, 162-3, 169, 172, 175, 184-91, 197, 201-4

   protective role, 9-10, 26, 76, 117, 128, 200

   representative role, 1, 3-4, 9, 12-13, 18-21, 24, 29-30, 39-41, 43, 46-9, 52, 62, 66, 69, 73, 76, 79, 90, 115-16, 121, 126, 136-8, 146, 148, 173, 175, 203-4

   sectoral, 9, 30, 31, 38, 43, 84, 103, 144, 185, 198

   traditional, 1-3, 5, 12-13, 15, 18-19, 22-4, 26, 28-31, 34-5, 38-40, 43-6, 48-51, 53-5, 59, 64, 71, 76-8, 81-4, 91, 102, 116-19, 122, 126, 133, 139-42, 144-8, 150, 153, 158-9, 165-7, 169-71, 174-6, 179-81, 185-7, 190, 193-4, 197, 199-205

   transmission belt, 17, 36, 57, 199

workers' lack of confidence in, 3, 16, 30, 33, 36, 41, 99, 126, 129, 135, 143, 167, 171
yellow, 65, 81, 89, 119, 196
transnational companies, 65, 68, 120, 123, 125, 140-2, 185, 188-200
  Japanese, 65-6, 71, 73, 94, 97, 129, 138
  Korean, 41, 68, 71-3, 114, 124, 129, 138
  Taiwanese, 41, 68, 72-3, 107, 124, 139
tripartite consultation, 19, 27, 32, 76-7, 88, 104-5, 145
tripartite structures, 32, 49, 54, 89, 103-5, 155, 157, 203
Tver, 196
unemployment, 18-19, 57-8, 66, 78, 205
United Russia, 31, 185
United Worker-Farmers Organisation of Vietnam (UWFO), 75
Vietnam Cooperative Alliance (VCA), 105, 130
Vietnam Chamber of Commerce and Industry (VCCI), 66, 69, 105, 130
Vietnam General Confederation of Labour (VGCL), 3, 10, 40-2, 66-7, 69-74, 78, 97-108, 112-13, 124-7, 130-7, 140, 142-3, 147-8, 151-3, 202, 204
victimisation, 34, 45, 50, 64, 69, 117, 120, 132, 139, 174, 186, 204
Vietnamese Confederation of Christian Workers (CVTC), 66
Vorkuta, 47
Vostretsov, Sergei, 54
Vsevolozhsk, 120, 185, 192-3, 196, 200
All-Union Central Council of Trade Unions (VTsSPS), 14, 22
wage table, 78, 95-6, 99, 126
wages, 1-2, 6, 23, 33, 37-8, 44, 52, 54, 56, 59, 61, 64, 68-9, 71, 75-8, 80, 83-5, 92-3, 98-9, 102, 106-9, 113, 116, 119,

127-8, 130, 140, 149-50, 154-71, 173, 176, 179-96, 201
  low, 2, 12, 31, 75, 92, 162
  non-payment, 17, 25, 27, 31, 51-2, 54, 56, 61, 67-8, 114, 117, 154, 175, 177
Wang Tongyan, 150
Wei Jianxing, 16, 87, 90
World Federation of Trade Unions (WFTU), 3, 204
women workers, 6, 17, 73, 76, 93, 190-1
worker
  activism, 2-5, 17, 28, 35, 45, 51-2, 54, 59, 75-8, 120, 132, 147-8, 174, 178, 202-3
  protest, 13, 17, 140, 202
  rights and interests, 2, 13, 18-19, 21, 28, 39, 46, 64, 90, 92-3, 116, 120, 126-7, 136, 146, 166, 184
working class, 1, 7-9, 11, 18, 20, 46, 57-9, 62, 137
working conditions, 1-2, 7, 9, 12, 27, 32-3, 63, 67, 71, 80, 83, 93, 101-3, 110-12, 125, 128, 136, 145, 147, 149-50, 154, 158, 175, 189, 195
working hours, 6, 19, 21, 63, 68, 76, 80, 86, 92, 94, 96, 108, 119, 125, 147, 150, 163, 167
World Bank, 26, 48
World Trade Organisation (WTO), 19, 59, 75, 106, 108, 137
Xinhe, 95-6
Yabloko, 31
Yamalo-Nenetsk, 163
Yeltsin, Boris, 16, 26, 29, 47-51, 110
Yiwu, 148, 149
Zeguo, 96
Zhang Chunsheng, 20
Zhejiang, 40, 95, 121-2, 137, 148
Zhongshan, 121
Zhu Jiazhen, 86
Zolotaryev, Petr, 185-7, 189, 191,